DIASPORA, IDENTITY AND THE MEDIA

Diasporic Transnationalism and Mediated Spatialities

URBAN COMMUNICATION
Gary Gumpert, series editor

Diaspora, Identity and the Media
  Diasporic Transnationalism and Mediated Spatialities
    Myria Georgiou

forthcoming

The Urban Communication Reader
    Gene Burd, Susan J. Drucker, and Gary Gumpert (eds.)

DIASPORA, IDENTITY AND THE MEDIA

Diasporic Transnationalism and Mediated Spatialities

Myria Georgiou
University of Leeds

HAMPTON PRESS, INC.
CRESSKILL, NEW JERSEY

Printed in the United States of America

Library of Congress Cataloging-in-Publishing Data

Georgiou, Myria.
    Diaspora, identity and the media : diasporic transnationalism and mediated spatialities / Myria Georgiou.
       p. cm. -- (Urban communication)
    Includes bibliographic references and index.
    ISBN 1-57273-723-9 -- ISBN 1-57273-724-7 (pbk.)
      1. Transnationalism. 2. Ethnicity. 3. Communication in human geography. I. Title.

    JV6035.G435 2006
    320.54--dc22

                             2006044371

Cover photos by Myria Georgiou, Gary Gumpert and Susan Drucker

Hampton Press, Inc.
23 Broadway
Cresskill, NJ 07626

For Clara and Aris

CONTENTS

ACKNOWLEDGEMENTS

When entering the local library in a neighborhood of North London, I come across familiar friendly faces in front of computer screens and around tables covered with Greek language newspapers. These are the faces of the many people whose names will not be mentioned here but who brought this book to life. I am indebted to the hundreds of participants who opened their homes to me, who shared their thoughts, family histories, and television viewings and who have welcomed me to community centers and to public and private events and celebrations. They showed me trust and I hope the final outcome is a fair interpretation of their everyday lives as lived and as imagined in diasporic spaces.

I am grateful to Roger Silverstone for intellectual encounters and discussions, which guided and inspired me through the years. A number of colleagues and friends, who read this work at various stages of its development, presented me with new intellectual challenges, but also offered me unconditional support. Madeleine Demetriou, Gareth Dale, Andreas Onoufriou, and John Roberts have been good friends and inspiring critics. Thank you all. I also want to thank Marie Gillespie and Kevin Robins for their valuable comments and suggestions when this book was at its early stages of development. A special thank you goes to Gary Gumpert, who has been a committed and motivating reader and editor.

Madeleine Demetriou, Gareth Dale, Andreas Onoufriou, and John Roberts have been good friends and inspiring critics. Thank you all. I also want to thank Marie Gillespie and Kevin Robins for their valuable comments and suggestions when this book was at its early stages of development, as well as Christine Ogan and Vangelis Kalotychos for the complementing words that appear on the back cover. A special thank you goes to Gary Gumpert, who has been a committed and motivating reader and editor.

Finally, I want to express my warmest appreciation to my family, who supported me through the making of this book. My parents, Clara and Aris, to whom this book is dedicated, have been my first intellectual and creative guides in life. They still are. Kevin has been through it all with me, in good and not so good times. My son, Leon, was born while this book was written. I cannot thank him enough for bringing new life to my work and for smiling to me even after long sleepless nights for both of us.

ONE ────────────────────

IDENTITY AND NEW SPATIALITIES

THE LAYERS OF DIASPORIC SPACE—
THE LAYERS OF IDENTITY CONSTRUCTION

The reconstitution and redefinition of space and spatial relations within globalization expressed in increased mobility, and growing interconnections of places through intensified mediation, have major implications for social, cultural, and economic life. Much provocative work has been done on space and spatial relations within globalization (e.g. Harvey, 1989; Giddens, 1990; Lefebvre, 1991; Massey, 1993; Castells, 1996; Massey, and Denton, 2000; Urry, 2000, 2002), inviting in-depth analysis of their social significance. This book focuses on one of the major consequences of globalization and of the reconstitution and redefinition of space within it. This book opens up the problematic area of identity and community construction across and beyond boundaries and investigates how and with what implications are identities and communities sustained across space. At present times, when ethnic identification and cultural difference are attacked for threatening harmony in national and global levels, understanding the actual formations and meanings of identity becomes imperative. The present study focuses on people who directly experience deterritorialization and reterritorialization—usually not by choice—and who develop and sustain distinct identities and social relations within and across nation-states. The emerging interconnected transnational space becomes a specific area of culture and social action closely linked to processes of globalization.

This book is about diasporization—the relocation of people in space and their ability, desire and persistence to sustain connections and commonality across the globe. Once, ethnicity was bounded, or forced to be bounded, in place. The ownership of specific bounded space was a key element for sustaining identity and community. Is the development of transnational communication and cultures a projection of a very traditional old ideology/imagination/longing for ethnicity—that is, seeking a place and a space that hosts ethnicity? Are diasporic populations seeking to reconfirm stability or manage mobility in global times? The struggle around the ownership of mediated space is not only a matter of power and control but also a matter of (symbolic) vitality and viability of postmodern ethnicity. Transnational connectedness depends more and more on information and communication technologies, inviting us to consider the diasporic appropriations of space in the context of media culture. Everyday culture has become media culture (Silverstone, 1994, 1999; Alasuutari, 1999). This book is about the construction of diasporic identities and the everyday administration of transnational community spaces in the context of the highly mediated everyday culture.

Diasporic peoples have a significant cultural, social and economic presence in advanced capitalist societies, even though this presence is not always acknowledged for its social significance and cultural and economic contribution. As the historical experience in the United States, the United Kingdom and other diverse societies has shown, diasporic populations sustain cultural continuity and distinct identities through time, while keeping links with their original *homeland*[1] and with populations of same origin spread across the world. Diasporic presence and the continuity of relevance of diasporic identity for multiethnic societies and across transnational spaces are significant in many levels, as will be discussed in the following pages. The continuous relevance of diasporic identity and identification shows how particularity sustains its significance within globalization, while being transformed through and universalizing ideologies of democracy, participation and free communication (Robertson, 1991; Georgiou, 2005b). Diasporic communication and cultures become a study area of growing importance as it reveals how identities become fragmented and situational, while remaining significant for the choices and restrictions that social groups have in terms of creativity, community and participation in cultural, social and political schemes. This is an area that can contribute to understanding how communities can be sustained, re-imagined and re-defined in global times and spaces and how they function as transnational networks. This research was designed to take into consideration the different spaces where diasporic life is lived. During its conduct, the importance of spatial contextualization and spatial connections proved to be even more significant for diasporic life and identity than originally thought. The layers of the diasporic space are the layers of identity construction. The home, the public, the city, (the nation), the transnational and the scheme of their interconnections and autonomies become the layers for identity construction and community building. Media and communication technologies cut across space, redefine it and frame symbolic community space and imagination.

Why Diaspora Matters

Diaspora has recently made a dynamic comeback in the debates around ethnicity, nationality and nationhood, boundaries and identity. A concept that has transformed over time, diaspora has returned to address and assist the understanding of migration, people's multiple sense of belonging and loyalties (Gillespie, 1995; Cohen, 1996, 1997; Dayan, 1999; Karim, 2002) beyond national boundaries. Diaspora has become 'an intermediate concept between the local and the global that nevertheless transcends the national perspectives which often limit cultural studies,' Gillespie argues (1995: p. 6). Diaspora implies a decentralized relation to ethnicity, real or imagined relations between scattered people who sustain a sense of community through various forms of communication and contact and who do not depend on returning to a distant *homeland* (Durham Peters, 1999).

Diaspora, as it applies to late modernity conditions, illustrates the hybrid and ever-changing nature of identities that are not inescapably dependent on homogeneity, purity and stable localization. Cultures' viability does not depend on purity; rather cultures survive through mixing (Boyarin and Boyarin, 1993). Identities in the diaspora become *diasporized*, Boyarin and Boyarin suggest, explaining that these identities can surpass dualisms. Clifford adds that diaspora does not signify only movement and transnationality but also 'political struggles to define the local . . . as a distinctive community, in historical contexts of displacement' (1994: 308).

In the context of Western advanced capitalism, diasporic populations' struggle for recognition and participation has gone beyond the linear and clearly defined experience of subordination and exploitation of the early days of mass migration. Though exclusion and exploitation are far from being experiences of the past, the diasporic condition has become much more complex and diverse, with some groups still living on the margin, but with most being in a position of *inside-outsider*. Many members of diasporic minority groups still struggle for recognition and inclusion, but others have already succeeded and established themselves in the mainstream. The Greeks and Greek Cypriots this book refers to are some of the groups that are well integrated in the British and American societies and they have thus partly overcome the *victim tradition* (Cohen, 1997). The diversity of diasporic formations and shifting ideologies challenge old understanding of identity and race in two ways. On one hand, some populations succeed in the host societies without losing their cultural particularity and become assimilated. On the other, success in the host societies often goes hand in hand with a growing sense of commitment and increased communication with the country of origin and the broader diasporic community (Bhabha, 1996; Brah, 1996; Anthias, 1998). The growing numbers of groups that find themselves living in multiple cultural, political and spatial contexts invite a reconceptualization of the diaspora. Such reconceptualization needs to address the global, transnational experience of diasporic groups and individuals who construct new and hybrid belongings, in relation to the country of origin, the country of settlement and through the routes of their diasporic journey (Gilroy, 1991, 1995; Clifford, 1997). The variety of diasporic cultural formations and spatial connections shows how diasporas are not bound in just one, stable and exclusive place, just one imagined community, but they are actually parts of various networks and communities while relating to at least two nation(-states)—the one of their origin and the one of their settlement. Diasporic experience includes at least one *journey*, mobility and, more and more, an everyday life that is informed by (and informs) more than one culture. Beck's suggestion for surpassing methodological nationalism and for analyzing social formations and practices beyond nation-centric discourses is challenging and relevant to the study of transnational cultures (2000, 2002). Multispatial and fragmented everyday lives require theoretical and methodological approaches that are not restrained within nation-centric analysis, but which, at the same time, avoid neophyte celebrations of postnational and postidentity fluid new worlds.

A SPATIAL PERSPECTIVE

The locus of our new reality and the cultural politics by which it must be confronted is that of space. (Fredric Jameson quoted in Morley and Robins, 1995: 37)

A space exists when one takes into consideration vectors of direction, velocities, and time variables. Thus space is composed of intersections of mobile elements. It is in a sense actuated by the ensemble of movements deployed within it. Space occurs as the effect produced by the operations that orient it, situate it, temporalize it, and make it function in a polyvalent unity of

> *confictual programs or contractual proximities. . . . In short, space is a practiced place.* (de Certeau, 1984: 117)

Space carries meanings, often conflicting and contradictory. It is fragmented and it is homogenous, it is consumed, like any other product in consumerist societies, but it is also involved in the production of work, transport, distribution and thus of culture and economy (Lefebvre, 2003). 'The concept of space links the mental and the cultural, the social and the historical. By reconstituting a complex process: *discovery* (of new or unknown spaces, of continents or of the cosmos)—*production* (of the spatial organization characteristic of each society)—*creation* (of *oeuvres*: landscape, the city with monumentality and décor)' (Lefebvre, 2003: 209). Space is real and/or virtual and imagined; its natural substance and boundedness are increasingly challenged as permanent characteristics. What space always carries are social meanings, and these are always plural. The meanings of the diasporic space are shaped in contexts of continuities, links and conflicts. The home, the public, the city, (the nation) and the transnational form the layers of the diasporic space where social relations, communication and action take place and shape the meanings of identity and community. Each of these elements of the diasporic space is an autonomous node and each has its own dynamics, its morality, economy, and its social and cultural meanings. The home or the city are not only defined in relation to the diasporic context or in relation to diasporic identities. They play multiple roles in the broader economic and cultural contexts of the locale, the nation and the global. However, in relation to diasporic identity and community they have a specific significance both in their autonomy and in their interconnection. 'Knowing where we are is as important as knowing who we are, and of course the two are intimately connected' argues Silverstone (1999: 86). It is this significance—in terms of symbols, meanings and communication—that is examined here.

In space, copresence and absences, participation and exclusion, as well as access, control and restrictions to economic and cultural resources—including communication technologies, media and network infrastructure—become both tools and contexts for constructing identities and for imagining communities. People experience the world from particular places and in the context of specific spaces. Places become nodes and spaces become contexts for drawing geographical and symbolic boundaries of *we*-ness and other-ness, for experiencing, remembering, imagining placement and displacement, for living the pains of deterritorialization, the promises of mobility and the opportunities and exclusions that come with (re-)settlement. Diaspora, as lived and as imagined, is largely dependent on the memory, experience and ideology of deterritorialization and reterritorialization. Diasporic populations live within specific locales—urban places especially—and in national and transnational spaces. The social interaction and communication within the diasporic communities, among dispersed sections of the same diaspora and beyond the limits of a diasporic community, all take place in space. Some of these spaces—also defined as ethnoscapes and mediascapes by Appadurai (1990, 1996)—are grounded in very specific places, such as the neighborhood, whereas others exist virtually and in nonplaces (Urry, 2000). Social interaction and relations are no longer dependent on simultaneous spatial copresence; there are also relations developing with the *absent other* through mediated communication. When place ceases from being a singular and restricting context for social relations, the experience of time and space becomes distanciated (Giddens, 1990) and diasporic communities break off the specificities and singularities of place and expand their potentials for communication and community. In this context, there is less and less a possibility for a neat equation between culture, community and geography (Gillespie, 1995) and increased potentials for 'imaginative geography and history' (Said, 1985). Diasporic family, community and global networks are increasingly sustained in connections and relations of *absent co-presence* become possible through mediated communication.

For diasporic populations, like for any other people, spheres of belonging begin with the intimate and immediate experience in what is called *home*. The domestic and the familial is the context where individuals start developing their sense of being and their position in the world. The home, being the starting point for identity construction and socialization, is only a node in a spatial scheme that expands to a number of spaces according to scale, levels of immediacy and intimacy, as well as in relation to imagination and social meanings. *Home*, however, in the case of the diaspora has a more complex meaning than in the case of other populations. There is a *home*, which equals the domestic and the familial, and there is a symbolic, imagined *home* that might be mythical, occupied, unreachable and/or connected to memories of exile and nostalgia. Images and sounds shared with other members of the home that bring closer together past and present, reconcile the inconsistencies between the lived and the imagined home.

Outside the home, particularity, similarity and difference get their meanings in relation to the others sharing that space; it is as much a matter of symbolic boundaries' construction between us and the others (Barth, 1969; Anthias, 2001) as it is about defining and imagining commonality and community. The public—the immediate, lived public outside the home—is the symbolic other leg in the binary private/public. It is the space where the intimate gets challenged by social rules and regulations, where identities are baptized and get their social meanings in a context of restrictions that surpass the immediate and protective familial sphere.

Everyday life in advanced capitalism depends on the separation of the public and the private. This separation–and its ideological basis—is incomplete and contradictory. The home/domestic is assumed to function as a private, protective, familiar sphere, yet it is inevitably linked to the public for the construction of the social meanings of its everyday. Everyday life— especially in advanced capitalist societies and as it is intensified with the expansion of communication technologies and the media—evolves around a paradoxical contradiction. On one hand, the dominant ideology promotes a clear division of the private and domestic from the public and common. On the other hand, the mediated public experience of consumption links the private and the public in a relation of inevitable interconnectivity. The walls of the home do not protect the private familial sphere from a clearly defined *outside*—the public—but they are flexibly molded inwards and outwards in appropriating products and information of the consumerist everyday. Consumption is primarily private and individual(istic), but its meanings are social and formed in the private-public dialectic.

The geography of social relations is changing as much as the relations between spaces. They often stretch out over defined spaces; yet, as Massey (1993) argues, social relations, movements and communication change, but they meet in places that become unique points of their intersection—geographical places become meeting places. One of those places, an important meeting point for diaspora, is the city. The multicultural and segmented urban is of key relevance in the production of diasporic cultures, especially because diasporic populations tend to concentrate in cities (Sennett, 1970; Sassen, 1999; Massey, 1999; Eade, 2000). Diasporic overconcentration in cities, often in parallel to a decrease of cities' native populations, raises many relevant issues, such as that of cultural visibility, social segregation and diasporic exclusion. Robins (2001) suggests that we should think through the city instead of through the nation; the city, he argues, is a more useful category of analysis, especially as it allows us to reflect on the cultural consequences of globalization from another than a national perspective. 'The nation, we may say, is a space of identification and identity, whilst the city is an existential and experimental space' (2001: 87). With reference to London—a reference that can extend to other culturally diverse metropoles—Robins argues that in the city people can re-think and redescribe their relation to culture and identity: '(T)he urban arena is about immersion in a world of multiplicity, and implicates us in the dimension of embodied, cultural experience' (2001: 87).

The particular dynamics of the city and of urban life, with its demographic diversity, its ethnic differences and its cultural heterogeneity allow diasporic populations, which are often excluded from the national representations and cultural production, to develop distinct, varied, co-existing and intermixing cultures. In the cities, different populations live together and, though not always in harmony, there is an overall popular awareness and consensus around diversity. The city becomes important for three reasons in the present discussion. Urban diversity allows more space for diasporic populations to develop and celebrate their cultural distinctiveness and particularity. Also, as the city is characterized by heterogeneity and co-existence of many different cultures, processes of cultural meeting and mixing take place. City demonstrates that cultural purity and closure are almost impossible and that all cultures are hybrid and dialectically linked to other cultural expressions around them. Thirdly, the autonomy of the city from the nation and the interconnection of cities in transnational networks show that diasporic populations spread across global cities sustain links and networks that are partly autonomous from the national contexts. Diasporic cultures are more urban and cross-urban cultures than national.

The city finds itself in a position of increasing tension with the nation. Especially in the case of global cities, cultural and economic autonomy directly challenges the boundedness and the dependence of the local urban and its people from the national context and its definitions of culture and (national) identity (Sassen, 2001). Yet, as the nation still stands as a bounded entity of concentrated power and control over economy and culture, it cannot be undermined or ignored. In the words of Lefebvre: 'a new space tends to develop, at a world scale, integrating and disintegrating the national and the local. A process full of contradictions, linked with the conflict between a division of labor on the planetary level, in the mode of capitalist production—and the effort to create another, more rational world order' (2003: 212).

The role of the nation, standing as the primary defining power of social and political relations in modernity, is increasingly challenged through recent processes of deterritorialization, mobility and networking (Urry, 2000; Hannerz, 2002; Beck, 2002). The national has been challenged by the regeneration of the local, which, in its particularity, learns from the diversity and the fluidity of the global, as this is primarily experienced in everyday life and through mediations and media(-ted) discourses (Appadurai, 1996; Friedman, 1995; Rantanen, 2004). The world gets more and more tied together (Harvey, 1989) and 'increasingly we are the decentered subjects of, and find ourselves subject to not simply the cultural unity of a particular ethnic community, but simultaneously, other infranational cultures as well as national, regional, transnational, perhaps even inter-continental cultures' (Smart, 1993: 144). Thus, it is not only the political power of the nation that is challenged, but also 'the imagery articulated with it (coherent communities and consistent subjectivities . . . dominant centers and distant margins) seems less convincing and appropriate' (Smart, 1993: 145).

In this book and in unraveling the elements of the diasporic space, the nation usually appears in brackets. This is the case for a number of reasons, none of them indicating an adoption of the premature and celebratory discourse about the 'death of the nation.' This visual (re)presentation of the nation aims at illustrating its position as an interruption and a disharmony in the scheme of the diasporic space. Whereas among the other nodes of diasporic space there is a—partial at least—continuity, the nation appears more as a disruption and a restriction. The nation, which in modernity is formalized as a nation-state, depends on ideologies and practices of clear-cut limits and requires the formation of identities and communities within defined borders and territory (Holton, 1998). As much as communication becomes deterritorialized, similarly the national boundaries become increasingly reinforced. The physical contains and grounds the mediated; the mediated 'freedom of flows' is not liberating but contested, as it is grounded by the constraining powers of the physical and the national (Bauman, 1998). The nation-state aims at sustaining its power and legitimacy based on ideologies of singularity—of singular loyalties, of the singularity of the national space ownership and of clear-cut borders. Diaspora challenges national ideologies, but it often finds itself trapped in them. The nation-state of origin requires loyalty and commitment, so does the nation-state of settlement. The nation-state in modernity—and this has not changed in late modernity as radically as is often claimed—forms its own project of progress and harmony based on social, economic and, inevitably, cultural assimilation of its population. It is in this context that cultural difference—as often expressed in diasporic cultural ideologies and practices—is marginalized, excluded and alienated within countries hosting diasporic populations.

The nation still needs to appear in the contextualizing scheme of diasporic belonging. Even as a source of restrictions and ideological polarization (e.g., expressed in discourses of nationalism, demands for singular loyalty, legitimating of national military power), it should be acknowledged as an element of the diasporic space for at least two reasons. On one hand, in democratic societies, national laws (should) protect (diasporic) minorities from discrimination, racism and exclusion and thus they (should) broaden their participation in multiethnic societies. On the other hand, restrictions, polarizations and exclusions initiated in the actual practices and ideologies of the nation play their part in the construction of identities. Identities are not shaped only through positive and creative processes of participation and communion, but also in processes of exclusion, marginalization and regressive ideologies—expressed in the mainstream ideologies of the country of settlement or of the country of origin, but also voiced from within the diasporic communities.

The national is a space of political and cultural restrictions and of negotiation and establishment of formal rights and duties; it is a space of a constant struggle between processes of diasporic social and cultural inclusion and exclusion. The space that is almost homologous to diaspora is the transnational. Transnational is not equal to the global, though it does relate to many common uses of *the global* in the literature. The transnational acknowledges the development and sustaining of connections and networks across geographical, cultural and political borders (Basch, Schiller and Blanc-Szanton, 1994), while at the same time it recognizes the interconnection and co-existence of the local, the national and the global. The transnational emphasizes the possibility for development of meaningful relations and social formations across borders and through the development of dense networks (Portes, 1997). As such, it is particularly relevant for understanding the processes by which migrant and diasporic communities forge and sustain multistranded social relations. The transnational is more meaningful than the global, especially in the context of the present discussion. It recognizes both the possibilities of networks and communities to surpass national boundaries, as well as the continuing significance of the national borders in partly framing and restricting social actions and their meanings. Furthermore, the transnational lacks the utopian connotations often attached to the global, which equate it to the universal.

It is in the context of transnationalism that contemporary theorizations of diaspora become useful in thinking of continuity, community and attachment across space. Although diaspora is a contested concept—having at times implied ethnic homogeneity and identity essentialism—in debates around globalization, transnationalism and communication, diaspora has been re-appropriated to recognize heterogeneity and diversity, transformation and difference (Hall, 1990; Clifford, 1994). Transnational diasporic communities challenge the binary opposition global/local, while their practices and multiple positionings invite us to think of counterhegemonic spaces and alternative forms of (selective) community participation and re-articulation of identities.

Diasporic identities are shaped in these different spaces, which are interconnected and sometimes distinct and competing. The diversity and different levels of intensity of spatial belongings reflect the multidimensionality of identities, that coexist, codepend and which cannot be holistic or framed within a single place any more. Even a single identity, like the diasporic, is not singular and remains viable only through the multiple interweaving of different spaces and relations of belonging. Additionally, for diasporic identity, spatiality is of particular importance, as processes of deterritorialization and reterritorialization shape them through experience and as context. Diasporic experience, either as lived or as collective memory, is the outcome of deterritorialization, of an interrupted relation of people with specific lands. As people are deterritorialized, they are reterritorialized in new lands, in new localities. As transnational movement and networks develop though, this reterritorialization does not only involve a new nation-state and a new (urban) locality, but also the country of origin. The process of reterritorialization takes place simultaneously in more than one place (Appadurai in Bell, 1999). Each place is constructed and deconstructed in relation to the other, through the pressures and the new possibilities created by new spatial politics.

MEDIA AND COMMUNICATION PRACTICES

Communication across territories and even more, communication at specific locations, has always been a process tightly interlinked with the construction of identities and communities. Mediated communication, as it initially developed through the press and later in radio, television and more recently in the Internet, has become a component of modernity itself. As Anderson's seminal *Imagined Communities* (1983) has initially shown, sharing common media advances the sense of belonging in a common project—that of the nation in his analysis. Media as means/technologies/contexts for communication in specific locations and beyond, have become institutions and organized mechanisms of great significance for constructing identities in local, national and transnational contexts within modernity. Interpersonal and nonmediated communication[2] have not lost their significance for identity and community; however, mediated communication has altered mechanisms, qualities and outcomes of communication processes in more than one way. When talking about 'the media' here I refer to the organized forms of mediated communication that involve more than interpersonal communication and its means. The specific focus is on electronic media—radio, television, and the Internet—as these media have overshadowed other older forms of communication systems—such as the press—with their popularity. Diasporic populations still read the press and engage with it but electronic media in their nature are more compatible with diaspora.

Electronic media, like diaspora, may cover small and large territories, shift between topics of interest, languages, and locations of broadcasting/narrowcasting, while they advance orality and visuality against the literacy demanded for press reading. In the years that this research was conducted, the numbers of participants who turn to press greatly decreased and those of people turning to the Internet and satellite television exploded. The press is still available in libraries and community centers and is always a welcome offering for a fraction of media users. However, the sociality and intense interactions that once took place around newsstands, now increasingly take place around television screens.

Electronic media saturate diasporic space, and mediated communication plays a growing role in defining the meanings, uses and appropriations of cultural and social space. Media might be more or less visible, but they are more and more present in the processes of representing and communicating identity and community. Especially as communication technologies increasingly allow fragmentation and diversity in mediascapes (Appadurai, 1996), they bring images of distant cultures close, they assist the development of *absent copresences*, they allow the recombination and the re-appropriation of the distant in relation to the immediate, they represent and mediate meanings of localities, diasporas, *homeland*s and communities. Media might lead to the rediscovery of diasporic identities, as they become the new carriers and carers of communal communication. Local media become a new kind of *gossip*, a more effective mediator of the word of mouth (Riggins, 1992). Diasporic media reinforce and rediscover the meaning of the locality, the community, the diasporic belonging of populations; they surpass the limitations of the body (Turkle, 1995) and place.

Broadcasting media and the Internet in particular, while using new technologies, bring together the different spaces of belonging in an unprecedented way (Jones, 1995; Holmes, 1997; Georgiou, 2006). Such media renew and reproduce diverse and multiple images of identity and community, only available as scattered and limited information to members of diasporas in the past. The media negotiate spatial and temporal limitations, simultaneously dealing with the roots and the routes of diaspora (Gilroy, 1995). Media suggest new ways of shaping belonging, beyond conventional restrictions between the real and the virtual (Turkle, 1995) in two ways: in the representations produced and in their consumption. Media cultures are formed around the growing significance of audiencehood. Everybody is a member of an audience—as much as everyone can be a member of the spectacle. As diasporic cultures and media cultures become more interwoved, the boundaries of the local and the global, of the public and the private are challenged and the limits of diasporic imagination expand across the globe and through transnational networks. As Abercrombie and Longhurst argue:

> Diffused audiences are both local and global, local in actual performance, global in that imagination—not restricted in space and time—is a crucial resource in the performance. Performances for diffused audiences are public and private. Indeed, they erode the difference between the two. (1998: 76)

In media cultures social interaction and relations are no longer dependent on simultaneous spatial copresence (Gillespie, 1995; Friedman, 1995;

Lull, 2000). The media renegotiate and represent diasporic copresence and a common past through images, which shape the (selective) renewed and contemporary collective memory and provide repertoires for the construction of new individual and communal identities.

Multicentered and Mediated Everyday Life

The everyday is shaped in the complex, interlinked mediated spaces of diasporic life. The local, the public, the urban, (the national) and the transnational are spaces where information is neither linear nor singular; they are spaces where possibilities for belonging, for choosing not to belong and for combining belonging in multiple communities emerge. They are spaces where the struggles for inclusion and exclusion are not between two sides—those of the powerful and the subordinate—but between different powerful and subordinate actors. Media actively get involved in everyday life debates of what it means to belong, of what identification with a group consists of, what the symbols of the imagined self, the Other and the community are, and how the boundaries around communities and places are appropriated.

Diasporic media can become powerful mouthpieces of the community they represent and they can create powerful images of self-representation for the group (Husband, 1994; Cottle, 2000; King and Wood, 2001). They can also become symbols of empowerment and potentially mediate a group's participation in the public sphere of the country where they live, in the public sphere of their country of origin and in transnational public spheres that emerge across boundaries. Such potentials for participation and inclusion in communities, for the widening possibility of being informed and part of an interpretative diasporic community are advanced by information and communication technologies. Digitalization has increased the potentials for the development of alternative, small-scale, community media—though so has the competition for audiences' attention. The cost for developing and sustaining alternative media has decreased substantially; so has their boundedness and spatial specificity.

Through the possibilities for production and consumption of different media, multisited and decentralized media cultures emerge. The meanings of spatial and temporal restrictions and boundaries are constantly challenged and redefined in media production and consumption—as images of a distant *homeland* are disseminated on satellite television, as the image of the distant family is reinvented on a homemade website, as the sound of a friend's newborn baby is mediated and at the same time immediately consumed on home video. The immediacy of access to images and sounds that once would be unreachable, the mediation of the experience and the way both are appropriated, allow the media to become part of the everyday. Media do not just 'fit in' a pre-existing everyday—they alter repertoires, methods and practiced communication. As Thompson (1995) argues for mediation's role in (re-)shaping social interaction:

> We can understand the social impact of the development of new net-works of communication and information flow only if we put aside the intuitively plausible idea that communication media serve to transmit information and symbolic content to individuals whose relations to others remain fundamentally unchanged. We must see, instead, that the use of communication media involves the creation of new forms of action and interaction in the social world, new kinds of social relation-ship and new ways of relating to others and to oneself. When individ-uals use communication media, they enter into forms of interaction which differ in certain respect from the type of face-to-face interaction which characterizes most encounters in daily life. They are able to act for others, who are physically absent, or act in response to others who are situated in distant locales. (1995: 4)

A TRANSATLANTIC CASE STUDY

This book develops a narrative and an argument about the continuous rel-evance of the increasingly mediated diasporic space for identity and com-munity. In doing this it draws from a transnational case study in London and New York. This study focused on the Greek Cypriot diasporic group, which is spread across the globe. This group has a substantial and distinct presence in London. Though in the American context, the specific group is small, it is fully integrated in the visible Greek community of New York; as such, it plays a cultural role within the multiethnic setting of New York City and the diverse American society. This diasporic group, settled and integrated in the two global cities, becomes an interesting case study for a number of reasons. As a group it sustains a distinct identity and communi-ty life in local and transnational scale, while constructing and rediscovering its particularity in the combination of intense local community and highly mediated transnational cultural life and communications. This is also a group that enjoys a rich and diverse collection of diasporic media produced in the country of origin, in the locale, in transnational spaces. Additionally, it is one of those groups that are found in the interesting position of in-betweeness, because of being defined as *white*.

   Greek Cypriots form one of the *white* minorities in London and New York. *White* minorities are understudied, as they do not fit into the traditional division between the white majority-black minority, dominating race and ethnicity studies (McDonald, 1972). White ethnicity raises issues that race and ethnicity studies tend to ignore. As much as non-white ethnicity is primarily defined in terms of visibility—the social and symbolic visibility of the color black in opposition to the taken-for-granted white—the definition of *whiteness* depends on invisibility. The hegemony of the social color *White* (Morrison, 1992; Drzewiecka and Wong (Lau), 1999; Stratton 2000a, 2000b) is reflected in perceptions about ethnicity being an identifier of the usually visibly different minority groups. What *white* ethnicity consists of and how it is formed are questions only recently raised. *White* identities, as well as any other, are contextual and the outcome of relations of power (Fanon, 1986; Frankenberg, 1997; Nakayama and Martin, 1999). Jewish became *white* after their integration in the American society, Stratton argues (2000a, 2000b). Populations such as the English in Britain and the WASPS in the United States, who were always identified as *white*, are rarely consider to be ethnic groups, but are seen as the norm, as a natural majority. Media are central in representing whiteness and racial hierarchies (Hall, 1981; Dyer, 1988; Gabriel, 1998).

As the ethnic/racial color *white* has long been understudied, scholars turn to everyday experience, its representation and enactment (Shome, 1999) in order to examine its sociopsychological dimensions. Shome (1999) emphasizes the discursiveness of *Whiteness* and its dependence on cultural space and time, as well as the importance of Eurocentrism for its establishment as the norm. Johnson (1999) subscribes to this approach, emphasizing in particular the role of communication for the construction of meanings of *Whiteness* and the *White*. These meanings, he adds, exceed the biological characteristics that constitute white skin. Like Jewish people, Cypriots became *white* in the diaspora and vis-à-vis other diasporic and migrant populations. Greek Cypriots embraced the dominant Europeanism against other non-European groups, gaining from the aura of the Greek cultural heritage. However, in their majority they arrived in the Western metropoles as economic migrants, like most migrants from the developing world. Adopted and projected *Whiteness* and Europeanism allowed Greek Cypriots—and Greeks—to position themselves in a higher place within the ethnic/racial British and American hierarchy.

Whiteness made integration easier and has had an impact in the formation of diasporic identities, not so much as an outcome of opposition with the dominant—*white*—majority, but primarily as a transnational, cultural project of particularity within *Whiteness*. Within the Greek Cypriot (hybrid) imagined community, diasporic identities are formed and informed by the change and the mobility that characterize different subgroups' experience through time and space. Change and mobility allow Greek Cypriot ethnicity to remain an unforceful and ordinary performance for most. Mobility and change even allow groups whose multiple identities challenge cultural traditions to negotiate identities, not to reject them. Their positioning in the locale and the diaspora varies. For the migrant generation, this positioning has being the outcome of a directly experienced—and usually painful—deterritorialization. For the new generations, North London and Astoria, New York City are their primary physical and cultural spaces of belonging, even if identities are still informed by the dominant diasporic discourse of deterritorialization.

London and New York: Greek Cypriot Diasporic Settlement

Cyprus became a country of extensive emigration, especially during two specific historical periods (Leeuwenbug, 1979; Oakley, 1979, 1989; King and Bridal, 1982; Costantinides, 1984; Mintoff-Bland, 1987; Hassiotis, 1989; Mettis, 1998; Koupparis, 1999). The first wave of large migration took place in the 1950s during the period of decolonization and the creation of the new Cypriot independent state. Poverty and deprivation, especially among rural populations led to mass migration to the former colonial ruler—Britain. Smaller waves of migrants took the American route. Migrants to the United Kingdom and the United States followed the small-scale Cypriot migration of the early 20th century. The second significant wave from Cyprus to Britain and the United States, followed the 1974 invasion of Cyprus by Turkish troops. With hundreds of thousands of refugees and the country struggling with the island's post-division economic restructuring, thousands were forced to leave Cyprus (King and Bridal, 1982; Anthias, 1992). In both cases, the already established ethnic networks in the diaspora become significant initial points of reference that enabled the economic and cultural integration of the new migrants. A more recent and much smaller wave of migration includes the expert migrants—that is, people who settled in the two countries after completing their studies there or after finding work as experts in managerial and scientific professions. This latest group is proportionately more numerous in the United States.

In the American case, Greek Cypriots settled within the already large and established Greek communities. There is limited accurate information available on the numbers of Cypriots settled in the United States; according to the most reliable estimates they number between 45-50,000 across the country (Zoupaniotis, 2004). More accurate data is available about the Greek communities (Greek Cypriots are often recorded as part of the large Greek American population). Greek Americans are estimated at over one million (Moskos, 1990) across the United States. About half of them live in the broader New York region, and at least 30,000 are based in Astoria, the northwestern part of Queens, New York City (Gumpert and Drucker, 1998). The Cypriot migrants of the 1950s and 1960s settled into a Greek community of migrants who had already established themselves in certain areas of the service economy, especially catering and tailoring (Panayiotopoulos, 1996). In time, Greek Americans have become some of the most prosperous and successful migrant communities. Since the last quarter of the 20th century, Greek Americans have gained both economic and political power, with some of them reaching the highest ranks of the economic and political ranks. Greek Americans—and within them, Greek Cypriot Americans—have developed a sense of ethnic pride and cultural power in the American mainstream as they embraced the hegemonic ideologies of nationalism, capitalism and *the melting pot.*[3] The group that settled on British soil has shaped its identity within rather different historical and cultural circumstances. London Greek Cypriots have landed in colonial/postcolonial Britain at times of mass migration from the (former) colonies. The cultural and political realities that led to the development of the British multicultural model meant that migrant communities were not required to assimilate and demonstrate loyalty to the nation as in the American case. The differences between nation-states are, at least partly, reflected in the differences observed in the two cities studied: New York City (Astoria, Queens) and North London. Astoria's demographics reflect the extensive ethnic segregation dominant in the American case, whereas the North London location reflects the intense meeting and mixing of various populations. Ideologies of nationhood are also observed in their small neighborhood scale at both locations. American flags are visible across Astoria, though British flags are a rarity in the culturally mixed North London, where diversity is celebrated in ideology and in practice. At the same time, the two localities have many similarities. They are both working class settings that serve as centers for diasporic populations living locally or in the suburbs. These urban localities host a collection of *ethnic* grocery stores, community centers, bars and restaurants. The commonality of the urban cultural interface extends to communication. Both locations are nodes in transnational networks. Technologies that connect the specific locations with other places—for example, Internet, satellite television—are very popular. Additionally, the urban locations as nodes consist of mechanisms that reinforce communication competency and intensity in a web of connections in local and transnational level. In both New York City and London, these include homes, local media, community organizations, entertainment industries, travel industries, and more.

Similarities and differences relate to national mainstreams and urban demographics, but also to ethnocultural and historical particularities. Those who settled in Britain found themselves among a predominantly Cypriot community, whereas the ones who reached the American shores settled into migrant communities dominated by migrants from Greece. Though in both cases Greek ethnicity and language have been key self-identifiers, the cultural domination of the Greeks from the mainland in the United States meant that the group defined itself primarily in the context of a (mainland) Greekness.[4] On the contrary, in the case of Britain, Greek Cypriots kept a distinct and strong sense of Cypriotness, firstly connected to Cyprus and secondarily to Greece (Constantinides, 1984). Saying that, identification with ethnicity and origin always shifts in both countries, depending on political and cultural contexts and developments.

Overall, Cypriot migration had Britain as its predominant destination. A large number of Greek Cypriots is concentrated and established in North London. Their established presence is, on one hand, the outcome of a numerical visibility—70 percent of the estimated 160,000-220,000[5] Greek Cypriots in Britain lives in London, mostly in the northern boroughs, and on the other, it is the reflection of an established and thriving community. In North London, Greek Cypriots live in predominately working class, multicultural pockets of the borough of Haringey, next to other minority groups that include Turkish Cypriots, Turks, Kurds, and more recent arrivals from Eastern Europe and Africa. Geographical concentration, marriage within the group, establishment of diasporic institutions including churches, schools and the media, as well as the extensive development of a local economy with shops, restaurants and businesses reflect the local dimensions of this community. At the same time, political lobbying for the Cyprus problem, participation of community leaders in British/American and international (diasporic) fora, strong links with Cyprus and the survival and reproduction of traditional values in life within and outside the group are some of the characteristics of a community that reproduces a distinct symbolic territory in local and transnational spaces.

Community and identity depend as much on the communal and the public experience as they do on the personal, domestic and private life. Thus, as the family is the dominant unit within the group—cherished and reproduced in new Greek (Cypriot) marriages—it becomes a strong cultural identifier and an everyday mechanism communicating traditional cultural values to the younger generations. As the support and the suppression of intense and intimate relations are sustained within the family, they become mundane references and somehow reproduce a sense of natural and inescapable particularity. 'There's no way I'd marry a foreigner (sic). He wouldn't understand our traditions, our lifestyle,' an 18-year-old British-born Greek Cypriot female participant says, emphasizing cultural continuity. Even when people end up in an interethnic marriage, they often reproduce traditional values and lifestyle. A 37-year-old male, son of a Greek Cypriot and an Italian and now married to a Serb, is an active member of many Cypriot organizations and networks. When asked if he was equally involved in the British Italian cultural life, he got annoyed: 'Do I look like an Italian?!' The high level of mass attendance in Orthodox churches and Greek Sunday school activities is another illustration of the cultural association of Greek (Cypriots) with a community life in the American cities and suburbia. This is even the case in many suburban neighborhoods, where mixed marriages predominate. Popular fiction books and films such as *My Big Fat Greek Wedding* (2003), Sedaris' *Naked* (1998) and *Me Talk Pretty One Day* (2001) and British Cypriot Eve Makis' *Eat, Drink and Be Married* (2004) reflect, in a satirical (even if stereo-typed) way, the density and continuity of Greek community life in Britain and the United States.

The extensive concentration in urban locales, which is reproduced in suburban middle-class second-generation habitats, keeps people in a vital and living relationship with Greekness and Cypriotness. Ethnicity becomes a lived experience every time people buy Cypriot bread from a local shop, every time they pass by the Greek Orthodox church, every time they talk to their Greek neighbor and every time they listen to the local Greek radio. At the same time, their diasporic experience is not only local, but it is not the same as the experience of people who live in Cyprus either. The shop that sells Cypriot bread also sells cheese from Turkey and fruit from the Caribbean. The local community center welcomes not only Greek Cypriots but also Turkish Cypriots. Greek Cypriots in the diaspora construct their identities in new terms, through new diasporic relations with Others, the Others that once lived thousands of miles away, or the Others that were once close but were called enemies. New hybrid ethnic-ities[6] are shaped at the meeting of the old and the new, the local and the global and they are not the same as the identities once shaped in a distant *homeland*.

Thriving traditional institutions in the two cities, such as churches, schools, family and kinship networks give the vague idea of community flesh and blood. They allow for bonding of the community, even if people interpret this bonding in different ways. 'We know each other. People care for each other . . . and even if they don't, at least they know of each other's existence,' is the interpretation of *community* for a 57-year-old Greek Cypriot. A 26-year-old woman gives a more negative interpretation, which, however, still acknowledges the existence of a community of people who care for each other's existence, even if this concern is negative: 'Everybody talks behind your back. . . Everybody competes with each other . . . Every wedding is a contest to make it look better and fancier than the next. . . .'

Community becomes meaningful in many ways. *The community* becomes a narrative and an (imaginary) context where commonly shared values and ethics are introduced and imposed in everyday life. As ethnici-ty depends on preserving a sense of distinct difference, community is the virtual and real entity where the boundaries between the insiders and the Others are confirmed. Furthermore, as the diasporic content becomes increasingly diverse, community turns into a symbolic and bonding context of belonging, where the sense of commonality is preserved. As much as traditional institutions and structures, such as the churches and the family, remain important for constructing a sense of common belonging and shared identities, new hybrid spaces and the media become increasingly relevant. Traditional institutions still have a significant role because, at the same time, other alternative spaces address diverse and hybrid expressions of ethnicity (e.g., pubs and clubs that have become Greek Cypriot hangouts). Then the media become the meeting point of the traditional and the hybrid, as they play the communication role that word of mouth once used to have; they mediate, translate and represent the multiplicity of a particular(istic) cultural discourse.

A HYBRID IMAGINED COMMUNITY?

Neither diasporic identity nor the media should be taken as stable and unquestionable reference for people who have the same origin or share Greek-looking names and surnames. I met people who think that Greek Cypriotness is completely irrelevant to their experience, though their parents migrated from Cyprus. I met others who defended their diasporic identity as a point of reference that they could not image themselves without, though they rejected the idea of tuning into any of the Cypriot media. Yet, most of the Greek Cypriots I met in the two cities would identify with neither of the two extremes. Most identify themselves as members of a community and admit they consume to a smaller or larger extent some media that relate to the diasporic community. In these people's words and in their everyday life, as observed and recorded, neither the community context nor the media are considered as unproblematic and unquestioned references.

As participants' crude honesty reveals in words and in actual everyday practice, ethnicity remains significant, as long as it is relevant and meaningful to them. One of them, a 38-year old British-born male solicitor, who works for a Greek Cypriot firm, illustrates this dependence: 'Greek Cypriots are always in contact, they socialize and do business together . . . we keep on with our culture. Younger people use the ideas and practices of the first generation when they do business . . . not as much as the older people do, but there's still a strong connection.' Many people highlighted in their talk and reconfirmed in their everyday life that they depend on the psychological, social and economic diasporic networks in local, national and transnational level. When young people turn to their parents for childcare support, they renew their own belonging in diasporic networks and initiate their children's *induction* to a particular community. When individuals coming from the same village in Cyprus organize outings and dances, they reconfirm their *diasporic sociality*. 'We have our dance twice a year. It's great. It's a great chance to reconnect with people we haven't seen in years. . . .We catch up . . . we gossip . . . we find out how our fellow villagers are doing,'says a middle-aged female member of a Cypriot village association[7] in words that reconfirm the meaningfulness of diaspora as everyday experience, practice and bonding mechanism.

Diasporic connectivity, commonality and community get their meanings as the divisions, exclusions and oppositions still shape the broader society and people turn to subgroups and communities for all different kinds of support (Guibernau and Rex, 1997; Modood, Berthoud *et al.* 1997; Tufte and Riis, 2001). The search for emotional and/or financial support, for stability and for particularity highlights the significance of community. But the meanings and the experience of community, like those of diaspora and identity, have changed radically in capitalist societies. And media have gained a central role for communication within the new imagined community (of the nation) (Anderson, 1983). Community has also changed in global times, in ways that challenge Anderson's dichotomy. He argues that mediated communication is central to the construction of imagined communities in capitalism, as opposed to the domination of face-to-face interaction in precapitalist communities. This dichotomy is challenged as the local remains—or has become—important for sustaining a sense of community. But as the local is not self-contained and completely autonomous in global times, community is not strictly dependent on face-to-face communication either. 'Ethnicity, once a genie contained in the bottle of some sort of locality—however large—has now become a global force, forever slipping in and through the cracks between states and borders,' Appadurai writes (1990: 306).

The study shows that a new form of community, a *hybrid imagined community*, is emerging. In this community, belonging is achieved, strengthened and renewed through mediated communication, but in parallel with immediate and face-to-face communication and while people belong to many other communities at the same time. When Greek Cypriots go together to local schools and community centers, when in their everyday media and in communication technologies' choices they get in touch with people in North London, Astoria, in Cyprus and in the rest of the diaspora, their sense of belonging is shaped at the meeting of local and transnational spaces. This imagined community is hybrid, as it is decentralized and its decentralization challenges the taken-for-grantedness of the nation and of nationalism. It is hybrid because in its transnationality it recognizes the inescapable multiple belonging of its members that are no longer members of a single community. In its hybridity, this community constructs new mechanisms to keep and renew people's belonging: these involve old community mechanisms and imagined community mechanisms. This is where the church meets satellite technology, where the Greek language meets computer language and Internet lingo.

The media have become major players for the emergence of a hybrid imagined community, and it is this community context where diasporic identities are shaped and reshaped. Electronic media, such as the local radio and television, the satellite Greek channels and the Internet, have become assertive players in the emergence of hybrid imagined communities, as they bring together the various spaces of belonging. As electronic media are both local and transnational, they surpass the boundedness of geographical positionings and allow people to shape belonging beyond singular categorizations: diaspora is constructed through experiencing being here, there and in-between (Gillespie, 1995; Baumann, 1996; Naficy, 1993, 1999). At the same time, the multiplicity of diasporic images presented in the media, the interactivity of the new media and the simultaneity in broadcasting beyond spatial limitations allow the daily renewal of relations between dispersed homes and transnational positions.

In their communal consumption, diasporic people appropriate shared representations, they construct codes of communication and set boundaries between Us and the Others. *We know, We understand, We share* (the media); the shared experience of communities as audiences gives content to their commonality; diasporic media renew the sense of sharing a common identity among dispersed populations; they shape a common cultural discourse. They help the development of *imagined presences* (Urry, 2000), of '[nonnational] communities of sentiment and interpretation' (Gilroy, 1995: 17). Media 'images can connect local experiences with each other and hence provide powerful sources of hermeneutic interpretation to make sense of what would otherwise be disparate and apparently unconnected events and phenomena' (Urry, 2000: 180).

The imaginative (co)presence, next to the real and immediate copresence, the daily interaction and participation in diasporic homes and publics, becomes the basis for constructing a multilayered belonging in an imagined community that crosses geographical boundaries. The mediated and the immediate come together into a hybrid imagined community; it is a community that is informed by changes in communication, in mobility and allegiances in local and transnational levels. It is a hybrid imagined community, as it is not bound within specific geographical boundaries. It is hybrid because it does not require exclusive belonging or holistic conforming to the community's rules. It is hybrid because it does not rely exclusively on the mediated imagining of belonging: it only becomes viable as it is informed by both the shared mediated discourses and the nonmediated discourses shaped by immediate and face-to-face communication, participation in traditional institutions and adoption/adaptation of traditional values.

Nevertheless, it is a community with boundaries—if not geographical, boundaries of the values and expectations of and from its members. For the hybrid imagined community, these boundaries have become more flexible and more reflexive because the interpretations of diasporic symbols are now more diverse; because they are challenged by discourses beyond the particular community, such as the mainstream media, nonethnic institutions and alternative contexts of everyday life. Representations have also expanded to include those produced by the group and by Others, representations produced in the local, the diasporic context, that of the distant *homeland*. Representations of diaspora are more decentralized in the hybrid imagined community; so are interpretations and appropriations. As there is increased decentralization in communities and fragmentation in everyday life, identities change. As will be shown, though, commonality still remains vital for most. Media and communication practices are in the heart of the everyday that is lived in local, national and transnational spaces and shaped through continuity and change.

The case study presented here illustrates how these processes take place in everyday life; how diverse subgroups renew their sense of belonging and perform their identities while using certain media and communication technologies; how people communally use particular media—an action that becomes a bonding activity by itself; how they negotiate both the boundaries of community and of the media to make them compatible with their everyday lives and their positioning in the local, the urban and the transnational space. This research seeks an ethnographic understanding of diaspora, identity and the media and is informed by the contextualization of media consumption in everyday life.[8] In order to understand the processes of diasporic identity construction and media consumption they both need to be positioned next to and against other identities and other activities of everyday life. Studying diasporic identities and diasporic media has a parallel starting point. People do not have to use diasporic media and they do not have to *have* diasporic identities.[9] To understand continuities, discontinuities, changes in identities and media consumption, I turn to concepts such as hybridity, community and connectivity. The diversity of the Greek Cypriot experience as lived in public and private, in diasporic and nondiasporic spaces, was studied ethnographically, taking into consideration generation, gender and age diversity especially, while being sensitive to people's other identities, politics, and lifestyle. This study examines how diversity comes together in the context of a community to produce and reproduce diasporic identities. It examines how media gain their everyday role in people's life. It investigates how their consumption allows the diaspora to (re)discover and (re)shape identities that are compatible and relevant to a transnational cultural and social present condition.

TWO ───────────────────────────

EVERYDAY LIFE

The Context of Diasporic Experience—
The Context of Research

> . . . *in the everyday our lives become meaningful, and without those mean-*
> *ings and without understanding those meanings and properly locating*
> *them within social space, we who participate (and also observe) will miss*
> *the dynamics of the social, and fail to comprehend its politics* (Silverstone,
> 1994: 164)

Everyday life is the context for social relations and network construction;
everyday life is where habits and routines get established, where individuals and groups become involved in struggles for control of cultural production and consumption, and where identities take their shape in interaction
with human (like members of a community) and nonhuman (like media
and communication technologies) cultural actors. Everyday life is a site of
contestation, a site of action, a site of subordination and alienation as much
as it is a site of resistance (de Certeau, 1984). Everyday life is a site where
creativity and authenticity fight an unequal battle (though not completely
lost) against forces of inequality and exclusion, which establish their control through the alienating systems of controlled consumption (Lefebvre,
1991). Marxists and cultural theorists especially have contributed in developing a sociological analysis of everyday life. The everyday is analyzed in
two ways. For those who emphasize capitalistic domination, everyday life
is a site where the results of economic relations become visible in alienat-

ing social living, class stratification and exclusion. From a more optimistic—and I would argue more dialectical—position, authors such as de
Certeau (1984), Lefebvre (1991), Bourdieu (1984) and Roberts (2003) see
everyday life as a site of conflict and contestation. This is where *the weak*
contest capitalistic domination and alienation in subversive and alternative
forms of production and consumption. Although such approaches emphasize the dominant alienating effects of capitalism, they still recognize the
potential for resistance. Lefebvre (1991) for example emphasizes the orig-
inality and the creativity in everyday life as a site where capitalism is still
challenged. For de Certeau, the emphasis lies on the complex dynamics of
consumption. Consumption, it is argued, is not just about alienation and
domination, but also about creative and alternative forms of resistance.

The everyday becomes a context for theoretical analysis, as it is a terrain where the dynamics of social action and interaction find their expressions, especially through consumption. Inevitably and increasingly, the
study of everyday life becomes interested in communication processes and
the media. More and more media and communication technologies are
integrated with domestic and public life, they mediate and inform daily
interaction and talk; they (re-)produce relations of time and space (Morley,
1991; Silverstone, 1993, 1994). In their representations they promote particular political, economic and social values and in their social use they
bring people together in sharing common discourses and shaping identities
in communal relations and communal consumption.

Everyday life is shaped and it is shaping cultural contexts in particular
times and at specific spaces. Increasingly the space of everyday life is
transnational. Consumption patterns and meanings, interaction and mobility and technological and communication flows challenge the boundedness
of everyday life at home, in the locale or the national context. The mundane becomes a terrain of contestation between the socioeconomic context
and the immediate lived cultural life. The present discussion primarily
draws from the analysis of everyday life offered by de Certeau (1984) and
Silverstone (1994). De Certeau (1984) emphasizes everyday life as a terrain of contradictions, oppositions, resistance and alienation, though he is
at times overly optimistic in his argument about the potentials of resistance. In discussing the potentials of resistance, Silverstone (1994) talks
about the dynamism of everyday life, while considering, more than de
Certeau, the overwhelmingly alienating power of capitalistic ethos and
consumption as initially discussed by Adorno and Benjamin. In this light,
Silverstone emphasizes the paradox of the everyday and how important it
is to study this paradox through empirical research:

And the terms of that paradox—the found object and the created
object—the imposed meanings and the selected meanings—the con-

trolled behaviour and the free—the meaningless and the meaningful—
the passive and the active—are in constant tension. These tensions can
be observed in everyday behaviour and traced through the study of the
individual and the group. They can be deciphered through ethnographic or psychoanalytic case studies—studies which must be firmly
grounded in the mutuality of empirical and theoretical understanding.
For it is in the dynamics of the particular that we will be able to identify, if not fully comprehend, the forces of structure: the forces both of
domination and resistance. (1994: 164)

In this book, everyday life is studied in its particularity and its ambiguity,
as it is shaped at the meeting of the working and the leisure time and space,
at the meeting of the private and the public, at the meeting of the individual and the communal. Everyday life is critically approached in its material invisibility, its vitality and its capacity for transcendence (Silverstone,
1994), which is neither singularly a context of resistance and autonomy—
a refuge from the power struggles for social control and domination—nor
a context where people simply learn to accept the dominant norms and
discourses without resistance. One of the main points that de Certeau and
Silverstone usefully highlight is the connection of everyday life with the
popular, particularly the media. Although de Certeau sees in the popular
tactics of resistance to the dominant power by the *weak*, this resistance is
not perceived as holistic and powerful enough to shake the dominant status quo. Against this background, Silverstone understands the popular—
and the broadcasting media in particular—within the *ordinariness* of everyday life, which implies as much resistance as it does conformity. The *ordi-*
nary and our understanding of the world are not only products of immediate experience, but they are also 'conditioned by our consumption of information, ideas and values that television and other media provide' (1994:
167).

The dialectic of production-consumption in the heart of de Certeau's
analysis is useful for understanding the incomplete and contested meanings
of consumption and engagement with the media on one hand and the
potentials of mediascapes becoming a site of contestation and creativity on
the other. De Certeau argues for the need to surpass assumptions about
consumers' passivity and subordination to established rules. At the same
time, he rejects any celebration of *social atomism*. Rather, he proposes an
analysis, which learns from *operational combinations* emerging in the meeting of production and consumption. Consumption is another production,
he argues. Although not everybody is equal within this process, different
uses and interpretations by consumers challenge the power of the original
producers; 'the strength of their difference lay in procedures of "consumption"' (1994: xiii). The definition of consumption in dialogue to production
is somehow and inevitably natural. People are consumers of representa-

tions, but they are simultaneously their producers. As thoughts, ideas and feelings are represented in language and culture (Hall, 1997), so do meanings and identities rely on representations, both linguistic and cultural; thus, identities are always mediated (Hall, 1997). Yet, the dialectic production-consumption is not just a matter of linguistic and sociopsychological processes. It is also a matter of cultural and social processes that are well grounded in the capitalist social system. In everyday life, people are consumers—consumers of goods, cultural products and symbols. At the same time, they become producers of meanings as they appropriate them in acts of social and communal consumption, in their contested position as consumers who make choices, who are excluded by certain forms of consumption and who might choose alternative products and forms of consumption at specific times or within specific social formations—for example, in the diasporic context.

The contestations and tensions in diasporic everyday life are multiple, building a web of relations that sometimes reproduce conformity—for example, to the national mainstream, capitalism's ethos, consumer culture, the diasporic traditional mainstream—and others enabling resistance—for example, to projects of national assimilation, of diasporic homogenization and singularity, and of consumer culture and capitalism. The position of the media—mainstream and diasporic—and technologies of communication can play part to both directions. Although mediation does not lead to either resistance or conformity alone, the increased diversity of the media available, the diversity in their spatial appropriation and the growing diffusion of communication technologies across different subgroups requires our attention and a reevaluation of everyday life for identity construction in transnational contexts.

About Representation

Identity construction always relies on representations (Lacan, 1977; Saussure, 1983). Representations begin in the use of common language, in signs and symbols that allow us to build up shared understandings and common codes for interpreting the world: 'in part, we give things meaning by how we represent them. . . .Meaning is what gives us a sense of our own identity, of who we are and with whom we "belong"' (Hall, 1997:3). Representations begin with language—the primary medium—but they extend into all other sorts of communication practices, including what is commonly called *the media*: the press, television, radio, the Internet. Media become important as systems of representation, but also as socially relevant cultural references—in their political economy, their content, their symbolic relevance for particular social groups. On one hand, everyday life is saturated by the images and sounds on screens, speakers and paper. On the other, media discourses have become some of the common denominators of everyday communication, in a way that sharing understandings about *Us* and the *Others* is often (expected or assumed to be) mediated by media discourses. Though the role of audiences in the construction of media meanings is now acknowledged, not all participants in the mediation process are equal. 'Meaning is a dialogue,' Hall argues (1997:4), but not between equals; '[meaning is] always only partially understood, always an unequal exchange.' Certain actors are more powerful than others, they seize hegemonic power of meanings (Butler, 1990) and thus produce and reproduce archetypes of identities, which are established as natural and correct and as models to conform to. Media producers, community leaders, institutions such as the churches and the schools have concentrated power and control over the production of identity and community archetypes. On the other hand, as Hall, Silverstone and Butler among others, remind us, the construction of meanings is incomplete; it is a process of ongoing contestation. It is in this space of incompleteness and tension that alternative systems of representation can be produced and where individual and collective understandings and misunderstandings can challenge dominant discourses and discursive singularities.

FOCUS ON THE MEDIA

If we accept that media have a 'cultural place' in the contemporary world (Alasuutari, 1999)—a place that is constantly contested, debated and involved in different power struggles between human and nonhuman actors—we need to examine how media get involved in shaping everyday life and identities. Media consumption extensively frames everyday life, as people learn about the world from the media, shape tastes through their consumption, develop common codes of communication while sharing media representations (Hall, 1997). Media consumption is not just an individual activity; as a social act it extensively frames the discursive construction of identities, sociality, the ability and tendency to form groups and communities (Morley and Robins, 1995; Dayan, 1998; Morley, 2000). Media establish their presence at home, as family viewing in particular becomes an everyday bonding experience (Silverstone, 1993). They establish their presence in public, as people shape their everyday communication around themes and representations they all share through media consumption (Hobson, 1989; Lull, 1990; Gillespie, 1995). The public and the private and the local and transnational come together in a relation of continuity and codependence as the media constantly cross set boundaries.

Spatial codependence becomes a codependence of spaces of belonging, because media come to inform, communicate and represent the people and the world they live in.

Diasporic media sometimes project a dominant model of identity as a holistic, essential quality of life. In their ever-presence, they repeatedly project particular perceptions and values that ascertain commonality and community. Media become involved in the everyday construction of images of Us and the Others, while fixing and (re-)broadcasting those images to members and nonmembers of a group. The electronic diasporic media especially enable their taken-for-grantedness, immediacy and simultaneity in everyday life in their structure and technical form (Silverstone and Hirsch, 1994; Cormack, 1998, 2000). Their ever-presence means they get involved in identity construction in multiple ways. In their availability and presence in everyday life, media become mechanisms for the emergence of imagined communities (Anderson, 1983), though their existence alone cannot lead to assumptions about their relevance to identity and community. Such arguments need to be investigated as diasporic media compete with mainstream media and other cultural choices. Furthermore, the potential users of the media have multiple identities, different lifestyles and their identities are not inescapably dependant on diasporic continuity and belonging. How do diasporic media remain relevant, if they do? How do they relate to community and commonality? How does the increasing interactivity and diversity of electronic (diasporic) media alter their outcome and their consumption? How do media culture(s) change limitations and possibilities for identities and belonging in the context of the everyday?

Both the centrality and the complexity of media consumption have been the focus of audience research. Such research is of key relevance to the present study, which aims at reflexively examining the theoretical and empirical agenda set within the field, as this relates to identity, community and diaspora. Diaspora links to social differentiation, particularity and identity. The fast-growing interest in diasporic media is the outcome of their increased role in projects of particularism, community and against exclusion and homogenization (Husband, 1994; Cottle, 2000; Karim, 2002). The study of diasporic media consumption, as a new area of interest, can expand the understanding of audiences, not only in width and in relation to diversity and the complexity of media consumption, but also in depth and in relation to media's role for sustaining commonality. At the same time, diasporic media studies need to reflexively learn from audience research and avoid homogenizing assumptions about the significance and the meanings of particularistic media. With this dual challenge in mind, this project is designed to study the relation between media, identity and community in a transnational context. This study focuses on the particular, the alternative, the contested experience of consuming particularistic rather than mainstream media; it does so while reflecting on similarities and differences, continuities and interruptions between the particular and the universal, the diasporic and the mainstream. Media cultures are shaped in people's diverse engagement with all kinds of media and communication technologies, whereas the meanings of particularistic and diasporic media cultures are shaped in the juxtaposition of different mediascapes and in the context of media literacy as a whole.

Many influential studies of globalization have acknowledged the significance of sustaining transnational diasporic communications for social formations and identity (Hannerz, 1996; Appadurai, 1996; Castells, 2001), yet very few studies have actually researched the practices and implications of diasporic communications (Ogan, 2001; Cottle, 2000; Aksoy and Robins, 2000, 2003; Mai, 2005; Siapera, 2005). The present study aims at understanding such communication practices and meanings in the context of everyday life. I focus on the activity of using the media, the relations developing around consumption, the appropriation of media in private, in public, in urban and transnational spaces. A choice to study the settings and the relations developing around the media and the dynamics of consumers' engagement with the communication technologies is made, over the study of media text. This is a choice that emphasizes the social character of media consumption, the social and socio-psychological dynamics of media appropriation and the ways consumption is ingrained in the structures of the domestic (Silverstone and Hirsch, 1994) and the public, in the networks that emerge in the meeting of the local and the transnational (Naficy, 1993; Dayan, 1999) and in the interplay among domestic, communal, and transnational moral economies. Though media texts are not irrelevant to the scope of this research, it is the choice of using (or not using) diasporic media, their appropriation as a communal act and their becoming part of everyday life that relate the most to the questions of identity construction.

In conceptualizing media consumption as a relation and the everyday as the context for research, the methodological choice cannot but be of qualitative conduct and analysis: an analysis that can generate contextual, 'natural occurring data,' as well as theory grounded in social processes (Silverstone, 1994). The present analysis is based on the study of the members of a transnational group who are media consumers: an audience, among other things. And while recognizing that the concept of the audience has been challenged (Fiske, 1982; Bryce, 1987; Ang, 1991, 1996, 1996; Seiter, 1999), it is also recognized that, while being redefined and contested, audience remains a relevant category for studying media consumption in the context of everyday life and as embedded in the public and the private realm. This project aims at strategically embracing a qualitative research approach and, more precisely, at incorporating ethnography, as the most appropriate methodology for its realization. Ethnography, generating from anthropology, has been used extensively in sociology and cultural studies, and it has shaped a distinct form within media studies (see, among others, Buckingham, 1987, 1993; Hobson, 1989; Morley and Silverstone, 1990; Fiske, 1990; Gillespie, 1995; Betteridge, 1997; Seiter, 1999). Ethnography has been adapted in communication research, mostly in studies aiming at contextualizing and grasping the multiple dimensions of media consumption (Lindlof, 1987; Lull, 1990; McQuail, 1997).

METHODOLOGY: PROBLEMATIZED THEORY

Discovering and Rediscovering the Audience

An ethnographic approach that focuses on appropriations of symbols and active formation of meanings, on social relations and identity construction, learns from theorizations of the audience as a participating party in a never-ending process of cultural appropriation. Studies such as Morley's *The 'Nationwide' Audience* (1980), Ang's *Watching Dallas* (1985) and Buckingham's *Public Secrets: Eastenders and Its Audience* (1987), to name a few key examples, directly challenged perceptions of the passive audience and suggested that audiences are participants in the construction of media meanings. Although these early studies engaged with the diversity of media consumption in relation to the social context and identity, they still reproduced economic determinism and ideologies of singular identities. The complexity of the social, temporal and spatial context as well as the diversity and multiplicity of identities have only recently been taken into serious consideration in audience research. The late realization of identity and contextual complexity relates to the dominant theorizations of the audience until recently. The insufficiency of cultural studies audience research is based on the phenomenological approach of audience, as a natural phenomenon rather than as a relation, argues Nightingale: 'The problem is that people are not audiences by nature but by culture. . . . We learn to act and to think of ourselves as audiences in certain contexts and situations' (1996: 147).

Nightingale makes four points in arguing about the reconceptualization of audience as a relation: (a) audience relations are relations of interaction linking the text, the media institutions, the medium and the system of publicity; (b) the consumption and the use of the media are necessary, but not sufficient explanations of audience relations; other activities are also crucial; (c) 'audience relations always involve the exercise of power—

someone always has the power to offer "audience" and someone else must respond by accepting or rejecting the offer' (1996: 149); (d) audience relations are operational, which means that they are linked to the structures they function within. Nightingale's proposal emphasizes relations of power: power structures 'govern' and audience relations and meanings are constructed within this framework. Heterogeneous, haphazard particularities of everyday life are transformed into personal narratives that conform to generic cultural ideologies. Relations of power frame media access and control of produced messages, they frame the range of choices and restrictions in media use and they define the range of audiences' interpretative tactics, including the level of their media literacy. Because studying the complexity of media cultures for analyzing audiencehood is recognized as the necessary analytical strategy, *the context* becomes more than an abstraction. Media consumption is always contextualized—it is a process always positioned in social systems, in time and space (Ang, 1991, 1996; Silverstone, 1994; Radway, 1987); it is 'embedded within a technical and consumer culture that is both domestic and national (and international), a culture that is at once private and public' (Morley and Silverstone, 1990: 32). Research on media consumption has challenged the functional approaches to audiencehood—that is, the analysis of activities around media use alone. It has investigated how media texts are articulated and multiplied through activities such as schoolyard talk and everyday gossip. 'The performed text outstrips the broadcast text in both significance and vitality, even though the two remain linked' (Nightingale, 1996: 148). Ang (1996) adds that media research is meaningful when it offers some critical understanding of the peculiarities of contemporary culture and she suggests that the media should be radically contextualized:

> We should stop conceptualizing television, radio, the press, and so on, in isolation, as a series of separable independent variables having more or less clearcut correlations with another set of dependent, audience variables. (1996: 68)

Ang's *radical contextualism* points out an important element to be taken into account in media research: the fact that we live in a 'media-saturated world' (1996: 72). It is thus extremely difficult, even undesirable, to separate the media from everyday life, and the researcher's task becomes more complicated, because the contextual horizon is endless. As a result, *radical contextualism* ends up in a contradictory form: on one hand, highlighting the need to take into account the context of media consumption, and on the other, admitting that no project can 'encompass such all-embracing knowing' of the 'eternally expanding contextuality' (1996: 73). Reflexivity and acknowledgement of the limitations of the ethnographic discourse become central strategies in dealing with the *eternally expanding contextu-ality*. The aim for contextualizing research and positioning the micro in a dialectic relation to the macro is a difficult one, but still a task not to be abandoned. One of the weaknesses of ethnographic audience studies is the inability to actually make the links between the micro and the macro, to manage to position research and analysis in the social, the spatial and the temporal context. Macrosociological questions about causes of events and the constitutions of systems and processes have been avoided (Clifford and Marcus, 1986). Williams (cited in Clifford and Marcus, 1986) suggests that in text construction researchers can integrate the macro into the micro: accounts of impersonal systems can be combined with representations of local life as cultural forms, both autonomous and constituted by the larger order. Learning from Marxist analysis which emphasizes that culture is the way people live their everyday lives in a structured system, we should con-struct texts that remember and remind readers that 'culture is not sui generis, but is class culture or subculture, entailing its formation in historic process' (Clifford and Marcus, 1986: 178).

A reflection on the historical, temporal and spatial context is particu-larly relevant in the case of diasporic cultures. The deterritorializing/reter-ritorializing experience of diaspora relates to uprooting, fleeing, colonial-ism and postcolonialism, the growing mobility of economic migrants, the experience of settlement in new countries, often accompanied by discrim-ination, racism, exclusion, but also by new opportunities for economic, social and cultural development and (re-)invention of identity. In the case of the Cypriot diaspora, the dialectic between pre-migration life in the divided Cypriot society—both in terms of political polarization and interethnic conflict—and settlement in the multiethnic Western metropo-les involves experiences of estrangement and alienation, but also of new forms of creativity, identity and community. The dialectics of past and pres-ent need to be taken into account when forming a contextualizing frame-work and a meaningful research plan for understanding diasporic identities and mediation.

Although the interconnection of the macro and the micro should be a continuous contextualizing background in the ethnographic text, ethnog-raphy's focus remains the particular and the cultural experience within specific locales (Geertz, 1973, 1988; Hastrup, 1992; Hammersley and Atkinson, 1995; Kuper, 1999). Gray (1987) emphasizes the usefulness of ethnographic open-ended approaches for studying specificities and partic-ularities. In the long and in-depth engagement with people's practices of consumption and everyday life, this research focuses on the particularity and the local context. In this research, a challenge has emerged: the chosen methodology should include strategies and practices to study both the local and localized everyday as well as the translocal and networked transnational. Adopting ethnographic methods and engaging in in-depth research within different locales is the best practice for studying particularity—as localized and as expanding across spaces. The study of the local in different locations allows an understanding of particularity, without assuming that this is necessarily and singularly local. Multipositioned ethnography can study the peculiarities of everyday life and identity as they are associated to specific locales, but also as they relate to networks, experiences and relations that expand across different locales (McDonald, 1993; Willis and Trondman, 2000). Identities and communities can then be studied in their root-ness and in their routed-ness.

In the diasporic case, the analysis of audiences is about identity as much as it is about communal practices and communitarian meanings that emerge in the engagement with the media. Audience research has addressed the formation of communities around the media even before the interest in particular, migrant and diasporic audiences developed. Abercrombie and Longhurst (1998) argue that members of audiences imagine each other as members of a community:

> Since the claim is that everybody is a member of an audience for each other's performance most of the time, the relationship between members of the audience is clearly going to be of more importance. In day-dreaming, people will imagine the presence of others who constitute the audience for their daily performances. Needless to say that these others are not just any others. They are significant others who are of like mind and have similar tastes and attitudes. One way of conceptualising the relationship between people who form part of this imagined presence is to describe it as a *community*. (1998: 114)

Abercrombie and Longhurst's emphasis on imagination and on the significant others is particularly relevant to the case of diasporic audiences. First, the construction of communities across space is primarily dependent on processes of imagination, which, as already argued, is increasingly mediated and involved in sustaining a sense of commonality in transnational contexts. Second, and in relation to audience research in particular, diasporic audiences have certain distinct characteristics. Most audiences—especially as they are only partly bounded within the imagined community of the nation—come together in communities of interests, as communities of consumers. In the case of diasporic audiences, an imagined community pre-exists; the assumption of commonality developed around media consumption is an ideology of community. Though elements of diasporic (imagined) commonality often emerge in media cultures, the ideology of community that frames media consumption makes this a case of particular interest. Not all audiences are the same and, as emphasized already, contextualizing media consumption within the social and ideological frame where it takes place is necessary for understanding its meanings.

THE ETHNOGRAPHIC PERSPECTIVE

Ethnography, originating in anthropology, has traditionally been used for studying cultures as a whole, whereas in media studies, ethnography has been primarily used for the study of one aspect of culture, that of media consumption (Seiter, 1999). Even though ethnographic media studies radically overcame the earlier media research orientation towards the study of media use in different kinds of laboratories, many of them still did not manage to create a framework for studying media consumption as a cultural activity, inseparable from all the cultural practices and discourses shaping and being shaped in the natural everyday setting and the broader social, spatial and temporal context. Media ethnography has sometimes become so narrow as to ignore the cultural and political context where media are consumed (Radway, 1984; Ang, 1996) and underestimate the sociological importance of talk and action. Nevertheless, media ethnography has also experimented with relatively new spaces and cultural discourses, such as the discourses shaped through daily interaction, conflicts and negotiations at home (Silverstone, 1994, 1996; Livingstone, 1998; Ang, 1996). Ethnography usefully has also engaged in long debates about the constructivist dimension of research and its interpretative nature, especially when it takes place in the 'familiar' context of the researcher's own culture (Rabinow, 1977; Clifford and Marcus, 1986; Hastrup, 1987; Hobson, 1989; Rosaldo, 1989; Hammersley and Atkinson, 1995; Hirsch, 1998; Seiter, 1999).

This study was designed as a critical, reflexive adoption of both media and anthropological ethnographic practice.[10] Ethnography is the methodological choice as it is one that allows us to study identity and cultural practices in the settings and rhythms where everyday life evolves (Lefebvre, 2003). Additionally, ethnography, as appropriated in media studies has advanced the understanding of the multiple and complex meanings of media consumption (Radway, 1987; Pasquier et al., 1998; Tufte, 2000). Media ethnography has rejected the pathologization of audiences often seen in the media effects' tradition and in other approaches, which see audiences as the receivers in a linear relation production/text/receiver Even though the media ethnographic tradition has advanced the analysis of audiencehood, it still has its limitations. The majority of this research still remains more or less framed within the domestic space, at least as a *natural space* where the actual empirical studies are conducted. The interweaving of the public and the private is studied in its domestic expressions. But actual research in the public as a space where everyday life inevitably expands has been rare (Hobson, 1989; Gillespie, 1995). The dialectical relation between the domestic and the public is discursive, mediated and direct. The media have challenged the boundaries between the private and the public, so has media consumption. As media consumption is conceptualized to exceed the actual media use, empirical research should be structured to the same direction. A parallel empirical study within and outside the home allows the collection of data from multiple locations—real, virtual and symbolic—and frames an understanding of media consumption as an inseparable component of everyday life.

The ethnographic perspective developed here allows a critical study of media consumption as a cultural process, of media consumption as part of everyday life and as a never-ending cultural experience. It allows the study of the audience as a relation and not as a phenomenon (Nightingale, 1996). The theorization of audience as a relation and of media consumption as a cultural process emphasizes the centrality of the relational and communicative dimension of media consumption—the importance of *who shares the media with whom* (Meyrowitz, 1985). In this context, the relations developing around media consumption rather than the texts being consumed form the focus. This research was conducted in and across various spaces, over a long period of time and while considering the diversity of relations within the Greek Cypriot diaspora. Ethnography, in its methodological openness, records and reflects on the diversity and the interconnectedness of the multiple spaces where the diasporic everyday expands. Visual and verbal material, recorded interviews and casual discussions in houses, bars and community centers (in-)formed a study that is as much about settings as it is about participating actors.

The book is based on intense ethnographic research that took place over a period exceeding two years. Most of the time (18 months) was spent in London. Less time was spent on the study of Greek Cypriot everyday in New York City, though past research with the Greek community of Boston boosted my understanding of the Greek Cypriot diasporic experience in the United States. The research combined a number of methods. Fifty qualitative semi-structured interviews took place in an equal number of households in the two sides of the Atlantic. Five families out of the 50 participated in ethnographic research that lasted from one to five months. This research included intense participant observation, with regular visits, participation in celebrations and outings and long unstructured discussions along the family members. Additionally, long-term participant observation took place in three community centers—two in London and one in New York City. In this case, regular visits, as combined with unstructured discussions and focus groups, helped me understand the continuities and the differences of everyday life conduct and media consumption in the private and public space. Participant observation, including unstructured discussions in clubs, cafés, schools and community organizations' gatherings have enriched my understanding of community life and of the performed identities and engagement with media and communication technologies in public.

THREE ——————————

DIASPORIC IDENTITIES
In Difference Lies Commonality

THE PROBLEMATIC CONCEPT OF IDENTITY

The meanings of identity have been shaped through popular narratives and ideologies of belonging, of nationalism and of inescapable commitments for so long that the analysis and deconstruction of the concept becomes an immense challenge. Identity is a problematic concept—a term always contested, as it has been used to mean everything and nothing, implying fixed qualities and inescapable belonging. Identity, as it has been applied to race and ethnicity in particular, has been celebrated in both its *purity* and its *impurity*, within national discourses of resistance to globalization or discourses of resistance to racism respectively (Smith, 1981, 1990, 1997; Ballis-Lal, 1986; Brass, 1986; Cashmore, 1988; Anthias and Yuval-Davis, 1992; Chambers, 1994; Bauman, 1996a; Ahmed, 1999). Identity became popular because as a concept it could be adjusted to fit the various meanings granted to it. Identity politics has become a new form of politics against the grand narratives of modernity and for the celebration of more inclusive—though often either unclear or essentializing—politics of difference. The contradictory meanings attributed to identity have often led to intellectual hostility to the concept. Gilroy, among an increasing number of scholars, questions identity and its connotations. Gilroy, however, following Hall, proposes a strategic and positional approach to identity, not an essentialist one: 'Identity provides a way of understanding the interplay between our subjective experience of the world and the cultural and historical settings in which this fragile subjectivity is formed' (1997: 301). An operational and deconstructing approach to identity is a necessary step in surpassing its problematic popular conceptualization (Gillespie, 1995).

A reflexive approach to identity is more productive than seeking *pure*, unspoiled concepts to replace it. Identity as a concept does not need to be fixed or holistic, especially since the process it aims at describing lacks these qualities. Although problematic, identity addresses a number of important social and cultural phenomena. As a concept, it implies belonging—a sense that can be as real as imagined, but which, in either case, is central to understanding people's political and emotional attachment to other individuals and groups. Furthermore, identity implies a level of continuity in terms of commitment, behavior and practice. Continuity does not equal stability; rather it refers to a process of *becoming* as well as of *being* (Hall, 1990: 223). Identity has to do as much with positioning oneself within a specific culture, following particular codes and practices, as it has to do with shaping a sense of belonging through appropriating and adopting the self and cultural discourses. As identities are not fixed and stable, they allow people to rediscover and redefine their content, not through an exclusive gaze to the past, but with a parallel focus on present experience and on the future of transformation and change.

The continuity implied in identity and its consequences requires the recognition of the significance of the past—as memory and as lived experience. Past and roots reflect important, yet sensitive, dimensions of identity. Addressing them, as Gilroy (1995) does in his concept of *the changing same*, means being equally insightful and reflexive. Fortier (1999: 41), following Gilroy and Calhoun, raises the issue when talking about the Italian migrants in London: 'Immigrant populations often project themselves in relation to specific origins that do not necessarily undermine multi-locality or transnational connections.' Similar to roots, people attribute important meanings to the past—a past that is shaped through memory and commemoration (Fischer, 1986; Boyarin, 1994; Ben Amos and Weissberg, 1999), myth and imagination but that, as a symbol signifies *where we come from, what heritage we share*. The meanings of memories and symbols usually vary for different individuals and subgroups, even though the collective memory and the power of the discourse around these events does, in one way or another, define individual and communal identities. Judith Butler (1990, 1993) talks about a binding power of such discourses and of such *statements* that frame everyday life. Such *statements* and *norms*, Butler explains, are powerful expressions constructing and framing identities, but they are not the essence, and the outcome of identities.

Identity and Power

Identities 'are subject to the continuous "play" of history, culture and power' (Hall, 1990: 223). Although dominant popular discourses want identities to be an individual and personal journey—a journey of free choices, especially in many postmodern popular debates—it needs to be stressed that identity construction is a highly political, contested process. Identities are shaped though struggles for power, as they are not freely and individually defined projects of self-awareness; rather they are social and discursive constructs (Foucault, 1974), developing around the negotiation and appropriation of hegemonic discourses of identity. "'. . . [I]dentity", though ostensibly a noun, behaves like a verb, albeit a strange one to be sure' (Bauman, 1996b: 19). The process of contestation and ongoing struggles is inherent to identities and their never-ending formation. If identities are always contested and changing, how do they remain viable? To look for answers there is a need to turn to politics of identity, to the social mechanisms for inclusion and recognition and to the construction of commonality and difference. Because identity is not only a description of a cultural process, but also a political concept, it inevitably relates to questions of power, hegemony and exclusion as much as it relates to individuality, sociality and belonging. Politics and policies of recognition and representation are of key relevance to the identity debate, even when the focus is on the cultural processes, the mundane and the everyday (Siapera, 2005).

Everyday life and culture are not celebratory spaces of freedom and creativity, rather they are always dialectically positioned vis-à-vis the processes that restrict freedom of expression and form hegemonic discourses (de Certeau, 1984; Levebvre, 1991). On one hand there are hierarchical discourses and normative cultural practices and representations of identity, and on the other there is divergence, as the meanings of identity and culture are fluid and contested (Song, 2003). Deviance and divergence often face punishment and marginalization:

> Identity is not only reinvented . . . it is at least partially given for different people in different ways and intensities. Bodies are marked as different and often as negatively different to the dominant cultural system, thus producing a dissonance or gap between one's practices and affects. (Boyarin and Boyarin, 1993: p. 704)

The marginalization of difference reproduces hierarchical forms of identity, pressures for conforming to normality and conceptions of identity authenticity circulated within and outside the group (Song, 2003). Authenticity implies pure forms, visible distinctiveness and permanent characteristics of identity. Ascription and inscription of identity, emic and etic meanings of identity and community interweave in the process of identity construction. Gerd Baumann's (1996) definitions of dominant and demotic discourses of community address the ongoing interplay of representations and meanings of identity and community within groups and between groups and the mainstream. Dominant discourses celebrate primordial, holistic and exclusive forms of belonging. The demotic ones, on the other hand, are the discourses emerging through ordinary action, interaction and experience; as such, they recognize diversity, hybridity and change within groups (Baumann, 1996). In everyday life, there is a constant juggle with both discourses that become as situational as identities themselves.

Identity As Performative

The reproduction of power through such processes of authenticating and fixing identities has been addressed in Foucaultian poststructuralist, postfeminist thought. In *Gender Trouble* (1990), Butler argues that a binary opposition—masculine and feminine—structures gender identities within systems of hegemonic naturalization of a binary relationship. In this context, gender becomes a performative repetition of roles and rituals that are already socially and symbolically assigned. Butler's *performativity* highlights that identities are not inescapably defined at birth, but as they are discursively formed, they become the outcome of the interplay of power in its Foucauldian conceptualization: 'Performativity is the discursive mode by which ontological effects are installed' (Butler in Osborne and Segal, 1997: 236). Identities relate to specific historical and social contexts; the meanings of identities are achieved through naming, through citations that become socially shared.

Butler's analysis has attracted much criticism for undermining agency, as she considers gender to be the outcome of repetitive acts. In her analysis, though, identities are never completely bound and fixed, for binary oppositions are challenged by alternative discourses. An example that Butler uses against the fixity of gender identity it that of drag/transexuality. Drag challenges the fixity and the binary character of gender and suggests fluidity, openness and resignification against the naturalization and essentialism of identities. Butler's use of the drag as an example of breaking off the binary (in this case male/female) is a recognition of the possibility of deviance. However, deviance is more occasional and peripheral, as the binary predominates. The binary reflects the significance of power and discourse in the process of constructing identities—in setting boundaries between Us and the Others within particular historical and social contexts. The possibility of performing identities alternatively and beyond the set hegemonic discourses is secondary in her analysis. Diasporic experiences studied here show that both hegemonic discourses of identity—the dominant diasporic, which emphasize essential particularism and the dominant mainstream, which focus on the commitment to the nation-state—are constantly challenged in the mundane practices of everyday life. Needless to say, that such challenges to the binary are unequally positioned vis-à-vis the dominant hegemonic discourses of identity (Onoufriou, 2002). This inequality between the normative and the hierarchical on one hand and the creative and diverse expressions of identity on the other highlight the significance of Foucaultian and Butlerian analyses.

The debates on the performative illustrate the discursive character of identity and therefore the importance of context and the potentiality for constant change. However, within these theorizations the question of identity's continuity and consequences remains:'[T]aking the temporal performative nature of identities as a theoretical premise means that more than ever, one needs to question how identities continue to be produced, embodied and performed, effectively, passionately and with social and political consequence' (Bell, 1999: 2). Goffman's (1959) influential thesis on performance can advance the analysis of the performative. His analysis is, in many ways, more dialectic than Butler's model, which has a tendency for the reproduction of an inescapable binary. Goffman describes social life as a kind of multistaged drama in which we each perform different roles in different social arenas, depending on the nature of the situation, our particular role in it, and the makeup of the audience. Goffman talks about frontstage and backstage performances, which allow individuals to negotiate how they present themselves, even though always within the limitations of these performances.

Theorizations of the performative have been influential on the study of ethnicity and diaspora. Stratton (2000a, 2000b) notes that ethnicity is becoming fundamentally performative, as it overcomes the constraints of descent and it increasingly depends 'on the subjective naturalization of culturally agreed upon signifiers' (2000b: 21). With reference to the American society and Jewishness, Stratton makes an argument similar to that of Butler about gender being naturalized through performance (1990). Jewishness, he argues, is performed and it is not necessarily the same as being a Jew, which primarily relates to descent. 'Jewishness, like other ethnicities, can in this way be thought as a set of attributes which are repeated and become naturalized as identifiably Jewish' (2000b: 21). Performative practices become central when drawing boundaries and the difference of communities, argue Dzewiecka and Wong (Lau) (1999). These practices give meaning to the community by symbolically and experientially marking its uniqueness. At the same time, as argued in this book, community becomes a unifying framework for bringing diversity into a common (transnational) stage where identities are performed and shaped. In the present analysis, identities are studied as the outcome of discursive relations of power, negotiations and redefinition of boundaries within specific historical and cultural contexts; they are analyzed as products of self-description and of representation of/for/outside the group,—as people perform identities *inscribed* to them and as they contest these *inscriptions*.

From the Individual to the Collective and Back

Identity is not only socially constructed; it is also shaped in the intermixing and meeting of the social and the psychological. Fanon's (1986) influential study of identity emphasizes the interconnection of psyche and society in the politically contested process of identity construction. His postcolonial analysis focuses on the process of suppression of the project of identity and self-fulfillment of the colonized subjects by the colonizers. From a psychoanalytical perspective, Fanon argues that ethnicity and race do not depend on pre-given identities, but are the products of images of identities that the Others—especially the colonizing powers—expect (colonial and postcolonial) subjects to adopt. Fanon's analysis and its dual focus on power inequality and the psychological dimensions of identity construction is a challenge for the study of identity and diaspora in postcolonial times. Identity construction includes emotional relations, deep psychological processes, but it is always constructed vis-à-vis the dominant, hierarchical ideologies and representations of identity and of social groups. Anthony Cohen's (1994) emphasis on self-consciousness for the construction of identities has a different starting point to Fanon's but it offers an equally valuable contribution for thinking of the self/psyche in relation to the social: 'We should focus on self consciousness not in order to fetishize the self but, rather, to illuminate society' (1994: 22). Cohen's analysis reminds us that there are *inexplicable* dimensions of identities that exceed the analysis of social relations. On the other hand, his analysis engages with the social relevance of identity and its distinct and dynamic involvement in group politics:

> The compelling requirement for a strong sense of self extends beyond individuals to groups, large and small. A sense of collective self may be qualitatively different from that of individual self, but the imperative need for identity is not less. A self-conscious perspective explains this imperative: groups have to struggle against their own contradictions, which lie precisely in the fact that they are composed by individuals,

self conscious individuals, whose differences from each other have to be resolved and reconciled to a degree which allows the group to be viable and cohere. (1994: 11)

Identity construction is both a private and a public matter, as it implies both an inner psychological process and the shaping of a shared and communal sense of belonging with others and against Others. The inner psychological processes are not adequate to sustain identities, which are formed in social contexts. Individual identities remain viable as public discourses give them meanings, as more people than one share common symbols and codes. 'The inner self finds its home in the world by participating in the identity of a collectivity. . . .The real me . . . is joined to the spiritual life of a community' (Kuper, 1999: 235).

ETHNICITY AND DIASPORA

Since the late 1970s, social sciences, and especially British cultural studies, have developed an interest in the study of identity as a social construct and as positioned within historical, economic and cultural systems. Identity became a distinct area of study, and identity construction in relation to media and mediated representations soon developed as an important sub-discipline. This interest was initially directed to class identities (Morley, 1980; Buckingham, 1987), but soon expanded to include gender, race and ethnicity, age and sexuality. Race and ethnicity studies focused primarily on exclusion, racism, minority misrepresentations and more recently to audiencehood (Liebes and Katz, 1990; Woodward, 1997; Tufte 2000; Mai, 2005). Ethnicity became a key concept in addressing cultural difference in multicultural societies and as a concept aimed at surpassing the essentializing and biological analysis dominating earlier analyses of race. Hall's (1988) analytical concept of *new ethnicities* emphasizes that ethnic identities are not defined at birth, that they are less dependent on blood relations and more on cultural belonging, and that they are hybrid and the outcome of the meeting of diverse cultures. Growing out of the tradition of cultural studies and the influential analysis of Fanon, new ethnicities explained how identities are constructed in historical, cultural and temporal contexts. As such, the theorization of new ethnicities became a starting point for the radical contextualization of identity in the context of diaspora and transnationalism:

The term ethnicity acknowledges a place of history, language and culture in the construction of subjectivity and identity, as well as the fact that all discourse is placed, positioned, situated, and all knowledge is situational. (Hall, 1992: 56)

Following Hall, Chambers (1994) refers to new ethnicities and expands the analysis to all identities. All identities are continuously formed throughout the journey of life and through processes that are never complete. Everybody is a stranger in unknown lands and that is part of human condition, not necessarily the outcome of displacement in the era of post-colonialism. Although Chambers' analysis tends to undermine the significance of power relations within and after colonialism and the particular importance of migration, at the same time it importantly positions the study of ethnicity within the broader theoretical debates on identity. Ethnic identity is not to be taken for granted as unique, everlasting and ever-important, as it coexists, codepends and competes with other identities. Acknowledging the ever-changing character of identity, its hybridity and positionality requires a reflexive and strategic operationalization that makes its analysis possible and meaningful. Hall (1991, 1992) has repeatedly emphasized that identity is a process. Along similar lines, Brah proposes an analysis that takes into consideration identity's change and multiplicity while defining *the process*:

> . . . Identity is neither fixed nor singular; rather it is a constantly changing relational multiplicity. But during the course of this flux identities do assume particular patterns, as in a kaleidoscope, against particular sets of personal, social and historical circumstances. Indeed, identity may be understood *as that very process by which the multiplicity, contradiction, and instability of subjectivity is signified as having coherence, continuity, stability; as having a core—a continually changing core but the sense of a core nevertheless—that at any given moment is enunciated as the 'I'.* (1996: 123-4, emphasis in the original)

Much of the analysis developing around diaspora and transnationalism at present originates in the above theorizations of ethnicity and identity. Ethnicity as a concept has been abandoned by many within cultural studies and sociology; it has been criticized for defining minority populations in relation to the mainstream and for assuming that minorities are marginalized and that they tend to close up into sectarian communities. However, other contemporary conceptualizations of ethnicity—also adopted here—argue against the tendency to abandon problematic and difficult concepts and rather to operationalize them through deconstruction and critique. Ethnicity is important as a concept that recognizes the social divisions and inequalities, as well as the cultural significance and implications of particularisms.

The study of ethnicity becomes more reflexive and interdisciplinary as it learns from diaspora and transnationalism studies within social sciences and the humanities. Old assumptions of race and ethnicity studies about the stability of the binary relation minority/majority and of the nation-state as the singular defining cultural and political context become contested. Similarly, ethnicity studies contribute to the dismissal of romantic approaches of identity, community and globalization within diaspora and transnationalism studies. As these areas of research meet and challenge each other's limitations, the study of identity, community and social interaction becomes more aware of issues of power in national and transnational scale, of social structures within and across societies, and of cultural formations that are neither stable nor stranded within the nation.

It is in this context that diaspora gets its significance as an operational concept. Diaspora, much more than ethnicity, recognizes that identities and communities are constructed in transnational spaces, in networks and through mediated links between various positions across the globe. Diaspora recognizes continuity in time and in terms of people's emotional and cultural attachment to a (imagined) community that spreads beyond national boundaries. Diaspora looks at cultural autonomy of groups that settle in certain countries but whose cultural and social capital is not defined in singular and necessarily subordinate ways by majorities and mainstream cultures. In its conceptualization, ethnicity shows how cultural belonging and creativity are socially constructed; it reminds us that relations of power, both within the societies where diasporic populations live and within the transnational communities, initiate, frame and restrain identity, belonging and participation. For these reasons, the concept of ethnicity is used here in dialogue with diaspora, and it is considered to be important for the cross-fertilization of the two concepts and the development of the study of identity, community and the media.

DIASPORA AND TRANSNATIONALISM

Diaspora has recently become a concept of contestation—being increasingly used in debates on globalization and transnationalism on one hand, and demonized as a new form of essentialism on the other. The concept of diaspora originates in Greek *speiro* (to sow) and *dia* (over). For the ancient Greeks, diaspora had more to do with migration as colonization rather than with uprooting and deterritorialization. In time, and for the groups that become the ultimate examples of *diaspora*—primarily the Jewish and the Armenians, but also the Palestinians and the Africans—diaspora signified a collective trauma, a banishment, 'where one dreamt of home but lived in exile' (Cohen, 1997: ix). With the historical and transnational Jewish and Armenian journeys of uprooting and prosecution becoming synonym to diaspora, the concept captured both the academic and the popular imagination. Recently, many peoples have been identifying—or have been identified by academics, politicians, policy makers—as diasporas, even when their migratory journey has not involved violence and prosecution. Diaspora has made a dynamic comeback in contemporary theorizations of migration and mobility, especially in the context of globalization: population dispersal and emergence of multicultural societies and transnational networks have invited a revisiting of the concept. The limits of diaspora have now expanded. According to Safran (1991: 83), diaspora is now deployed 'as a metaphoric designation' to 'describe *different categories* of people'—'expatriates, expellees, political refugees, alien residents, immigrants and ethnic and racial minorities *tout court*'. In introducing such a flexible conceptualization of diaspora, Cohen and others have been criticized for diluting the significance and the uniqueness of the concept. From another but relevant point of view, the use of the concept has been criticized as assuming a continuous role of an original *homeland* and an inevitable continuing attachment of spread populations with each other and with an original *homeland*.

Diaspora has become one more of the concepts standing on an intellectual thin line as it is accused of reproducing essentializing tendencies of identity. Yet, at the same time, revisiting diaspora as a concept has helped to address new and old phenomena, such as the growing relevance of transnational (mediated) networks, the success of transnational media that grasp the interest and the imagination of people spread across the globe, the continuing attachment of dispersed populations to distant others and to distant locations of origin. Diaspora, like identity, needs to be deconstructed and revisited in the context of globalization, increased mediation, multiple belongings and the sociopsychological processes that lead to engagement with communities and social formations. Diaspora can be a useful concept for understanding the insistence and the meanings of transnational networks of emotional, economic and cultural connections. In order to do that, it needs to consider the meanings of identity and community in the context of continuing inequalities and of growing political and social exclusions in national and transnational spaces. Diaspora does not need to imply uninterrupted continuity, inescapable belonging and ethnocentric analyses of society and globalization.

Dismissing concepts such as diaspora, identity and community altogether might be an intellectual challenge invited by processes of societal fragmentation and diversification. No matter how attractive this intellectual challenge might be, the dismissal of key sociological concepts inevitably romanticizes transnationalism and media cultures. In such analyses of the post-identity literature, social formations, relations of power, restrictions and struggles for recognition, participation and particularity are replaced by the romantic image of free-floating individuals who move between social, geographical and cultural spheres of a newly founded liberating cosmopolitanism. Against the dismissal of social categories and analyses in the name of a postsociety academic fad, a significant trend in research struggles to understand and conceptualize continuity, change and the growing complexity of identity and community in transnational times. In this literature, diaspora is revisited and reappropriated to recognize mediation, heterogeneity and diversity, transformation and difference (cf. Hall, 1990; Dayan, 1999; Morley, 1999; Iordanova, 2001). As it will be indicated, the diasporic condition has been shifting and the centrality of the nation-state and the *homeland* has been challenged. The changes in the construction of social networks and identities in late modernity, the increased social and cultural diversification of Western societies and the possibilities for decentralized and participatory communication, point to both the usefulness of the concept and to its limitations. Belonging, choosing not to belong, being excluded from belonging are all present conditions that need to be taken into account in defining diaspora and its meanings. The diasporic condition is contextual and it relates to the changing global cultural and communicational maps, as well as to the social and physiological processes that set symbolic (transnational) boundaries.

The continuity and the sense of commonality across transnational communities reflected in the concept of diaspora are crucial for a discussion on transnational participation; continuity and sense of (imagined) belonging do not imply homogeneity and essentialism; rather they imply commonality and identity, shaped in the tense heterogeneous space of an imagined community. In this context, migration, diasporization and hybridization allow us to think of new forms of alternative and subversive politics in their diverse, mundane and unintentional expressions and in their potentiality for challenging hegemony and power relations within minority communities and in the relation between minority communities and the mainstream (Bhabha, 1990; Kearney, 1991). As Guarnizo and Smith (1998) remind us, counter-hegemonic practices and discourses do not necessarily challenge relations of power in linear ways and with the same effects for all *the excluded*. Inequalities and conflicts within diasporic communities remain, while the voices of minorities within minorities are often and still silenced and suppressed—for example, women, sexual minorities, the elderly. As will be shown here, the inequalities *within* and the persistence of hegemonic relations and narratives do not erase the potential role of oppositional narratives and practices in expanding participation and democratizing transnational communities.

THE CONTEXT OF COMMUNITY:
THE CONTEXT FOR NEGOTIATING IDENTITY

Community is the context where the similarities and the differences that constitute *what we really are* and *what we have become* (Hall, 1990) turn into a shared discourse. This discourse includes representations of identities produced and consumed communally in a way that the sense of belonging and the symbolic boundaries of Us as insiders and the Others as outsiders are actively and continuously produced. Within the community context, shared characteristics—language, religion, family values, food tastes, and so forth—get their meanings and construct images of *We-ness* and *Otherness*. Furthermore, within the community context the difference between people sharing the same ethnicity is justified; the inevitable diversity characterizing identities can be shared and celebrated, as long as there are symbolic boundaries framing it. The commonality can be the outcome of the shared difference, which creates a communal/shared space for imagining. This imagining strengthens the boundaries between Us and the Others and dramatizes the sense of what is close and what is distant (Said, 1985).

Community is neither real nor fictional. Its boundaries are rarely structured; in most cases they are imagined. But people refer to community as a commonly shared concept—as a taken for granted consistency. As difficult as it is to define, as problematic as it is to theorize, it is equally difficult to avoid community (Calhoun, 1980; A. Cohen, 1985, 1994; Rutherford, 1990; P. Cohen, 1993; Bauman, 2000). Anthony Cohen argues that community as a concept needs to be taken seriously, as it carries important meanings for many people (1985). As with identity, community requires a strategic and reflexive operationalization and theorization. Community is used here cautiously and reflexively; conceptualizations of community as a taken-for-granted notion, as a clearly defined structural or cultural reference that has a meaning everybody understands, shares and embraces are rejected. At the same time, this study learns from theorizations such as P. Cohen's (1985) and Anderson's (1983) that turn community into a useful tool and a constructive theoretical concept for the analysis of diasporic continuity, identity and their consequences. Additionally, community is hereby linked to its demotic (Baumann, 1996), *emic* definitions from the meanings and significance people give to it.

Cohen (1985), inspired by Wittgenstein, proposes to seek *use* of *community* rather than lexical meaning. In that way, the tension is relieved and the focus turns from structure to culture. Cohen recognizes that *community* has various meanings for different people, as a set of values, as an ideal, as an existing social formation. For Barth (1969), Barbesino (1996) and many others, community exists and becomes distinctive because of the boundary. Such theorizations aim at a relational understanding of community, which, however, needs to consider the qualitative and relational components of community—identity, communion, imagination. The differences in conceptualizations of community reflect the diversity among case studies as much as they reflect the problematic character of an emotionally and popularly biased concept. The vagueness of the concept itself becomes less important as the focus turns to the symbolic value of community, crucial for the construction of identity. As Cohen argues, community:

> . . . is a largely mental construct, whose 'objective' manifestations in locality or ethnicity give it credibility. It is highly symbolized, with the consequence that its members can invest it with their selves. Its character is sufficiently malleable that it can accommodate all its members' selves without them feeling their individuality to be overly compromised. Indeed, the gloss of commonality which it paints over its diverse components gives to each of them an additional referent for their identities (1985: 109)

Locality and ethnicity are not the necessary basis upon which community relies any more, as Cohen suggests, especially as new connections and attachments emerge across and beyond geographical and bounded locations, in virtual and networked spaces. Even when community emerges in the form of fan clubs and special interest groups, its strength still lays on its highly symbolic value. People share common symbols framing processes of constructing spaces of belonging and commonality. At the same time, the ways people interpret and operationalize symbols varies extensively, leaving individuals and community subgroups enough space to give to community meanings that are malleable, significant to them and that do not require full and constant commitment. 'Community has many meanings, it involves different sets of experience for different groups of people, and indeed for the same people at different times,' argue Crow and Allen (1994: 183), highlighting the flexibility of community and identity.

The key dimensions of community that make it meaningful to people, beyond its vagueness and its diversity, can be highlighted under three headings: (a) co-presence, which might be real, virtual or tele-presence (Barbesino, 1996); (b) memory, which is communal and selective and relates to the imagined We, the imagined Others and the common myth of roots and routes (Clifford, 1994); and (c) future outlook, which is necessary for existence and which has to do both with the reproduction and the renewal of community. All the three dimensions rely more and more upon the media. In his analysis of imagined community, Anderson (1983) emphasized the role of the press for the construction of the nation. Looking beyond the restrictions and the limitations of the press and the nation and towards more diverse communities that emerge and are renewed in a world increasingly dependent on information and communication technologies, the media continue to mediate images and narratives for communities, shaping images of Us and Them, of *homelands* and localities, mapping spaces of copresence and designing outlooks for the future. As such, community in its local and transnational formations and expressions cannot be but of great relevance for this project. For the Greek Cypriots, identity and diaspora are tightly interlinked to community, as a symbolic—and not only that—social and spatial context. But as much as people rely on community, they playfully negotiate and continuously redefine it. As the sense of community is shaped in the context of everyday life, inevitably it depends on the contradictions that come with it.

Community Between Imagining and Living: Beyond Idealization

The concentration of many members of the Greek Cypriot community within particular locales explains why everyday face-to-face sociality is dominated by relations within the group. Everyday life is mediated by local coexistence, interaction and visual reproduction of a bounded community. The awareness of living among other people with the same background is cherished by many members of the group; their talk reflects the sociopsychological appreciation of community that is considered as secure and familiar, especially within the diverse Western metropoles. 'Something might happen to you. It's good to have somebody around that you can trust,' says a female interviewee, 35. Two other female interviewees reproduce the same sense of community: 'At the beginning, when we first got here, it was very important [to live in an area with many Cypriots] . . . the thought of having friends and relatives around made us feel more secure . . .' (female, 47). And a 36-year-old, married to a Welshman, explains how she insisted her family should remain within the *ethnic enclave*: 'I grew up in the Greek Cypriot culture. I feel comfortable with them [Greek Cypriots]. I like the sense of community.'

For others, though, the choice of location reflects a tense relation with the community, or the diversity of their identities. For a 43-year-old female participant, it is her middle-class identity and her choice to be single and live alone that defines her residential choice. It is a choice that also reveals her diasporic in-betweeness: 'I prefer to live at a certain distance from the community. I couldn't live somewhere where there is no Greek [Cypriot] context at all. But, at the same time, I wouldn't like to live somewhere where it's full of Cypriots'. Another participant of the same age and status explains emphatically why she moved further away from the heart of the local Cypriot community: 'I didn't want to be part of a ghetto!' Mobility and residence away from the initial settlement characterizes younger generations' choice, especially those achieving a middle-class status. For many young single people and families, geographical and social mobility go together. Their choice to move reflects a *decontextualization* of diasporic experience from the intense, everyday and working-class performance of a certain form of ethnicity characteristic of the migrant generation. For them, moving to suburbia reflects the hybridity and multiplicity of their identity, their choice to be part of the mainstream, while keeping at the same time a selective relation with the diasporic community nearby. For these younger generations, communication and sustaining of networks with other members of the group living in the same locale, the same country, another country or a far away continent becomes increasingly mediated and electronically sustained.

Social and residential mobility does not undermine the diasporic community in its local expressions. 'As soon as the first group of Greeks moves to a suburban area, a Greek Orthodox church is established there too! Then many more follow', says one of the participants in New York. Similarly, in the British context, a female participant explains diasporic continuity among younger generations: 'There's still extensive ethnic concentration; people need to live together. To have a church close by. They get married in the Greek church, use the Greek media and the Greek schools. Third and fourth generations still go to Greek schools and community centers. Greek Cypriots are not fully integrated and need their different identities. And there is a very strong sense of identity among them'.

Mobility and critique of what is considered to be an ethnic community characterizes the talk and choices of many young people. As already argued, critique does not necessarily lead to disengagement, though in many cases it does. The contradictions in talking about community show the complexity of community engagement and the shifting of its members' position. When asked if there is such a thing as a Cypriot community, the participant who earlier argued for the importance of living in a Cypriot local context says: 'When I was younger I would say yes [i.e. there is a community]. But now, I think community is a myth. People only help their own. People have changed a lot. It's a massive generalization to say that Greeks help each other more than others [ethnic groups]'.

Conflicts and contradictions are revealed in the words of some younger members of the group, who feel excluded and marginalized as their personal choices and multiple identities are rejected by the dominant community ideologies of the group. A lesbian participant's words show how her sexual identity partly defines how she constructs her diasporic identity and how other people see her in the diasporic community context: ' . . . for the people who don't adopt the mainstream idea of tradition it's difficult. I feel more like an outsider. There are expectations from everybody. . . . ' Making unconventional choices of lifestyle increases the ambivalence of people who choose not to conform to the community norm. It is an ambivalence that reveals a diasporic in-betweeness. Ambivalence also reveals the strength of community as a reference; even when people construct a lifestyle away from the community, they often continue to partly depend on it. In the words of one of the disillusioned participants:

> There is a sense of community, but it's not homogenous. It's a community but with different parts. Something unites them: their language, culture, but not all the people are the same. I don't know if I am really part of it. Those who are part of it must feel they belong. I don't know if I belong. . . . I don't belong with the English either.

Such critical approaches to the community—especially the local one—reveal the shift towards new ethnicities. There is disillusionment but still not complete distanciation from the community project. A 35-year-old accountant gives community meanings that reflect his in-betweeness and expose the demotic deconstruction (Baumann, 1996) of community. His critical perspective, though, leaves space for his own particular sense of belonging:

> What does community mean to me? A collection of people of Greek Cypriot origin. A collection of people being together out of a need to survive . . . It provides shelter for those who would have a hard time outside a Greek Cypriot community. Some other people have invested in different things, like for example common interests. Others are in it because they desperately need it for politics and other interests. You have the peripheries as well. People who are Anglicized. Those who don't even know or do not want to know about LGR . . . Am I part of it? Yes and no . . . Historically I'm part of it . . . .

In the everyday context of his professional life, which is predominantly white, English, middle-class male, his ethnicity can be a negative element, he argues. Or, it might become positive. In words that reveal the performative character of identity, he says: 'In the market you have to have a selling point. If you are Greek, you better say you are one and be proud of it.'

As the diversity of everyday experience in the Western metropoles increases, community is reproduced and sustained in the sharing of a number of key issues that capture diasporic imagination beyond internal difference. Some of these issues remain high on the agenda for the younger generations and sometimes they even become increasingly important in time and as the ultimate symbols of identity and community boundary definers. For the Greek Cypriots, the issue that is almost universally defined as a key reference of diasporic commonality is the ongoing division of Cyprus. The relevant comments of participants, the widespread interest they show when there are political developments on the issue, the series of various community events that deal with it and its domination in the agenda of both the local and the transnational media confirm that the Cyprus problem is an overarching identifier of commonality across subgroups and generations. The way people express this concern in everyday life might vary— and it is expected to vary as their identities are different—but, in all its different expressions, it remains a shared concern. For the younger generations, such issues that become transnational and abstract—that is, the Cyprus problem, Greek Orthodox religion, common history—overshadow the particularities and the much more essentializing elements of diasporic identity expressed locally by the migrant generations. The expansion of communications across dispersed diasporic populations means that the sharing of narratives and images that signify a selective and theme-based identification with a *homeland* and the broader diaspora increasingly gain importance. Local and national lobbying in the two countries initiated by migrant-generation organizations rarely grasps the interest and imagination of the younger generations. 'I've never been in a march [against Turkish occupation of Northern Cyprus]. It's fine that people do it, but I consider it a waste of time', says a British-born Cypriot. 'Community organizations are dominated by first generation men. They are so macho and traditional, they discourage fresh blood from joining' says a female participant, 35, in New York. More widespread among the younger generations is either a privatized political engagement with the problem, or a long-distance selective form of activism—for example, signing petitions, financial support of transnational Cypriot lobbying activities.

Community and Communication Beyond the Locality

> [T]he process of communication is in fact the process of community: the sharing of common meanings, and hence common activities and purposes, the offering, reception and comparison of new meanings, leading to the tensions, achievements of growth and change. (Williams, 1961: 10)

People turn to community to idealize and demonize it, to rely on and to escape from. As already mentioned, the meanings of community are neither stable nor shared by all. Community changes in times of global complexity (Urry, 2002) and of extensive spatial interconnections (Morley and

Robins, 1995; Sassen, 1991, 2001). Once it was considered to be the answer to the anonymity of the city, a holistic space defining people's existence (Park et al., 1925[1984]), then it became almost synonymous with locality (Bell and Newby, 1971). Within the context of globalization, community has been reconceptualized as the reply to global anonymity:

> The face-to-face communities that are knowable, that are locatable, one can give them place. One knows what the faces are. The re-creation, the reconstruction of imaginary, knowable places in the face of the global postmodern which has, as it were, destroyed the identities of specific places, absorbed them into this postmodern flux of diversity. So one understands the moment when people reach for those groundings. (Hall, 1991: 35-6)

Here Hall conceptualizes community as the expression of local particularity against universalizing processes of globalization. No matter how much people turn to local communities to find a refuge from the chaotic global anonymity, the survival and the viability of local particularity is now inescapably dependant on the global trends (Robertson, 1991; Morley and Robins, 1995; Sreberny-Mohammadi, 1996; Hannerz, 1996). Local communities' politics of culture and communication learn from the global and the emergence of new global and virtual communities, which depend on fragmentation, diversity and co-existence of people beyond the conventional face-to-face communication (Jones, 1995; Holmes, 1997). The local communities have changed in times of globalization, as communication and mobility have expanded across space. People do not inescapably belong to and depend on local microcommunities, ethnic or otherwise. They simultaneously belong to other communities, they move between spaces and everyday mobility—physical or mediated—opens up scenaria of identity in ways that challenge the taken-for-grantedness of the local and the bounded community context. Local communication, as much as transnational communication, becomes immediate and mediated, because the media appear as a link of individuals and subgroups in easier, more direct and accessible ways; the symbols of community are available on the airwaves and on the screen. Calhoun (1998) emphasizes the role of new media technologies for time and space distanciation that led to redefinitions of communities on a more democratic and less oppressive basis. As people are more mobile and communication more diverse, local communities become less closed and bounded value/social systems. Communities such as the transnational diasporic reflect the condition of increased mobility and interconnectivity across space.

Media cultures renew local communication practices and the local public sphere 'through the stimulation of cultural innovation, identity and difference' (Bassand *et al.* quoted in Morley and Robins, 1995: 41). But as local identities become more critical, they cannot but be interconnected and in dialogue with transnational and global cultures. 'Contemporary cultural identities must also be about internationalism in a direct sense, about our positions in transnational spaces' (1995: 41). Local communities are often revitalized because there is a sense of connectedness with other distant communities—communities they can be associated with. In the case of diasporic communities in particular, even when rooted in particular locales such as those of London and New York, the sense of belonging to larger, emergent transnational communities feeds the local *versions* with new energy. Diasporic communities, which include the local and the transnational, become resources for inspiration and of perspective for the future of local communities.

With this multidimensionality in mind, community is here operationalized in its dual sense. On one hand, it is positioned in the local context, especially as it applies to the demotic meanings of everyday life. On the other, it is conceptualized in its imagining, as this exceeds the local and achieves its meaning through transnational interconnections and cultural formations.

Mediated communication becomes as central as the immediate and direct in a community that surpasses the dependence on face-to-face communication, as Anderson (1983) suggests and many others after him (Silverstone, 1994; Morley and Robins, 1995). In Anderson's imagined community, it is the press that brings the nation together. In hybrid imagined communities, which are not bounded any more within specific, manageable and predictable boundaries, it is the electronic media that take over, bringing together people who might be in geographical distance or proximity. Electronic diasporic media undermine the domination of the imagined community of the nation (Papastergiades, 1998; Werbner, 1999), as they offer alternative spaces of belonging in everyday life. At the same time, electronic media daily renew the sense of belonging in a global community, which is saturated by difference and diversity. Mediation of communication, as it is argued elsewhere (see especially Morley and Robins, 1995; Robins and Webster, 1999), implies 'estrangement from the real' (Morley and Robins, 1995: 39), a further distanciation of the mediated Other. As the media come between the experience of different people, they might *smoothen* its *rough edge*, but at the same time, they might create a sense of sharing that, no matter how imagined, still shapes identities. As hybrid imagined communities rely on both mediated and nonmediated communication, the imagination is continuously informed and enriched by the immediate experience and vice versa. Nonmediated communication takes place in the locality, in face-to-face communication and in participation in various localities, as physical and imaginative mobility increases (Urry, 2002).

DIASPORIC PARTICULARITY
AND MULTIPLE IDENTITIES

Homogeneity can signify unity but unity need not require homogeneity.
(Gilroy, 1993b: 2)

Ethnicity has been increasingly acknowledged as a key element of identity
and community construction in multicultural societies. Shared discourses
of commonality reconfirm and sustain identity and community; commonality, however, does not equal homogeneity or singularity of identities. We
all achieve our identities through membership in a large number of groups
(Tajfel cited in Husband, 1994), and each group is broken down to more
or less permanent subgroups. Diasporic identities are always positioned
and dialectically shaped in relation to other identities, such as gender, age,
class, generation and sexuality. Like ethnicity, no identity is independently
shaped or has a pure form; co-existence and struggle is the constant condition of identity formation. Thus, individuals and groups construct their
diasporic identities in everyday life, in social interaction and economic relations and always in the context of the multiplicity and complexity of identities and their meanings—for example' a female working-class lesbian's
identity differs from a middle-class, financially independent woman's in an
intercultural marriage. At the same time, this interweaving of identities
means that diasporic identity itself is very diverse, and the tensions around
difference take place within diasporic groups as much as they do between
the particular communities and the mainstream.

The diversity within can be ever-expanding if identity is put under the
scrutiny of deconstruction. A never-ending deconstruction, however,
dilutes the social and psychological meanings of identity and its consequences for culture, social encounters and formations. Gender and generation are the two main themes discussed here in relation to the diversity
within. These two identities/identifiers formed in dialogue with ethnicity
will be discussed in showing how diversity and commonality do not always
contradict each other, but rather they become the components of multifac-
eted identities in the context of imagined communities.

Generation: A Key Signifier
of Diasporic Identity

. . . Generations, in immigration discourses, are the living embodiment of
continuity and change, mediating memories of the past with present living
conditions, bringing the past into the present and charged with the respon-

sibility of keeping some form of ethnic identity alive in the future. (Fortier, 2000: 55)

When studying diasporic populations, it soon becomes apparent that the migrant generation that left a distant *homeland* and settled in an unknown land relates differently to the origin, the journey and the country of settlement compared to the generations born and raised in a country that was already *home*. For the first generation, being part of a diasporic community is considered and experienced almost as natural. Because they experienced deterritorialization and reterritorialization directly, they relate to the *homeland* and a transnational community through physical contact, in the sustaining of transnational networks of friends and family and, very importantly, through memory and reconstruction of an imagined past in dialogue to their present diasporic condition.

Continuity and the Memory of Deterritorialization— Reterritorialization

Diasporic continuity, involves a process of *becoming* rather than of *being*, of a *changing same* (Gilroy, 1993a); it is sustained in identities that are the changing *outcome* of the meeting of diasporic roots and routes (Clifford, 1994; Gilroy, 1995). For the migrant generation especially, such continuity depends on the shared experience of deterritorialization and reterritorialization, but also on the communal memories and myths that informed the imagination of the shared diasporic *journey*. Experience and memory form the dual standpoint that brings the past and the future together in the core of diasporic imagination of commonality and thus of identity.

The construction of unity around the reproduction of shared imagination and of the imagined common past was revealed in one of the community settings where this research took place. Most of the first generation habitués of the Cypriot Community Center in London migrated in the 1950s and the 1960s and have developed a shared discourse around *migration* and *the journey*: a journey that, in most cases, started from a state of deprivation in rural Cyprus, followed by a lonely boat trip to an unknown land, the arrival in an unfamiliar place with no money and no knowledge of the English language and culture. The struggle that started with the *journey* and that has probably continued for decades becomes an important aspect of self-identification in everyday life for the older male habitués of the community center. The life story and the recollection of *the journey* becomes a mechanism for (re-)producing community boundaries and for performing identity in public, diasporic community spaces.

Life stories become a narrative through which many men introduce and present themselves; it is a code for shaping a common language with insiders that excludes the outsiders. In everyday talk in the community center, a selective representation of the self as a member of a migrant group often takes over in the form of a long, nostalgic narrative discourse. Violent and forced uprooting, usually caused by conflict and economic deprivation, are directly experienced moments in the process of diasporization and ingredients of collective memory (Naficy, 1993; Morley, 2000). War, political division and exile as components of the collective memory of many groups such as the Cypriots, the Jews, the Palestinians, the Armenians and the Iranians, become symbols integrated in the ideologies of diasporic particularity, identity and are produced and reproduced in narratives that reconfirm belonging in a distinct transnational community. As the narratives of resettlement in specific new locations usually accompany the memory and talk of uprooting, the imagination of transnational diasporic particularity interweaves with the imagining of the unique routes each particular group has followed. The specific elements of reterritorialization become important ingredients for imagining particularity: the historical memory of resettlement in specific (urban) locales feeds the imagining of the distinct diasporic routes, as much as the memory of uprooting feeds the imagining of the common roots. The memory of undesired deterritorialization reminds the members of the group that the original *homeland* is not an ideal place to return to—it carries memories of pain as much as it carries the myth of *home*/Heimat (Morley, 2000). At the same time, the memory of the collective resettlement in new locales, in urban metropoles, is a reminder of the changes that have occurred in the diasporic journey. The duality of diasporic memory of routes and roots has shaped the Greek Cypriot identities in the diaspora as identities of integrated particularity, or what Song (2003) calls conditional belonging:

> The notion of conditional belonging is useful, because it illustrates how partial, fragmented, and multifaceted the experience of 'belonging' can be. What is also striking about the idea of conditional belonging is that individuals who feel this way are staking a claim; they are refusing to accept the view that they do not belong to Britain because they are Chinese. . . . At the same time, assertions of conditional belonging point to the ways in which African Caribbean and Chinese people resists any easy and blithe notion of belonging in multicultural Britain—for the reality is that such belonging is not total, uncontested, or unambiguously embraced. (2003: 58)

Identity Reproduction in Everyday Life

For many members of the migrant generation, relations within the group dominate everyday life. Strong diasporic economic activity keeps many members of the group within the community, though less so in the American case, where there is extensive social and economic dispersal. Even when employed outside the physical and symbolic diasporic territory where the specific group predominates, most social encounters take place within the group. This is the case when socializing with friends and family, when attending one of the community organizations' activities, when participating in public community events—for example, christenings and political meetings, community associations' dinners. Though this generation reproduces Greek habits, traditions and values much more forcefully than the younger generations, their identities are still hybrid. In the words of a British participant: 'Cyprus is our home country and Britain is our home, if you can make the distinction. We feel that Cyprus is our home country but . . . then again, when we go there we realize that it's not our home.' This comment reveals as much the diasporic experience as it reveals the feeling of *strangeness* often marking the migrant generation's experience in both countries. Similarly, a migrant in New York says: 'We love Cyprus, it's our homeland. We'll do everything we can for it. But this country—[the] U.S—offers us the life we enjoy today. You can't underestimate how important this is.'

The migrant generation can be critical to the present condition in the country of origin, but it can also invent a diasporic discourse of nationalism and essentialism, which is either nonexistent or on the decline in the *homeland*. Essentialism and the quest for commonality within a group with different origins redefines complex cultural and political relations, such as that between Greeks and Greek Cypriots. The complexity of this relation cannot be analyzed in a few lines,[11] though it is worth mentioning that within the transnational context, Cypriot [national] particularity diminishes. This especially applies to the American case, where Cypriots are few within a large population from Greece. A performative celebration of Greek history and of Greek cultural and political achievements throughout time takes over Cypriot distinctiveness and its political and cultural particularity. Such celebrations of a glorious people, Greeks, is particularly visible and flamboyant in the United States—for example, with the demonstration of flags, religious symbols, ancient Greek symbol-decorations in houses and shops. Numerous Greek flags and children learning in schools and churches how to praise Greece in songs such as one heard in a community celebration ('I'm holding my flag high up and I sing for Greece, which I love so much') reflect the exaggerated aesthetics of performed Greekness. In Britain, such pride and a selective gaze to the ancient Greek past are mostly expressed in formal and informal community education, everyday talk references to Greek greatness and to other ethnic groups' comparative inferiority. Such discourses playfully and in contradictory ways reproduce the community boundaries while showing conditional respect to multicultural societies and Western capitalist values. In the

American case, a strong sense of ethnic pride and association with Greek culture and heritage is not considered as contradictory, but an all-American value. A female participant's words explain how the particular and the national coexist:

> You can't separate ethnicity from being American. You have the cultural melting pot here. People have their distinct celebrations but they live together. All Americans are used to criticize their own government. Cypriots, like other groups of course, also have distinct interests.

A 19-year-old male student identifies himself in the context of an all-American integrated diversity: 'I have the privilege of a Greek cultural heritage and I'm proud to be American'. The diversification and hybridity of people born in the diaspora distances them from the country of origin. Often, direct contact between the diaspora and the country of origin becomes a reminder of the distance between the diasporic transnational project of identity and that of the *homeland*'s national project of global homogeneity. Criticizing cultures and attitudes of people living in Greece and Cyprus is common. A female student, 20, says: 'We have been brought up in a pluralistic society. The paradox is that Greeks [of Greece and Cyprus] have given us Greek Orthodoxy which teaches us to love each other, but when it comes to other ethnic groups this value is abandoned.'

Youth and Shifting Identities

Teenagers, who tend to seek acceptance and integration within diverse peer groups, relate differently to diaspora than older and migrant generations. As many participants in their 30s say, in their early youth they resented many elements of Greek culture and community public life. As they grow older, many participants admit that they shift their identities, appreciating more cultural references and values associated with their ethnic background. A sense of responsibility for reproducing values and symbols of Greekness takes over a conditional and often resentful position towards the community, many of them say. For the generations born and raised in the diaspora, *code switching* between different groups and situations is common lived practice. Waters (quoted in Song, 2003: 108) refers to the words of a second-generation Haitian from New York:

> When I'm at school and I sit with my black friends, and sometimes I'm ashamed to say this, but my accent changes. I learn all the words. I switch. Well, when I'm with my black friends, I say I'm black, black American. When I'm with my Haitian-American friends, I say I'm Haitian.

Such forms of shifting in identification and performance of identities have been observed in the present study as well. Interestingly such code switching depends on the hegemonic or minority position of the group within particular locales. Young people in both New York and London coming from areas where the Greek and/or Cypriot representation among the local population is limited, reveal such shifting more frequently. In areas where Greek and/or Cypriot presence is large, confidence in projecting a Greek (Cypriot) identity within multicultural environments and social groups dominates. In these cases, the performed identity is more about combinations than about selective identifications as either/or. For example, in multicultural parties and social gatherings, a particular performance of North London Cypriotness, which is more compatible with multicultural youth culture, was observed. This involved the adoption of a strong local accent beyond ethnic particularity, distinct dressing codes and musical preferences that combined Greek and British/American pop cultures.

Intergeneration Relations and Identity

Generation is not only a definer of difference within; it is also a point of meeting and dialogue. Commonality and community are shaped in the dialogue between different generations and in the negotiation of community meanings and boundaries. Continuity is reproduced in family relations, the communication of traditional values and the use of the original language in the familial context. The initiation of younger generations in the public life of a community, through attendance of Greek schools, church, community clubs, and increasingly in their intended or unintended use of diasporic media, become mechanisms of reproduction of values and customs and shape spaces for intergenerational dialogue.

In the ethnographic research conducted in one of the Greek Cypriot homes participating in this study, reproduction of identity was observed in everyday talk and practice. Greek is the dominant language spoken in this home; it is a language the two daughters understand and speak almost fluently. The parents make sure that their daughters receive formal and informal Greek education; this includes going to Greek school and church and participating in discussions on Greek history, mythology, traditions and politics at home. The girls actively appropriate all these in ways that fit into their own sense of Greek Cypriotness, their age, gender and lifestyle choices. In other familial contexts observed, children resist and reject their parents' insistence in reproducing diasporic discourses, values and language. Intergenerational conflicts are not uncommon. However, in this case, the two girls celebrate it, though in their own terms. The reasons rest primarily on the social context of their everyday life. The close relations within the wider family and kin, which includes at least a dozen cousins of their own age, means that their identities are shaped in a communal context of performed ethnicity. Beyond the familial, the context is similarly dominated by Greek human and nonhuman references. The schools attended by the two young members of the family have a large number of Greek students. Their close friends are mostly Greek and they tend to go out to cafés, bars and clubs popular among the Greek youth. The communal performance of identity expands from the domestic to the public. Most public places of leisure and entertainment are hybrid and reveal how identity is actually communally performed and constructed. One of them, the 18-year-old girl (Girl 1—G1), explains:

G1: One Greek goes, then they all go! Greeks like to stick together . . . it's because we don't really like the rest of the population . . . (laughs)

Q: Why don't you like them?

G1: (serious) They have their own culture, they have their own people.

Q: What are the things you do with your Greek friends that you can't do with non-Greeks?

G1: For example, if the weather is good, we'll go to the park and make *souvla* (σουβλα—Cypriot BBQ). We enjoy doing it; nobody else would. It's because we all do it at home with our families. . . . And we go to the park and do things like we know how to . . . prepare the salad, BBQ the meat. . . . It's silly, but that's what we grew up with and we try to keep it up. . . . Then if you are only with Greeks you can speak in Greek. If there are others, you can't. We're not racists but this is the way things are. . . . With the Greek music as well . . . you can talk about Greek music with other Greeks. We do speak to everybody [Greeks and non-Greeks] in school but then we choose to hang out with the Greeks. It's the same with other cultures. The black people, they all go out together, because they go to the same places, they like the same music.

Q: Are there Greek Cypriot people of your age that reject all these?

G1: Yeah . . .

Q: What do they do?

G1: They act differently. . . . They are ashamed to be associated with the Greek culture. They don't want people to know they are Greeks. . . . But they grow out of this eventually (laughs). They aren't ashamed to be Greek. They just prefer to do other things, show off. But we all know that we are the same. We have the same upbringing, the same way of thinking.

This teenager's lifestyle reveals dimensions of diasporic identity as captured in Gilroy's (1993a) conceptualization of *the changing same*; change relates to experience within the diasporic group and the multicultural local community (Back, 1996; van der Pennen, 1998; Steinberg, 2000). When she celebrated her eighteenth birthday, she had a party in a Greek taverna. Not only her Greek schoolmates were invited, but also many non-Greeks. The non-Greek schoolmates, who grow up in a place of significant Greek presence, were more comfortable with the party activities than I was; they danced to the Greek pop music and they enjoyed Greek cuisine. Apparently, it all was very familiar to them.

In intergenerational relations, especially within the family, traditional values and the symbolic boundaries of the community are reproduced. The same two girls, both teenagers, discuss their attitudes relating to future choices, such as marriage. With confidence, the older girl (Girl 1—G1) and her sister (Girl 2) explain why marrying within the group is the only decision that would be right:

G2: I want him [future husband] to be Greek for the religion, the tradition, for everything . . .

G1: Definitely Greek! We want to get married to Greeks because we want our kids to grow up like we did . . . having our cousins around . . . you know, the Greek way! The Greek way is the best, you see! (laughs) We are so close . . . we spend so much time with our cousins and our friends.

Q: What would happen if you ended up with a non-Greek partner?

G1: It would be difficult . . .

Q: Do you think this 'preference' will continue with your kids?

G1: If my kids bring me non-Greeks, I'll kill them! (laughs)

Interestingly, an almost identical discussion took place in a Greek café in Astoria, New York, when a group of teenage girls were asked similar questions. They confirmed their confidence in reproducing Greek families and they as well thought that communication with other Greek youth (and potential husbands) is much easier and somehow natural. While arguing that ending up with a Greek partner would be their own independent choice, both groups clearly show that they know this is what their parents want. One of the girls in New York says: 'I'm going out with an Italian guy now. My mom is fine with it. But she's fine because she knows it's not serious. When I get older this will change.' When one of the girls' mother is asked if the tendency for endogamy will continue in the generations to come, she confidently says:

I think there's no question about that. If you see in history . . . things that we didn't know until recently and we learned through television . . . people were leaving Greece and Cyprus many many years before and even though at first they would marry non-Greeks, they would still managed to preserve their ethnicity . . .

Gendered Diasporic Identities

Gender is another key element, next to generation, that plays a key role in the construction and performance of diasporic identity. Women, who are usually ascribed the role of the carriers of the particular culture, the morality, the language and traditions within the family and the domestic space (Loizos and Papataxiarchis, 1991; Gillespie, 1995; Franklin, 2001), have a different relation to diasporic particularity than men who tend to move more flexibly across particular and multicultural public spaces.

The discourses of community and the narratives of diasporic continuity often reproduce male hegemony within the group. The roles ascribed to women and the restrictions in their participation in public life form relations of subordination, inequality, but also initiate tactics of resistance within. One of the participants working for a community organization in London is fluent in Greek and dreams of moving to Cyprus one day. However, she refuses to unconditionally adopt the Greek traditional gender relations. She is engaged to an English man and defends her choice by saying: 'Greek Cypriot men look for their mothers in their wives'. She argues that most Greek Cypriot girls rebel against their parents' traditional expectation. 'But it's not the same with boys. They learn to be treated like masters by their mothers and expect that from their girlfriends and wives. But young women are not willing to accept this attitude, that's why there are many split-ups'. Her own construction and experiencing of gender identity in essential for the way she deals with ethnicity in her life. Her particular gender identity influenced her choosing a partner outside the group. And it is reflected in conflicts with her migrant father. 'My father calls me "Εγγλεζουδα" (*Englezouda*—English girl). I ask him why. Just because I don't always say: "yes father", "whatever you say father"?' However, there is no clear-cut division between conforming to traditional values and breaking away from them. She defends her choice of an English partner, but she adds:

At least he's not Muslim. That, neither my family nor I could accept. I am not that strong, if you know what I mean. You see, it's easier with an English man because they are not religious or anything. With Asians[12] for example, the religion would be in the way, making it dif-

ficult to work. Either you or him has to sacrifice culture and religion.
And personally, I'm not willing to do it.

Young women within this group sometimes find themselves in a tense position of inside Otherness, as their values, lifestyle and ideologies often contradict the dominant ones. This is particularly visible in the case of young middle-class women, who have more choice of moving in and out of the community. Marginalization and exorcism of difference is directly experienced by men and women of sexual minorities. Often this conflict pushes many away from the community. A lesbian web designer explains her distanciation from the community's public life: 'The main problem is that the community and the church are very closely connected. You have to adapt to certain traditions and values to belong to this community. Otherwise it becomes closed and hostile.'

Gender and generation emerge as two key identities constantly inter-weaving with diasporic identities and individuals' positioning in relation to community. However, they are not the only ones. Gender and generation should not replace the old domination of class as an analytical category of ethnicity. They, like all identities, need to be studied in their complexity and coexistence. Bhabha (1990) proposed that we should take into consideration multiple subject positions, which include gender and class, but also race, generation, sexuality and geopolitical locality. Robin Cohen goes even further (1994: 205) proposing: 'Gender, age, disability, race, religion, ethnicity, nationality, civic status, even musical styles and dress codes, are also potent axes of organization and identification. These different forms of identity appear to be upheld simultaneously, successively and separately and with different degrees of force, conviction and enthusiasm.'

FOUR

LIVING IN MEDIA CULTURE
In Consumption Lies Identity

The particularization of production and consumption taking place within locales and in transnational spaces has multiple implications for diasporic populations. Geographical and national restrictions in distribution of media and their messages are challenged, especially with satellite television and the Internet—the transborder media par excellence. Technological convergence also means greater, easier and simultaneous access to multiple products across space. Television and radio produced in the original *homeland*, in the locale or in other places where diasporic populations live are available on computer and television screens, and it is a matter a time before they are transmitted via mobile phones. Digitalization has led to the emergence of new media players—commercial, amateur, once marginalized and silenced. Digital media are not restricted by airwave scarcity anymore and they are more likely to slip through the gaps of policy inadequacies to fully control technoscapes and mediascapes. Old marginalized players reappearing as vocal and visible challenge singularities of diasporic ideologies and dominant discourses of identity either in their extremism or their alternative creative expressions of difference within. At the same time, commercial players destabilize the singularity of the nation-centered, state-controlled ideologies of community and reinforce ideologies and discourses of commonality that emerge around consumption of commercially produced diasporic media.

With the expansion of digital and satellite media, new producers who destabilize the old status quo in diasporic communications have emerged. Two-way or multi-way communication and production that is not constrained in the country of origin and/or the locale are some of those major challenges. Needless to say, such challenges do not guarantee democratic and inclusive participation for all. In many ways, diasporic media depend for their success on ideologies of similarity over diversity, because such ideologies often maximize audiences. Many commercial new media reproduce ideologies of national homogeneity across boundaries as this suits their project of maximization of profits. Also, many of the new diasporic media are no more than evolved forms of old media systems and tend to reproduce ideologies of dominant powers—for example, states, diasporic political elite and conservative diasporic institutions such as the church. The most characteristic example is that of state-run satellite television. The project of assimilation of diasporic populations within a national project and the reconfirmation of their loyalty towards the original *homeland*—in terms of political and financial support—is the dominant ideology behind state-run television broadcasts for the diaspora across the globe. On the other extreme, some media invest so much in addressing particular interests of certain subgroups that lack any sense of reflexivity. Such cases can mostly be found on-line, in discussion groups that sometimes decontextualize issues when they bring them from the national to the transnational space—for example, in the discussion of 'national interests' without considering international politics, or stigmatization of Others based on a national historical past. Next to these homogenizing and segregational efforts, there are on-line diasporic projects concentrating so much on the production and sustaining of virtual versions of identity and community that their ideology becomes an ideology of disconnection from the off-line. Examples of such cases are some elitist intellectual diasporic projects that want to disconnect from mainstream—often conservative and nationalistic—diasporic ideologies. Often, the producers of such projects become so focused on virtual cultures and virtual images of identity and diaspora that they end up ignoring the off-line lived diasporic experience. Alternative ideologies to the diasporic dominant imaginary can become abstract and irrelevant if disconnected from the off-line; not surprisingly, such projects engage very small minorities within the diaspora.

This brief outline of the dominant trends in the ideology of diasporic media illustrates the diversity in diasporic mediascapes. Some of these examples also indicate the problematic character of mediascapes and communication technologies that do not necessary advance communicative, communitarian and creative projects of identity and community. Silverstone (1999) raises concerns about the structural amorality of the media that create a distance by masking it as closeness, while keeping people apart through connection and making Others' difference less visible by bringing them too close. Robins and Webster (1999) set a similar set of issues:

> It is not that we doubt the efficacy of the new technologies—indeed, we accept that it is entirely possible, even probable, that virtual technologies will sustain such new patterns of communication and community. Our problem is, rather, with the kind of social space or spaces that the new technologies are bringing into existence—this comfortable space of collaboration, dialogue, understanding, intimacy, reciprocity, and so on. Informed as it is by a sensible imagination of mutuality and consensus, we regard it as a banal space. The new virtual space is a pacified space . . . it is a tendency for the world to lose its substantiality and otherness, and thereby its human resonance and significance. Thus, we suggest, virtual culture is driven by the desire to suppress the complexities, difficulties and divisions that characterise real geographies. (*ibid.*: 239)

Such concerns focusing on production raise important issues about mediated proximity, about the consequences of increased mediation in bringing together dispersed populations in communities and in participating in the construction of identities. As will be shown here, consumption becomes an area where media and their messages are appropriated through engagement and negotiation. In consumption, and in its dialectic relation with production, mediated proximity, closeness and distance take their actual meanings.

MEDIA CONSUMPTION AS A RELATION

A mother and a daughter are having one of their usual arguments—the teenage girl spends hours on Instant Messenger, chatting with her friends. What are they talking about? Gossip, boys, going out to one of the trendy bars of Astoria, *Byzantium*. Her mother is angry with her. She doesn't know which is worse—the time her daughter spends on Instant Messenger or the fact that she goes to *Byzantium*. 'Don't get me wrong. I'm happy that my daughter has Greek friends and likes Greek music and stuff. But I'm not sure she's meeting the best kind of people where she hangs out.' Teenage access and use of technology, with limited adult control, and the appropriation of public ethnic space by young generations become some of the hot topics in the lips of many Greek Cypriot parents in the diaspora. These are the people who hope their children will sustain a strong sense of Greek

Cypriotness. These are the people who know that, beyond ideology, lived identity and sociality takes different directions. The blame is often directed to technology and 'the freedom of the new country.' These are the same two elements adults praise when it comes to their own everyday and their dual connection to their distinct community and the society they live in.

Technological developments have multiple implications for the diasporic everyday life. These include the challenge to national boundaries and any assumed affiliation to singular communities, but also they involve tensions in-between. Diversification of communication in private and public life destabilizes hierarchies between majorities and minorities, the national and the transnational, but also hierarchies within groups.

The analysis of diasporic consumption here is informed by de Certeau's arguments discussed in previous chapters. Whereas the powerful parties—those who have the control of the market and the unequal share of the economic and cultural capital—have strategies for establishing dominant and hegemonic discourses through production, the powerless have their own tactics—methods of resistance through consumption. What people consume can make all the difference in the construction of their identities. Diasporic media consumption might facilitate the emergence of discourses that lead to the reinvention and redefinition of particular identities. As media consumption is never singularly defined by particularistic media, nor is it shared in its characteristics across a group, the construction of identities in media cultures is complex and involves different communication processes, appropriations of various media and involvement in the production of various mediated discourses on the consumption side. Where and with whom people consume diasporic media is also important—media consumption is a social act, an act grounded in social contexts. Are individuals and subgroups in the periphery of the group, with family and friends, alone in their bedroom, overhearing diasporic radio programs? The social and communal experience of media consumption can explain the significance of the media for identity. Thinking about the social context of consumption means challenging assumptions about the linearity of the relation between media consumption and identity construction. If media are grounded in particular social settings and integrated in certain social relations, the connection of media and identity is more about interweaving rather than about causality. Changes in mediascapes and social settings can destabilize identities. In this context, the social relations around media become central. In Meyrowitz's words:

> . . . While we tend to think of our group affiliations simply in terms of who we are, our sense of identity is also shaped by where we are and who is with us. A change in the structure of situations—as a result of changes in media or other factors—will change people's sense of us and

them. An important issue to consider in predicting the effects of new media on group identities is how the new medium alters who shares social information with whom. As social information-systems merge or divide, so will group identities (1985: 54).

The questions of *where* and *with whom* highlight the significance of spatial and space-defined relations. Media consumption takes place in space, in the private and the public, in the real and the imagined community space that expands in transnational spaces. Places are neither defined as independent entities nor as bounded within clear-cut national and geographical territories. Similarly positioned relations are not just rooted in place; relations and communication expand across space and the social contextualization of media consumption requires considering relations that surpass the face-to-face and the national.

Breaking Off Homogeneity

The media, like other institutions within diasporic communities, tend to assume and celebrate an ideology of singular and common identity shared globally and across communities in London, Boston, Sidney and the original *homeland*. This ideology is rarely developed as a distinct political project; rather, it is reproduced in essentializing assumptions within the media about a sharing of common language, morality, interests and cultural capital across dispersed audiences. New communication technologies partly enhance such ideologies, as they create possibilities for simultaneous and common broadcasting beyond spatial and temporal boundaries. Yet, the tendencies within the media to assume audience homogeneity are counteracted by the process of mediation and by the particularities of diasporic media cultures. Transnational communication is more about relations than about conditions and phenomena. Some of those key relations are: a relation between production and consumption in the construction of mediated meanings; a relation between different actions of the audience across and within space; and, most importantly, a relation between the shared communal consumption and the construction of communal (mediated) symbols and meanings.

The present discussion focuses on the role of diasporic media in processes of constructing identities and sustaining communities. Diasporic media, it is argued, become important cultural references, both as agents of cultural representations as well as in the act of consumption. Consumption itself is a bonding experience shared across generations and different subgroups within a community. People watch programs together; they talk about them at home, at school, at work; they reproduce sitcoms' jokes and sing songs they hear on the radio. Diasporic media become part of the ordi-

nariness of everyday life; they are integrated in everyday routines and relations and sometimes achieve surprisingly central community roles. A
British-born mother explains how she solved the riddle of the growing fluency of her children in Greek: 'Of course [they are fluent in Greek] . . . all
they do when they visit their grandparents is watch Greek TV.' Similarly,
for teenagers and young adults, listening to Greek pop programs on the
radio becomes a rite of passage: knowing the latest Greek hits is a necessary precondition for being included in age groups, for fitting in, for being
invited to club nights. Greek pop music consumption becomes a bonding
experience among young people in the locale, but also between them and
other people in Cyprus and the rest of the diaspora; it teaches the Greek
language and it mediates contemporary Greek values and lifestyle in everyday life.[13]

Mediation theories (Martin-Barbero, 1993; Silverstone, 1999) have
already argued for thinking of media as a process and in relational terms,
for thinking of the interweaving between media institutions, media content
and consumption in the construction of their meanings and their role in
people's lives. At the same time, empirical research on audiences and consumption has illustrated how media are appropriated in daily performances and in the particular practices of engagement with them (Lull, 1990;
Gray and McGuigan, 1993; Nightingale, 1996); how various fractions of
the audience, located in diverse social, geographical and temporal contexts,
make sense of the media in different ways (Morley, 1980; Gillespie, 1995;
Ang, 1985). The original empirical research for this study reconfirms this
diversity and illustrates its nuances. Additionally, it focuses on the particular sociocultural parameters that characterize media consumption within a
community, across transnational spaces and in relation to diasporic—alternative to the mainstream—media.

The possibilities for expanded and diverse communication inherent in
new communication technologies shape new geographies, new ethnoscapes
and mediascapes (Appadurai, 1996). Yet, communication technologies do
not only blur the boundaries between the local, the country of origin and
the diaspora; they also blur the boundaries between different media. Both
conventional and new media adopt new technologies and converge in their
effort to reach larger audiences, minimize their cost and maximize the
range of their delivery. As a result, media focus shifts constantly between
the local and the transnational in order to meet more efficiently delivery
aspirations, as well as the needs and interests of dispersed audiences. New
and old technologies are implemented, on one hand, when they serve the
needs and goals of the producers, and on the other, when they can fulfill
audiences' demands for broadcasting from the country of origin, the broader diaspora and the local community. Local channels, like London Greek
Radio (LGR) and the London-based cable channel Hellenic TV, adopt satel-

lite technologies to rebroadcast programs from Cyprus, and use analog technologies and conventional phone-ins for their locally focused output.

As media cross geographical boundaries and allow direct access to
information from the country of origin and the broader diaspora, they
become compatible with the diasporic. Diasporic communities—even if
diverse and with particularities in different cases—have always relied on
networks, which have expanded from the immediate locale to the global.
In the diaspora, the construction of common imagination, partly dependent
on sharing images and sounds, has been a key element for sustaining community (Dayan, 1999; Naficy, 1999). New communication technologies
have taken even further the potentials for developing diasporic cultures of
mediated, transnational and partly free from state control communication
(Naficy, 1999; Tsaliki, 2002; Alia, 2002). Political and financial networks
have been expanding in professional web sites and in blogs produced within North London and Astoria, in different fractions of the diaspora, or in the
country of origin. At the same time, the invisible, banal and ever-increasing
exchange of e-mails has confirmed and expanded the immediacy and
everydayness of diasporic communication. E-mail has been developing as a
powerful competitor to the telephone and the mail—the older technologies for sustaining transnational relations through mediation—and has
taken transnational communication further. Family photos traveling from
Cyprus to the diaspora and the other way around are among the most popular attachments exchanged among dispersed families and friends. With e-
mail, the exchange of everyday mundane news has increased. Friends who
live in Cyprus, London and New York exchange details of a night out and
of intimate everyday experiences. The immediacy and availability of the
Internet mean sharing the ordinariness, routines and common activities of
everyday life, which reinforces a sense of belonging.

The expansion of mediated communication, of the invention and reinvention of relations and interests within the local and across the global are
not only enhanced in the interactive media technologies and outputs. In
locally produced radio and television, sounds and images of local
Cypriotness are broadcast, constructed and affirmed. In programs from the
homeland and other places across the diaspora, dispersed populations listen
to how people in the country of origin talk and watch how they dress. The
mediated construction of images and sounds of a community in its local
and transnational scale replace outdated, inconsistent and scattered images
and sounds. Diasporic media thus have tendencies for affirmation, closure
and construction of clear-cut identities. On the other hand, as they expand
connections and networks across boundaries and over time, new potentials
for diversified and participatory communication emerge.

The insistence and expansion of the transnational communication
flows within the diaspora and between the diaspora and the *homeland* do

not undermine the local. The local is the immediate context of everyday life, which gives meanings to media as cultural signifiers. In local information and advertising, in phone-ins, gossip and locally relevant social services programs, the dailyness of ethnicity unfolds, and audiences find expressions of their specific identities. The local media are run by individuals coming from the neighborhood, they are situated in known locations and they present and talk about local personalities; thus, they allow audiences to imagine the media as their own and the mediated local space as starting in the local radio headquarters and including their home and the local community center. The local (mediated) space grounds the community in a familiar place, beyond global anonymity:

> The face-to-face communities that are knowable, that are locatable, one can give them place. One knows what the faces are. The re-creation, the reconstruction of imaginary, knowable places in the face of the global postmodern which has, as it were, destroyed the identities of specific places, absorbed them into this postmodern flux of diversity. So one understands the moment when people reach for those groundings. (Hall, 1991: 35-6)

In the demotic discourse, a participant makes a similar point. In this case, too, the process of imagination as central in constructing commonality is implied:

> We listen to people [on the radio] who we share a lot with. We live in a foreign place, so when we hear a voice from our *homeland*, a voice from someone we know, it makes us very happy. (male, 53)

The search for grounding and familiarity that the local offers is reflected in the media consumption practices of the group being studied. Although most of the subscribers of the cable channels in both sides of the Atlantic say that they primarily watch them for their broadcasts from Greece (and, when possible, Cyprus), they repeatedly express a desire for local content. According to an 18-year-old interviewee, this applies to the London-based cable channel Hellenic TV: 'I wish they had more community programs. All they do is show old films over and over again.' Some attempts of Hellenic TV to produce locally focused programs attracted positive comments. The most famous of them (*Πρόσωπα*—Faces) presented prominent figures of the community. 'It's a good program. We get to know more about these people we've heard of for years,' says a male participant, 46. Similarly, one of the most popular media in New York is Hellas Radio. Much of the appreciation expressed is supported by arguments regarding its identity as a medium: members of the audience believe the station's producers belong to the local New York community and argue that the agenda of the station evolves around the concerns, interests and tastes of the Greeks and Greek Cypriots living in the locale.

On one hand, people belonging both to local communities and to global diasporas shift their consumption between local and global products and desire output from both. On the other, members of diasporic groups are consumers and members of multicultural societies. Thus, they might choose BBC1 for watching the popular soap *Eastenders* and the mainstream ITV for the news, while they might listen to LGR for a favorite music program and watch satellite television for the news from Cyprus. As participants' words indicate, they do not use particular media out of a sense of duty. Rather they turn to them because they are sources of information and entertainment and because they easily become part of everyday rituals and routines and tools for communicating and liaising with each other: just like they do with all media (Rothenbuhler, 1998).

MEDIA CONSUMPTION AS CULTURAL ACTIVITY

Media consumption becomes communal when shared interests and family socializing predominate at certain times of the day, and it becomes segregated as diverse interests and tastes take over at other times. More than one television set, more than one radio and stereo, and increasingly more than one computer per household serve families' diverse media preferences. In most of the homes where satellite or cable Greek (Cypriot) channels are available, the television set in the living room is switched onto one of the diasporic channels in the evenings, and a mainstream channel is on in another room. Similarly, the radio in the kitchen is usually tuned to a Greek language channel, while another one, usually in the children's bedroom(s), is switched onto one of the commercial mainstream—usually music—radio stations. Most of the diasporic homes, not unlike other homes in western metropoles, are not only television-saturated; they are media-saturated overall. When television is not on, the radio is; or even sometimes both—not to mention the PCs, game consoles and telephone that additionally, and often in parallel, mediate everyday communication within the home and between the home and the rest of the world.

People move between channels and media as they move between rooms and symbolic spaces. Younger generations enjoy the most of the spatial, communicational and cultural mobility and flexibility. For the young technology-literate generations a playful mobility in and out of their ethnicity and between diasporic and nondiasporic mediascapes and virtual

scapes is a daily experience—as they go to multiethnic schools, live in culturally diverse neighborhoods, as they consume media and technologies
that tend to be blind to ethno-cultural difference and more sensitive to
gender and age identities—for example. games, or pop music (Lee and
Cho, 1990; Berland, 1992; Gray, 1992; Bodroghkozy, 1995; Robins and
Webster, 1999). In the domestic familial space, diasporic cultural commonality predominates; its importance decreases as the younger members of
the household move to more private spaces such as their bedrooms. There,
age and gender identity particularities predominate. These might meet
diasporic identity—for example, in the consumption of popular radio programs among young Cypriots—but they might not. In the practice of
everyday life, especially for the younger generations—the fragmentation of
identities and parallel cultural spaces of belonging becomes visible. When
teenage boys get together to spend an evening around Playstation, diasporic identity subsides and processes of construction of age and gender
identities become more significant.

Young Greek Cypriots are in general more selective that other age
groups in their diasporic media consumption choices. This fact, though,
does not signify a decline in particularistic media consumption; it signifies
the shared importance of the particular and the mainstream/universal in
young Greek Cypriots' lives and the changing patterns in media consumption overall, which becomes more diverse and fragmented. As such, it indicates a parameter of a diasporic identity that is Greek Cypriot, but
inescapably integrated with identities relating to age, class, gender, national societies and (transnational) consumer cultures.

Considering young people's privileged social, spatial and symbolic
mobility, the shifts in their relation to diasporic media comes as no surprise.
Young members of the diaspora start their lives in a family context, where
their parents usually consume diasporic (language) media. Most of them,
in their early childhood through to their early adulthood, despise these
media, which in their eyes reflect a version of Greek Cypriotness they
reject; they are more eager to be part of the mainstream. This is no generalization, but a dominant discourse among the young participants in this
study. As second and third generations grow older and settle down—very
often in new Greek Cypriot families—they turn back to diasporic media.
The same people who admit that at a younger age they rejected these
media, confess that they turn to them in order to keep in touch with the
community and renew the values they feel diasporic media represent. The
dominant community discourse that many young families adopt—even
though always selectively and critically—reinforces the power of diasporic
traditions and values for cultural identity. Young parents often talk about
their concerns with morality and the values they want to transmit to their
children. Unsurprisingly, cultural symbols connected to ethnicity, such as

language and religion, become reassuring values and bonds with their children and to a community parents imagine their children becoming part of.
Media expose children to those cultural references and the language their
parents seek to reproduce. And they do it in the mundane, unpressured
way that fits everyday life. As Cormack argues with reference to the Irish
language media products in post-independence Ireland (2000), the projects that have proved successful are the ones that are not didactic but integrated in everyday popular culture.

Diasporic media become pertinent as they offer relevant and contemporary cultural references for people to actively renew and reinvent their
identities and sense of belonging. Concerns about the loss of the sense of
belonging and sharing are continuous sources of unease among diasporic
communities. Diasporic subjects have always been concerned with the
temporal and spatial constraints that leave much of the cultural references
connecting them to the original *homeland* fading in the past. Communication and transportation technologies have directly addressed these diasporic concerns (Cohen, 1997; Dayan, 1999). The images of the *homeland*,
experienced directly through traveling and mediated in television, radio,
the Internet, are now part of people's everyday cultural repertoires. In
studying media practices, I came across examples of male viewers organiz-
ing their evening routines around their devoted daily viewing of satellite
television news broadcasts; I overheard women talking about a Greek soap
over coffee; I repeatedly heard sitcom jokes being shared by first and second generation members of the group. During the interviews, I heard people calling CBC-SAT[14] 'the television channel of the *homeland*,' the channel that *speaks* the ethnic language, the channel that constantly informs
people about what is happening in Cyprus and entertains them with some
of the most popular programs across the community—primarily sitcoms
and soaps. In the words of a male interviewee, 49: 'News is great. Now we
know what's going on in Cyprus. Before we didn't have a clue.'

MEDIA CONSUMPTION AS NEGOTIATION OF AUDIENCEHOOD

Patterns of diasporic media consumption often indicate a love and hate
relationship between audiences and these media. Some wholeheartedly
applaud them, but the majority praises and hates the media at the same
time. Diasporic media are not permanent and unquestioned references.
They are contested, and their presence in everyday life is continuously
challenged, especially as mainstream media increasingly become acceptable and preferred cultural references among members of minorities, as

they move between spatial and social spaces and as they form their (mediated) social encounters. This comes as no surprise, especially when the generations born in the diaspora are concerned. Younger generations often feel much more at ease in communicating and consuming media in the mainstream dominant language, while participation in mainstream media cultures is taken for granted. Yet, many of the anecdotal material indicate that media consumption becomes more and more a matter of combined and diverse media practices rather than of an either (minority)/or (mainstream) exclusive participation in one media culture. Particular media remain relevant across subgroups of different generations—and often grow to be more important than in the past—even if their permanence and dominance in the domestic and across the public space is increasingly contested. People's own words indicate that mainstream and minority media are part of the same media cultures of diversity.

Words and practices show constant negotiation and unease in defining a clear-cut position as members of audiences. Even within the migrant older generations, these negotiations are common. A 70-year-old female immigrant with poor English admits that she has endless arguments with her husband, as she often wants to watch 'English' television, whereas he insists on watching Greek television all the time:

> My husband always watches Hellenic TV. But I do get bored sometimes and I ask him to switch over an English channel for a while. He gets angry and tells me: 'That's my language. That's what I want to watch and listen to.'

Negotiation comes with hybridization in media cultures: both mainstream and minority media consumption patterns and interpretations of representations are increasingly informed by each other and they interweave in new ways. When the homosexuality of the famous British Greek Cypriot artist George Michael was revealed after his arrest in a public lavatory in Los Angeles, many expressed dissatisfaction about the 'unacceptable' bias against him in diasporic local media. Some participants argued that it is completely inappropriate for these media to judge his actions, apparently drawing from the British press values of objectivity and neutrality. At the same time, they demanded that diasporic media show respect toward George Michael, who is one of the most successful members of the community beyond the limits of the group. In this paradoxical way, critics of the Greek coverage of the event wanted neutral coverage on one hand, but expected the media to adapt a community role of responsibility on the other.

The patterns of consumption of minority and mainstream media are equally hybrid. A discussion with a group of students, aged 12–16, revealed this hybridity in their contradictory narrative. When asked what they usu-ally watch on television, they mentioned a long list of mainstream British and American soaps and sitcoms. Yet, this reality was highlighted by shades of diasporic media consumption in the process of confrontation. When a male student admitted that he listens to the Local Greek Radio (LGR), one of his female classmates mocked him: 'Old women listen to LGR!.' The sis-ter of the latter, though, revealed her sibling's own habits to the group: 'Oh, really?! You forget that you watch sketches [sitcoms] all the time on CBC . . . in Greek!' In her reply to the revelation, the student in question embarrassingly defended herself: 'I just watch them when they are on and when they [referring to her parents] don't let me switch over to another channel . . . '

Such patterns of media consumption and audiencehood show some of the mechanisms that reproduce diasporic media's relevance. As already argued, such media meet interests, entertainment and information needs and become bonding cultural references. Furthermore, particularistic media are ingrained in everyday culture of extensive mediation. Cypriots use the media—both mainstream and minority—a lot. Satellite, digital and cable commercial television packages, as well as VCR and DVD players are very popular across the group, across the Atlantic and across generations. Greek channels are often part of the satellite or cable television package; however, diasporic television is found in just a fraction of the households that receive the commercial cable, satellite and digital channels. On one hand, diasporic media consumption cannot be understood except in the context of broader experience of mediation, and on the other, a minority community's media cultures cannot be understood if separated from the general patterns of media use in Western societies. The range of similarities in the practices of the groups studied on the two sides of the Atlantic does not only relate to their diasporic connections, but also to the fact that in both cases the local groups form part of Western metropolitan capitalist cultures and economic contexts. The words of a 24-year old council employee indicate that media choices relate both to her working-class habitus and general patterns regarding the media in the West:

> We got cable because overall it's cheaper entertainment. It would cost much more to go out every evening, or even every weekend. So, we choose to pay and get the various entertainment choices cable offers. . . . But the Greek channel, no we don't have it. . . . I can't stand it, it drives me crazy.

The extensive media saturation and sophistication of media consump-tion characterizing this community's domestic terrain and its everyday dis-courses have played their own part in diasporic media establishing their popularity. Particularistic media might be popular, yet media consumption is very diverse within different subgroups, as the previous quote reveals. As will be shown in more detail in the following chapters, media preferences relate, among other things, to class, gender, generation, spatial location, and they are situational and shift to fit in the routines, choices and restrictions of everyday life. Furthermore, different media play different roles as they require various levels of participation, concentration and effort, financial ability, access and familiarity with information and communication technologies.

As this research and others in this area (cf. Gillespie, 1995; Drucker and Gumpert, 1997; Aksoy and Robins, 2003) show, people always use a combination of different media: mainstream and minority, print and electronic, digital and analog, local and global, old and new. Not a single person out of the hundreds participating in this research uses diasporic media alone. Interestingly, though, all of them are exposed to the particularistic media: either because they choose to use them, or because other members of their households and work environment use or talk about their content. The apparent variety observed in media consumption within most diasporic groups (Georgiou, 2001, 2003, 2005a; Sreberny, 2002; Karim, 2002; After September 11 Research Project, 2002; Naficy, 1993) reflects the richness of everyday life and the inherent diversity within diasporic communities.

Apart from gender and class, and more than any other identity, it is generation, combined with age, that define the level of member's engagement with the diasporic media cultures. It is true that older members of the migrant generation, whose fluency in English is still limited, are the ones who use ethnic language media more than any other group. 'It's great to listen to your own language. . . . It's like being in Cyprus,' one of them says. Young generations' relation to diasporic media like their relation towards many diasporic cultural references (Kassimati, 1984), is much more ambivalent and interesting for understanding hybrid identities and the construction of communities in the diaspora. It is very common for young Greek Cypriots to criticize diasporic media and to mock their parents and grandparents for consuming them. Yet, and as the classroom anecdote above and the extensive ethnographic research conducted with young members of the group revealed, they often do use and enjoy them. In other cases, they refuse to consume any kind of diasporic media. They despise them for being an obstacle to their integration in the societies where they live, for being tasteless and of doubtful quality, as well as for underestimating their audience's intelligence. A third case, which is not in contrast to the previous two, is the exposure of young people to diasporic media, not by choice, but because they are part of the background of their everyday life at home, at work, in public places.

Taking this ambiguity into account, it is interesting to note that certain media products are most successful within this group and across diverse subgroups in transnational scale. Such programs usually belong to genres that are easily consumed and easily translated: music programs on radio and sitcoms on satellite channels from Greece and Cyprus being the most characteristic examples. The reason for such programs' success is twofold. On one hand, they follow the patterns of successful western media products. Many of the (musical) sounds, images and themes—especially in sitcoms—are not much different from other mainstream products of similar genres. Yet, such diasporic programs are not just like any mainstream media. There is another dimension to their success. Their representations, aesthetics and recipes for success are in many ways universal, but they are also particular. Pop music and sitcoms become inclusive symbolic mediated spaces, as in their broad consumption, commonality can be imagined across borders and generations. The sense of humor that travels from generation to generation also travels over airwaves. The aurality and visuality of broadcasting do not demand fluency in Greek. The sitcom drama presenting conflicts between universal themes of love and conspiracy on one hand and particular Cypriot values on the other become repertoires that are rather similar to lived experience. In their temporality, normality and taken-for-grantedness, media and consumption as part of popular culture are not only compatible with everyday life, but they are also part of it. The media speak the everyday language, they produce and reproduce everyday humor, as the repeated comments of many participants emphasize.[15] Media representations, agendas and narratives inform the discourses of ethnicity and in their dailyness they produce and reproduce symbols of identity and community. As Urry argues, the media form a new 'public stage' and 'alter the very possibilities of interaction and dialogue . . . producing new ways of conceiving of self and identity and generating fundamentally new performativities' (2000: 180).

FIVE

HOME, HOMELINESS AND MEDIATION

Home is the initial habitat of ethnicity, both in its real shape as a place, as well as in its symbolic imaginary form (Morse, 1999). Home is the symbolic and real place that becomes a synonym to familiarity, intimacy, security and identity against the unknown, the distant and the large. 'Home, of course, needs to be understood in both literal and metaphorical senses. The defense of home is a defense of both the private spaces of intimate social relations and domestic security—the household; as well as of the larger symbolic spaces of neighbourhood and nation—the collective and the community,' Silverstone (2004: 442) argues. Media destabilize the role of the home in achieving ontological security. '[B]oth [the domestic and the collective home] are threatened by the media extension of cultural boundaries: both laterally, as it were, through the globalisation of symbolic space, and vertically through the extension of accessible culture into the forbidden and the threatening. In both cases home has to be defended against material breaches of symbolic security' (Silverstone, 2004: 442). For diasporas, extended cultural boundaries might be enabling for the construction of new and multiple domestic and collective homes. At the same time, and as cultural boundaries stretch, stability and ontological security become even less adequate synonyms for home. Home in the case of diasporic populations is always ambiguous and incomplete. It is never as fixed and permanent as the ideal perception of *the Home* assumes it to be: private, safe, fixed, a shelter to return to. In a way, this idealization of home does not correspond to any kind of home anywhere in late modernity, where symbolic and real boundaries of space and privacy are blurred (Morley, 1999; Silverstone, 2004). But in no other case is the change of Home more obvious than in the case of diaspora. The diasporic home is not necessarily synonymous with a house, it is not necessarily singular. Which house would that be anyway? Which *one* home is home?

GAZING INTO THE PAST— IMAGINING THE PRESENT

In the case of the Greek Cypriots, would it be the house in North London or Astoria, the beach house bought in Cyprus, or the parents' house in a Cypriot village rarely visited? A British-born young woman, who poses for Nassari's (1999) photographic exhibition on identity and personal totems,[16] explains her chosen item. It is a photo album with pictures from her grandparents' occupied village—Akanthou. She defines the meaning of her chosen object and the representations it carries: 'It's where I'm from, even though I've never visited the place. That's all we've got left, just pictures, we don't even have the memories.' A very similar projection of homeliness in still pictures capturing the past was also observed in a New York home.

   While visiting a Cypriot home in Astoria, New York City, two images struck me as I walked in: a large photograph of Kyrenia's[17] castle and a huge enlarged reproduction of a holy icon from the owner's village church. And then, of course, there was the television tuned to a Greek channel. 'Our memories stop in 1974,[18] my hostess repeated a few times later on. 'Our memories stop at the point we were forced to leave our village.' Migrants, refugees and exiles have always carried pictures, photos of loved people and places through their journey. Still pictures, satellite broadcasts, bites, digital sounds mediate memories and the latest repertoires of identity that are carried along, downloaded, watched on screens. The pictures from the land of her origin, hanging on her New York home, remind my hostess of her sacred connection, a connection that is repeatedly referred to as frozen in time and place.

   Home is the container of memory and cognition, Silverstone argues (1999). But for the diasporic home there is no sequence, as different generations, different individuals sharing common ethnicity name different places as home. This is the inescapable ambiguity of the home as imagined symbol. It can never be complete, as it can be here, there, in both places, or nowhere. Another woman photographed by the same diasporic photographer, John Nassari (1999), says: 'When I go back to Cyprus I feel like a foreigner, but here in England I feel like a foreigner too. It's the same wherever I go, I'll be a stranger. . . .' Many people talk of a sense of strangeness in more than one places. The condition of strangeness, more than anything, symbolizes the nostalgia for the old permanent and fixed home, of the sequence in the placement in space and the assumed continuation of the significance of one place through time. Massey (1991) questions the stable and inward-looking nature of the home and argues that a sense of place does not depend on its stability and purity; rather it depends on its unique position as a point of intersection in a wider context of relations. Nostalgia, strangeness and the sense of loss (Seed, 1999) intensify the efforts of making a house a home (Morse, 1999). The search for ontological security becomes one of the main reasons for reinventing close family relations, relations that often become even more intense in the diaspora than they would ever be in the country of origin.

The extensive focus on constructing a diasporic home, along with the relations that it implies—relations among its members, relations to the inside and the outside world that a construct with walls and windows shapes—give home[19] its meanings. In this respect, home is the starting point, where diasporic bonds and relations initially develop, where people learn their first words in the *ethnic* language—both the spoken and the unspoken. Experience of diaspora in early childhood, within the home, critically marks the sense of belonging. Boyarin and Boyarin, when discussing the process of constructing ethnic identities in childhood, argue: 'Contact with other people who share the name of a given identity and seem to feel organically connected to a community can produce a sense of nostalgia even in one who has never been near the things that that community does' (1993: 704).

Within the home, diasporic identities are constructed as the hierarchy of family relations and the dominant culture of the family shape roles and moral values. Silverstone and Hirsch (1994) note the significance of the domestic in the modern world as a place enhanced, mediated, contained, even constrained by our ever-increasing range of information and communication technologies and the systems and services that they offer the household. Media shape cultural scapes and mediate interpersonal relations and thus, domestic hierarchies and moral values. On one hand, media invade the privacy of the home (Morley, 1999), making it impossible for the insiders to shape their values and lifestyle without the outsiders' intervention. On the other hand, they mediate for the members of the household the experience of the outside world, before going 'out there.' Media produce representations of the world outside the domestic space, but also of the home itself (Morley and Silverstone, 1990).

PRESENT CONTINUOUS

Let's return to my host in Astoria and her struggle to persuade herself and me that her old village and the frozen images of the past are the most significant references for her own identity and her family's identity. The constantly switched on television, usually tuned into a Greek satellite channel, challenges her ideological declared closure and represents a different perspective of the outside world—the Greek world she so eagerly wants to belong to. 'What has Cyprus turned into? . . . And Greece as well . . . so much immorality, so much nudity, so much blasphemy,' she says referring to her viewings on Greek television. Sometimes I think of covering Panayia [the icon of Virgin Mary] with a cloth or of moving the icon so that she won't face the tv.' The constant feeding of images from the present *homeland* in the media challenges frozen time, brings contemporary reality closer. Resistance to the present realities of Cyprus, an attempt to protect oneself or to hide from its realities is a blessing and a curse for the diaspora; it is certainly a clear indication that diaspora is not just an extension of a nation. It indicates its ambivalent position in relation to the *homeland*: my hostess still chooses to have Greek television, she still switches it on. The frozen memory she constantly talks about is not actually that frozen. She seeks information—the images and sounds—from contemporary Cyprus and Greece, even if it not always pleasant. The imagined commonality in the *mediated* images and sounds that travel across boundaries is shared in instant and simultaneous time. The communion, which Anderson (1983) talks about, is found in the imagining of comradeship that lies on the uneasy meeting of the past and the present, as lived and as imagined in the original *homeland* and in the global diaspora.

The media bring another temptation home. Though their representations are sometimes hated, they still allow people to imagine they go to places without leaving their home. In media cultures, audiences can also choose with whom and where they go (Moores, 1993). No other example is more obscure or revealing than the devoted viewing of the weather forecast in Cyprus. A participant in New York says:

> My husband always follows the weather in Cyprus—on tv and on the Internet. It's so funny! I ask him: 'Why the hell do you watch the weather? You're not in Cyprus, you're thousands of miles away!' (female, 38)

The words of a woman in London give an explanation of this strange habit.

> If it wasn't for CBC I wouldn't have remembered that it's *Kataklysmos*[20] today. I saw the celebrations on tv and it was lovely. . . . it looked so nice and warm, everybody was at the beach. . . . I wish I was there. . . . (female, 47)

Images of commonality and of a *homeland* that was lived in the past and is imagined at present are shaped in everyday viewings. This participant's words show how television images remind her of important common cultural references; in present engagement with the media memories are given *real* present substance. Mundane information, such as the weather forecast, activates processes of imagining of how Cyprus looks like now and what people do at the specific temporal instance. The television weather forecast of a distant *homeland* becomes the container and transporter of imagined copresences across the globe. The construction of memory is intrigued by a sensual and sentimental relation to the *homeland*, a relation that is attached to old traditions, to an idealized village, to habits and rituals connected to specific seasons and weather conditions (Loizos, 1981). Visual culture is a culture of imaginative travel and mobility (Urry, 2000). The circulation and consumption of contemporary images of everyday life in Cyprus reinforces the construction of an imagined past, which, in contrasting the *homeland's* present, strengthens diasporic belonging: the fact that the origin is a strong referent but only in its imagined, past and constructed version.

The Domestic and the Familial: Constructing Commonality Around Television

When diasporic media, along with other cultural references, become integrated in everyday life, various scenaria of family relations, moral values and consumer culture co-exist and clash. The new technologies might coexist with some old social forms and they might even reproduce them (Williams, 1980); they might incorporate each other or challenge each other's limits (as it very often happens around the intergenerational arguments about the choices of television programs, music and games). Diasporic, like all media, are not homogenous; neither do the members of the household passively digest all representations in the same way. The shared consumption, as well as the conflict around diasporic media, can become a dialogical, vivid space for the construction of individual and familial identities.

The homes visited and the people participating in this research are different in many ways; however, some important similarities were observed.

The first and most striking similarity is the place of television in the house. A television set—often one of many—is strategically positioned in the room where members of the household spend most of their leisure time— the living room or the kitchen. This is the case in all participating house- holds. The television is always switched on and in most cases it is not switched off even when interviews take place or guests enter the house. Television seems to be the necessary background in the domestic setting when not watched, and comes to the foreground when something that the members of the household want to watch is on. The continuous presence of the switched on television might seem an unwelcoming signal in the eyes of the untrained visitor. However, after becoming familiar with the diasporic Cypriot home, it soon becomes apparent that socializing among family members and with guests often takes place around the television— as it is watched, discussed, ignored and naturalized in the domestic setting. Silverstone argues that television's taken for grantedness is involved in the construction of social spaces and spaces of belonging that involve the domestic and the public:

> Television and other media are part of home—part of its idealisation, part of its reality. . . . Yet the 'box in the corner' is, in our dependence on it, a crucial link to the shared or shareable world of community and nation (Anderson, 1983) and, as such, acts to extent the boundaries of home beyond the front door. Television may be received 'at home' but 'home' itself is both constructed through, and constructs, other reali- ties, and television is implicated in all of them. (1994: 29)

Transnational diasporic television does not only act as a community link; it acts as a reconfirmation of the multipositionality of diasporic home and its connection to numerous publics. Diasporic television is local and it is glob- al; it is consumed next to national and global mainstream television; it is a window to a number of worlds, which compete and which are appropriat- ed in their coexistence.

For the substantial number of homes I visited, everyday life is saturat- ed by media—media in the background, in the foreground, media as initi- ating and setting agendas in face-to-face communication. This happens in unforced and casual ways, as people sit on their couch and as they have a drink. Everyday communication requires knowing of and about the media and collectively consuming them. For entering this highly mediated domestic sphere, I had to adjust my media consumption. I got cable televi- sion and started watching popular mainstream and diasporic soap operas. Not adapting to the dominant media culture becomes an alienating factor in everyday communication, as one finds herself excluded of much of everyday talk. In a way, more than the media content, it is the media culture that people share. And in the case of the diasporic media, it is this alternative to the mainstream media culture that members of a community share, or are expected to share.

The practices and the meanings of diasporic media consumption are not very different from those that apply to mainstream media. For example, gendered genres such as news and soap operas are similarly gendered in the case of the diasporic and the mainstream media consumption. Also, younger people use the Internet much more than older members of the group; this goes for the use of both Greek and American/British sites. Thus, there are two important points to be highlighted here. Diasporic populations are integrated in media cultures as much as most people who live in highly mediated, advanced capitalist societies of the West.[21] It is this extensive and taken-for-granted mediation of everyday life that establishes and confirms the significance of diasporic media for identity and community. Media (diasporic, like other) saturate everyday life and mediate communication between consumers. Diasporic media are powerful cultural references exactly because they are integrated in everyday life. What makes them distinct is not the fact that their audiences are very different to anybody else, but the fact that they are used by certain people and not others. They are involved in projects of (transnational) particularity and in the construction of distinct imagined communities.

Media are consumed and appropriated in social relations and in the context of everyday life. In this case, the centrality of the family, reproduced in generation after generation, creates a context for the continuation of a sense of common belonging that primarily relies upon familial relations. In the case of the Cypriot diaspora, it is very common for parents and children of different ages to live under the same roof. Often children only leave their parents' home to start their own family. And even when family members do not live under the same roof, the family still functions as the smallest dominant unit within the community that mediates individuals' initiation in its public activities. Most often grandparents are the primary source of daycarer for children. Usually, different generations of the same family go together to church, public celebrations, and attend community center activities. And more than that, on a daily basis they all find themselves positioned in front of the same television set.

The Construction of a Communication Space at Home

> *We watch more Cypriot television here than we do in Cyprus. All we do is watch Cypriot TV.* (Female interviewee, 47, London)

In the majority of households observed, diasporic media are extensively consumed, though not necessarily by choice. For most young participants, diasporic television and radio are linked to their familial setting and they are usually the choice of their parents. 'I hate LGR, but my mom always has it switched on!' a teenage girl says. Often, and especially as observed in the homes where extensive ethnographic research took place, young family members' consumption of diasporic television and radio is the outcome of a consensual agreement with parents and grandparents. For many young participants, such consumption signifies familial harmony, as well as their disempowerment within the home. Many, especially the youngest, often complain that they do not have any choice but to watch Greek television. No matter how much and how often young people declare their dislike of diasporic media, in practice they engage with certain media products and sometimes they develop genuine interest in them. The key difference to their consumption in relation to the migrant generation is not that of no consumption vis-à-vis too much consumption, but selective consumption of diasporic media, which is an integrated fraction of their overall media consumption vis-à-vis extensive consumption by the migrant generation.

A family of four—the parents and two teenage children, one girl, one boy—observed over a period of six months, lives in a household where media technologies dominate: four television sets, two stereos, numerous portable radios, four mobile phones, two computers. The consumption practices vary among its members, with the mother consuming diasporic media the most and her teenage son the least. Most of the time the family members consume media individually or in pairs. In the evening, though, there is at least one hour of communal television viewing, which includes both mainstream and minority media program consumption. All family members recognize and praise the role of diasporic media, even if their communication practices do not always reflect this ideology. They all think that diasporic media are among the most effective and professional organizations in the community.

The high level of media use and media literacy of this family explain the negotiation of practice and ideology that takes place around media talk and media consumption. The parents of the British-born boy and girl acknowledge the fact that their children's identities are different to theirs. In relation to their children's limited diasporic media use, which somehow contradicts their strong sense of Greekness,[22] the parents say that diasporic media consumption is not necessary for ethnic awareness. They are media literate enough to know that trying to force anybody to watch or listen to particular media is ineffective. They also know that the variety of media on offer minimizes the success of small and less commercial media, including the diasporic. More than anything, they understand that each family member's media preferences are individual and unique. The individualistic fragmented media consumption in this household seems to be in accordance with dominant consumption practices in western metropoles. But it is combined with a consensus that assumes that only a fraction of this consumption is communal and for the whole family. This seems to be the case with church attendance and with visits to the extended family as well. The mediated in this case becomes the link of the familial to the community and of the domestic to the diasporic public life. It is selective and much more limited than in other cases observed. Will diasporic links and diasporic media consumption decrease and disappear when the teenage members of the family move out of their parents' home? This is a possible scenario. There are, however, alternative scenaria reflected in the partial engagement of the younger generations with the diasporic cultural context.

In another home, television viewing shows how for the younger generations diasporic cultural engagement becomes partial while remaining present. The owners of this second household have three children and two grandchildren. Their two adult sons live with them; their daughter is married to a Welsh man and lives in her own home with her husband and their two children. The children spend every afternoon and evening at the grandparents' home as their grandmother takes care of them when they are not in school and when their parents work. Most of this extended family's members spend a substantial amount of their time together in the large kitchen. The television set has a prominent place in it. The grandfather is a fanatic of Greek television. This causes arguments with every other member of the family. However, when it comes to the grandchildren negotiation takes place. The grandfather has reached an agreement with his grandchildren for alternating between programs that each likes. Inevitably all of them watch programs they wouldn't otherwise choose. The coexistence and the negotiation that takes place around viewing and around familial relations create some interesting dynamics. The children improve their Greek, which is the outcome of the close relation with their grandparents and of their satellite television viewing. The grandfather familiarizes himself with the British culture, even when he doesn't want to and even when he doesn't understand it. His grandchildren interpret the language and the cultural codes when they watch together British soap operas. This space of cultural and intergenerational exchange reflects the hybridity of diaspora. In the everyday interplay mediated by relations of love, the members of this extended family develop their multiple connections to close and distant, diasporic and mainstream cultural hubs.

Such hybrid expressions of identity were also observed in two other participating households in New York City and London. In these two cases, teenage children are actively engaged in public diasporic life while remaining critical participants in cultural activities and practices initiated by their parents and community organizations. In both homes the cultural capital of the families is one that promotes education, but also cultural particularity. In this context, media—both minority and mainstream—are seen as having multiple functions: for entertainment, information, education, socialization. 'I look up Greek web sites when I want to find out about new [music] releases. There're some really good ones. I want to know what's out there and Internet is a way to find out' says a 16-year-old in New York. A girl of this age group in London praises the role of the local Greek radio for its charity campaigns. She still makes fun of some of the producers, whom she thinks are unprofessional and unable to see beyond their Cypriot past. Nevertheless, she has no problem admitting that she likes some of the radio programs and that she even watches news on the Cypriot satellite channel, though usually not by choice. Interestingly, she, like most participants of all ages and generations, talks passionately about Cypriot politics, especially in relation to Cyprus' ongoing division.

In all the cases discussed, there is an obvious continuity observed in the affiliation of the older and younger family members with a community, even if this is often criticized and even despised. None of these people, young and old, had any dilemma in naming their ethnicity; they all consider themselves to be Greek (Cypriot). The common elements that surpass difference are the strong familial relations and the participant (mediated) domestic everyday. A playful engagement with diasporic media culture explains particularistic media's ongoing relevance, at least for some members of the group. In the words of a young participant in London:

> People my age are forced to watch Greek TV, to listen to the radio [Greek radio stations]. But then, they end up liking them. For example some funny programs like *Kafenion*,[23] we all get together on Friday night and watch it. We can relate to it. It's like having your parents on TV. It's this kind of stereotype of them, but it's funny! . . . Then again, with LGR, many young people listen to it, especially at night when they go to bed even if they don't admit it. . . . LGR has started all these Greek club nights and stuff—events that people go to. If it wasn't for LGR they wouldn't be happening. It's great, because, in that way people get together and they do so through the radio.

MEDIA CONSUMPTION AND MOVING IN AND OUT OF THE DIASPORIC CONTEXT

The central role of television and its mediating power for communication between family members and with guests does not mean that nondiasporic media are peripheral in everyday life. All kinds of media contribute to representing the world—they show what a home should look like, how the ideal mother-daughter relations should be, what food should be consumed. Media of all kinds, in their presence and their shared consumption, become the cultural and material referents necessary for harmony and ontological security. The practice and the talk around media culture have been recorded in a number of visits and interviews that took place in 50 households in London and New York. The majority of the participating homes are media-saturated in general, not only television saturated. That means that usually radio is on and listening is communal during the hours the television is switched off—for example, in the morning or early afternoon. Radio's use becomes individual, gendered or age-defined when tastes and interests predominate over family dynamics. The case with the Internet is similar. The Internet is predominant in everyday life, especially for the younger generations and age groups. Though it is difficult to observe, as its consumption is usually individual and privatized, it is a constant reference. In this case, the consumption and communication exchange on-line is syncretic and primarily involves e-mail exchange (and chat) with other members of the diaspora, friends and family in Cyprus, as well as non–Greek Cypriot friends. Access and use of web sites is also mixed, reflecting the constant intersection of interests and communication practices between the mainstream and the particular.

With reference to all media consumption, use becomes communal—especially television viewing—when shared interests and family socializing predominate at certain times of the day, and it becomes segregated as diverse interests and tastes take over at other times. More than one television set, more than one radio, at least one VCR, a DVD and a stereo, serve these diverse media preferences. People move among channels as they move between rooms. This mobility is mostly experienced by the younger members of the household. It is like their moving in and out of their ethnicity in other contexts. Ethnicity predominates in the main family setting, but its importance decreases as they move to more private, especially teenage, spaces such as their bedroom.

Intergenerational Dynamics

Overall, this research indicates that among the people born in the diaspora, particularistic media use is more limited, following a trend opposite to that of the first generation. As participants admit, and as their everyday practices confirm, diasporic media use does not disappear. Long-term ethnographic observation, as well as shorter encounters with the participants, shows extensive media consumption. Media presence is so extensive in the domestic space and everyday life that meanings constructed around media exceed their consumption and *invade* many aspects of everyday life. When young people' parents criticize 'English values' during the communal watching of a BBC soap opera, children are introduced to another set of values, a set of Greek Cypriot values.[24] As the Cyprus problem is discussed day after day on Cypriot satellite broadcasts, it constantly reintroduces it in the political agenda of the diaspora and reinforces its position as a concern among family members.

No matter how present diasporic media are in everyday life, words and practices reveal that diasporic media use is critical and relates to diasporic identity, other identities, as well as to the particular context where media consumption takes place. 'I don't listen to radio in general. Also I can't relate to LGR. I would listen to it if there were debates and controversial discussions for our community. If there was something juicy and challenging,' says a second-generation female participant. Another British-born social worker explains that she listens to LGR for the Greek music because she enjoys it, though she avoids news and discussion programs: 'I guess I'm not too confident with my [Greek] language skills. I prefer music to talk.' A more outspoken participant is very clear regarding her rejection of LGR: 'Its crap! Also I am not able to follow politics and language. I like some of the music but I hate Greek pop, Euro-pop, and phone-ins. I would be interested in listening to challenging discussions. But I like listening to LGR late at night for the music. Also for community affairs and for Greek and Cypriot recipes.' A female participant in New York says that her use of Greek media is very selective as she does not think most of the programs are worth her time. All four women's comments indicate a revealing similarity in their critical perspective, making obvious the distanciation of the younger, educated middle-class from diasporic current affairs and debate programs. They distance themselves from media's first-generation and extensively Cyprus-oriented ideology, demanding programs that address bilingual audiences and consumers who are accustomed to the British and American media style and quality. At the same time, though, music and Greek cuisine programs are more compatible with their own diasporic identities, which reflect a selective *commitment* with the rest of the diaspora.

The critical perspective that members of the younger, middle-class groups adapt toward diasporic media also reflects their critical approach to the media in general. A male participant explains why he does not watch Greek television: 'I find it pathetic. People doing the programs have no creativity or imagination. If I watched an English program and it was as bad, I'd switch over. Why should I watch something bad just because it's Greek?' Similarly, a 18-year-old female student rejects Greek radio because she feels that it is incompatible with her values and identity: 'The way they [the radio producers] see Cypriot women is outdated. They don't realize that Greek Cypriot women have changed.' As already argued, the critical stand of many interviewees—especially of the younger generations— reveals their resistance to media discourses they feel underestimate them, either as media consumers, and/or as people who have different diasporic identities to the dominant community ideology. A 48-year-old expresses this dissatisfaction: 'I can't stand LGR. They think that everybody is thick!' As he goes on, it becomes obvious that he looks down on the migrant generation that dominates the community's public life. 'LGR's only listeners are the women who stay at home and the machinists,' he says in a comment that sums up the stereotypical image of the migrant.

Diasporic media become synonymous with a migrant culture that many young people want to disengage with. 'I'm very happy that Greek radio is there . . . for my mom and my grandma. . . . I don't know how they'd spend their time without it. . . . For myself? . . . I don't know if it makes that much of a difference' says a 29-year-old woman. Similarly, a well-educated female participant, 43, notes: 'It's good that the radio is there. People do listen to it. Especially people who don't feel comfortable with English. But I personally can't relate to it.' Comments of this kind are constantly repeated across the transatlantic diasporic space, reflecting not only the generational but also the class divisions within the group. Diasporic media, as expressions of a particularistic project sometimes seen as competitive to integration, become symbols of the past in the eyes of young people who are eager to succeed in the society they live in. As often becomes the case with particularistic identities, there are contradictions and tensions around the cultural boundaries that people feel they should fit in. Ambivalence towards ethnicity and the particularistic culture is the norm for the young and the well-educated participants. Needless to say, ambivalence in words goes hand in hand with the ambivalence of lived culture: the choice of friends, media consumption, religious practices, the choice of where and how to start a new home and a new family. It seems that more than *either/or* choices sare of the *this and that* kind.

Most young participants' approach to diasporic media is compatible with the dominant values of the Western capitalistic societies they live in; cynicism and "use and value" approaches predominate. Greek radio might not be a constant companion, but it is there to inform and function as a mediator with the broader community in its local and transnational scale. Many young Greek Cypriots tune into evening programs to find out when a forthcoming Greek club night is on or to catch up with the latest hits. They recognize diasporic media's significance for gaining access to information that is not available elsewhere. 'I just came back from a funeral. I found out about the man's death and funeral arrangements from listening to LGR,' a female participant says. Otherwise, she distances herself from it. Her words is a cynical reflection of the divisions in terms of class and cul-

tural capital within the diasporic group: 'Most programs address machinists. But since I've university education, I expect something more.'

Against the younger generations' liberal, critical and cynical perspective, the migrant generation praises the media for their role as mediators
of diasporic culture and for reinforcing the relations across the local and
the transnational community. The migrant generation's dominant appreciation of diasporic media reflects some key elements of diasporic identity.
The first most obvious point is the homology between the media and
migrants' nostalgia for a distant home. The emotional and patriotic representations of a home and of an unquestioned sense of belonging to the
original *homeland*, which dominate the media, are usually welcome by
this generation. Another significant element of the migrant identity—
though this does not apply to all people—is their particular relation to
capitalism and individualistic values of the host society. As most come
from rural communities where early capitalist values dominated cultural
and economic life, loyalty and commitment to a community reflect a
familiar discourse. Finally, this generation has a demotic awareness of the
need to establish mechanisms that enable community continuity. In the
media they see one of those key mechanisms that replace relations of spatial and familial intimacy of the past. 'Through LGR we learn a lot. We
learn about the new music, about traditions, it helps children with the language' (female, 38).

Even if the communal domestic viewing of diasporic channels in the
households of the first generation is the norm, the particularistic media's
future is threatened. The majority of the participants born in the diaspora do not choose to gain access to any of the diasporic television channels,
even if they often claim they want to. In the case of the present sample,
households with no interest in diasporic television are in the majority
comprised of interethnic families. In Britain, these are also the households, that, in majority, have only terrestrial television. A significant difference of the American case vis-à-vis the British is the availability of
Greek programs on cable community channels. Access to such programs
is free, as long as the household has cable connection. As a result, some of
the middle-class participants say that they occasionally switch over to
Greek programs for news, sports or entertainment. Limited access or use
of diasporic media in most cases, as this research reveals, is not always a
matter of choosing or not choosing diasporic media against the mainstream. In some of these homes, television consumption is more limited
in general, revealing a cultural difference—a difference that does not necessarily relate to diaspora, but more to middle-class identities. Overall,
though, it seems that the more media-wise a household is, with a larger
range of media available, the more diverse media use is, including diasporic media consumption.

NETWORKS OF HOMES

New communication technologies, such as satellite and cable, bring the images of different places with specific cultural significance together, at home: images of London and New York, images of the transnational community, images of Cyprus and Greece in this case. These images can reflect the diverse sense of Home and the desire for a sense of Home. More than anything, they can bring together the diasporic homes—in plural—into a new relation; they become nodes in networks that are culturally distinct and transnationally connected.

One of the things that the participants take for granted in their talk is the strength of diasporic networks—their relations with other Greek Cypriots. Although most homes I visited housed nuclear families, the extended family, kinship and friendly relations position the domestic in a fluid relationship with the public, including other households. People visit and spend hours in each other's homes, often without any previous arrangement. Visits, especially from relatives, rarely come as a surprise and visitors are usually welcome to share dinner and television viewing with the family, as my own experience shows and as my observation of participants' socializing reveals. This mobility between different houses brings the community home and creates different dynamics compared to other homes—that is family units organized around their domestic privacy (Morley and Silverstone, 1990). It also reveals the ambivalence of the diasporic home, which, as argued already, has multiple and situational meanings; it cannot be defined only in terms of privacy, but it actually extends into many spheres of belonging.

One of the participating families is very characteristic of the networked transnational community. Friends and relatives living in the neighborhood, in other cities and in other countries—for example, Cyprus, Greece, South Africa—pay regular visits to this family. When the family members go out or on a trip, they usually pay back the visits. Their domestic activities, such as having dinner or watching television, mediate their socialization and bring the domestic and the public closer together. Greek media and Greek food are the two kinds of commodities mostly consumed in this household, even though media consumption is rarely exclusive or extensive, except for the father of the family, who, following male viewing patterns of the group, consumes the media the most.

Media consumption practices are also influenced by this extended sociality: media are communally consumed and television talk becomes an everyday bonding experience, not only between family members, but also with other members of the immediate—usually Greek Cypriot—social network. As communal media consumption takes place, especially the evening television viewing, younger and older members of the same family—and perhaps some from other families—share their time, talk about their viewing and communally construct the discourse of their everyday communication. In this shared space, at this shared time, the common *language* of communication is shaped around common experiences—or through the conflict of different experiences—and in the struggle of different generations to speak the same tongue: a meeting of Greek and English.

A number of arguments can be made in relation to the processes of diasporic identities' shaping and reshaping in the domestic space, especially in relation to media's dynamic and contested presence. In their diversity, all these families—and the individuals within them—identify as British Greek Cypriots, Greek Americans, Greek Cypriots, Greeks, Cypriots. In these different self-identifiers, Greekness and Cypriotness are present as continuing and persistent ideological referents. Such self-identifications reveal a diasporic awareness, an awareness and admission of diaspora's relevance to everyday life. Such awareness is visible in the close-knit families, relations of support and companionship that accompany individuals throughout their lives, diasporic networks and the establishment of new Greek Cypriot families—or interethnic families that are still ethnically aware. As one of the young participants' words reveal when talking about the Cypriot BBQs, the Greek songs and the television jokes that Greek Cypriots share, it is the small and common everyday things that renew the sense of belonging.

As younger and older generations, men and women, working class and middle class diasporic subjects share the common everyday small things and perform routines, habits and rituals, they construct shared discourses, ideologies and reconfirm their belonging in a community. Roles and values that signify diaspora—in its stereotyped understanding and self-understanding are reproduced in everyday life. Thus, female gender roles that require women to be the carriers of the family diasporic culture and male roles that require men to be the mediators of the public into the domestic, become diasporic identifiers experienced by the older and learned by the younger from an early age.

Diasporic awareness and active belonging in families and networks is not incompatible with aspirations for social success in the British and American societies. Most working-class migrant parents have aspirations for their children's success, and indeed, most of them do reach educational and professional achievements that fulfill their parents' dreams. This duality that the devotion to the values of the diasporic community and those of the broader society implies, signifies the shift of the diasporic experience from generation to generation. This same diasporic context leads to an intimate distanciation from Cyprus, its people and its culture. Although the diaspora feels a connection to Cyprus—and some of them to

Greece, too—and although they consume diasporic media, their interpretation and their appropriation of images, information and ethics implies a critical distance. They relate to Cyprus in the context of a hybrid imagined community, but they do not *belong* to Cyprus. People's practice and talk about the media, although critical, reveal their expectations: expectations that relate to a role in the community—both the local and the imagined—for disseminating information, images, narratives, for being educators and mediators in everyday communication. All these indicate that within the diaspora there is a sense that particularistic media are indeed actively involved in the processes of learning, teaching, producing and consuming identity. In their diverse expectations, which primarily relate to age, gender and generation, participants reject the media if they do not fulfill these roles.

SIX ───────────────────────────

THE PUBLIC(S)
Diasporic Constructions and Divisions

> . . . *the place where we come and go, and meet—the street, the café, the station—is more important and genuinely more interesting than our homes, houses, places connected one with another.* (Lefebvre, 2003: 90)

The domestic might be the space where identities are initially constructed, but everyday life conduct depends on the continuation of the living scapes, including both the domestic and the public. The spatial interrelation and interdependence of the private and the public have often escaped the attention of audience research, which tends to study media use as bounded at home. Such focus fails to capture the continuation and the complexity of the public and domestic experience of individuals and families, which are of key relevance to the study of identities, especially when referring to group identities. On the other hand, studies of ethnicity have the opposite preconception: they tend to study the public and only to discuss the domestic as an element of problematic social conditions—that is, in relation to poverty and to crisis in family life. The reason for emphasizing the need to study the public space and public life within media studies in particular generates from the conceptualization of media consumption as a cultural process. This exceeds the narrowly conceived activity of receiving the media and acknowledges the participation of audiences in the production of meanings and the persistence of media discourses in everyday life (Silverstone, 1994; Ang, 1996). Although the arguments about audience participation in the construction of media discourses are by now theoretically and empirically well established in media studies (Morley, 1986, 1995; Radway, 1984; Lull, 1990), the fascination with the domestic remains.

The public is not singular but plural (Dayan, 1998). It is a diverse space, and different publics have different meanings and various implications for their socialization. Public spaces, which are primarily defined by their culturally distinct character, such as churches and community centers, serve as unifying contexts for bringing together diasporic diversity and turning it into shared experience. Other spaces, such as shopping centers, schools, libraries and even the street, challenge bounded ethnicity promoted and practiced by diasporic institutions and enrich and diversify identity. People's public positionings relate and depend on their ability to communicate multiple identities, suitable and necessary for communicating with others. Publics also involve inequalities in access and struggles for establishing individuals' and groups' presence. Not everybody is equal, as publics have their rules and people take and are given a place in them. Gender inequalities in public are probably the most obvious example of the struggle for power and visibility. For example, men often mediate Greek Cypriot women's participation in activities outside the home, as Greek Cypriot men move freely in public space while women's public socialization is more restricted from an early age.

The identities that are initially constructed at home are "baptized" and reconfirmed in the public. Without the rituals of public performance, identities are doomed to fade away, especially when socialization surpasses the familial domestic framework. Diasporic identities remain relevant as and when they are social and performed identities; as they are tested, contested and debated in the cultural and social context. As individuals become exposed to the public, their identities become public performances—performances that relate to the context and the expectations of the others around them, those within the group and those outside. In adopted behaviors, in their attitudes and in their roles, individuals take their social, public position; they shape their identity and they are subject to processes of identification that they take or are forced to accept. Diaspora becomes participatory in the public; it becomes a public reconfirmation of commitment to a common project. It comes with rules, restrictions, boundaries and a set of values. Public performance and public reconfirmation of diasporic identities brings the personal and the communal closer and leads to approval and achievement of a sense of belonging. Some performances, which might not conform to social or communal expectations, might also lead to disapproval and even exile. Though the public is the space where rules and consequences of belonging become clearer, the extent of tolerance, acceptance and rejection of difference is not predictable. Public discourses, ideologies and perceptions about tolerance, duties, rights and belonging confine and expand the limits of performed identities.

Media are involved in giving meanings to the public(s), in framing public discourses and in naming the consequences of adopting and adapting behaviors and identifications. Media bring together the private and the public by mediating the image of each one in the other. The home will never be completely private again, as the television has become the continuous mediator and translator of what is beyond the walls of the house (Silverstone, 1999). At the same time, the representation of domestic life, intimacy and privacy in the media has brought the private in the public; individualism, privacy and spatial separation are values saturating public life ideologies in western societies. As boundaries and definitions of the public and the private are challenged, so is the role of people in them. Roles, behaviors, performances are learned and negotiated when communicated. The media communicate common themes and representations and propose cultural expressions of identity and community. This sharing can establish commonality and educate people in the common spoken and symbolic language that communal identities require. When entering the public, people already have consumed its mediated images and norms, the expected expressions of identities, the boundaries between Us and the Others. The consequences of conforming, or not, to these expectations and boundaries are reflected in participation and exclusion from social and community life. Oldenburg (1999) describes the significance of places such as cafés and community centers as the 'third places'—beyond household and work—where communities are sustained. The public space is where identity, initially constituted in the domestic familial space, is instigated as socially relevant. It is in such public spaces that the heterogeneous articulation of symbolic products is given communally shared meanings.

THE DIASPORIC PUBLIC SPACE

Both in the British and the American context, diasporic Greek (Cypriot) institutions and organizations are numerous. As already mentioned, among the most important are the churches and the Greek schools. In greater New York City alone, there are more than 50 Greek Orthodox churches and in London more than 20 Greek afternoon/Saturday Greek language schools. Additionally, hundreds other organizations—political, cultural, professional, of people who share the same village origin, neighborhood centers and more—form the map of the [exclusive] diasporic cultural space.[25] This map is often signposted by posters covering the diasporic territory. Plays, concerts, political meetings and celebrity visits are announced in colorful posters, written in Greek or in Greek and English. The posters signify a form of visualized mediated everyday culture but also the evolution of the word of mouth, a key form of community communication. Although schools and the churches have a particular importance—as symbols and as real spaces—for Greek Cypriots, a number of other institutions achieve a greater and more persistent role: places that are meeting points, spaces of activities and of communal celebrations. Most of these places are found in the areas with the highest concentration of diasporic populations.

Cafés, bars and music clubs often turn out to be more significant in identity construction than formal community institutions. Such places are found in North London and in Astoria and the successful ones become trendy and visited by certain subgroups on a regular basis. Bars and cafés frequented by young people are a very characteristic example. Such places are hybrid in nature. For example, many are mainstream pubs and clubs that attract primarily Greek Cypriot clientele during some days of the week. Musically, they tend to combine Greek and American/British tunes. The ones owned and visited by a primarily Greek (Cypriot) clientele tend to reflect and express dual loyalties. An extremely popular café in Astoria has Greek themes integrated in the decoration, while declaring that 'United We Stand' with a large sign illustrated with the American flag on the front door. Dual loyalties are not only political; they are also cultural. The same café allows its primarily Greek clientele to smoke illegally and turns a blind eye to underage drinking.[26] At the same time, its staff is multiethnic and no assumption is made for Greek being the dominant language in its premises. Such public spaces are common and popular among the youth, but they are not all the same. For example, in Astoria, next to the mainstream Greek cafés there is an alternative one. Like the others, this also declares its allegiance to Greek culture, with its food, its music, its backgammon-playing clientele. But, unlike the others, it attracts alternative youth and its Greek musical choices are not as mainstream as in other bars. The divisions of the diasporic public spaces are vertical and horizontal. The growing diversity of places to visit turns the diasporic public space into an attractive choice that hosts various tastes. As a participant, 36, who grew up in Astoria explains:

> When I was young (about 10-15 years ago) there was nothing Greek we liked to do. It was just the things our parents liked to do—restaurants, *kafenia*,[27] community associations, nothing attractive, accessible or interesting. Now there're so many things that kids love to do and go to. There're cool places—cafés, clubs . . . well-known Greek DJs, concerts. . . .

An additional consequence of diversified diasporic cultural choices is that combinations of various activities, of cultural references and interethnic dialogue become naturalized. The same participant reflects on increased diversity in relation to the past: 'Now, kids [i.e. youth] combine things—they listen to American music and Greek music. They have Greek friends and American friends. They do it all. I don't know how they do it, but they manage.' Nonexclusivity explains the success of the diasporic public for younger generations, who are used to juggling different cultural choices and move in and out of cultural contexts and communities.

Another element of the diasporic public space's hybridity is reflected in the flexible transformation of places in order to host different use groups and different activities. A popular Cypriot restaurant in the heart of Astoria functions as a business most of the time. However, it occasionally hosts high-profile political lobbying events for Cyprus, and it offers its premises for weekly use by a Cypriot choir and a traditional Greek/Cypriot dance group. The diverse uses of its premises mean that this restaurant is frequented by a large variety of users: families, politicians and individuals involved in politics (primarily male and middle-aged), children of all ages attending the dance lessons and women of all generations (members of the choir and mothers of the dancing group' children). Many of this place's users travel from suburbia to the heart of the diasporic community of Astoria to attend the various activities. The local diasporic space of Astoria becomes the hub of diversified and dispersed diaspora.

Activities taking place in the diversified diasporic public space often reinforce ethnicity and a sense of belonging to a community through face-to-face contact. When studying the diasporic public space, however, and when participants are asked how they find out about events or about the latest Greek music, it becomes apparent that even face-to-face interaction is extensively mediated. Activities of community organizations are advertised on local Greek radio and press; they are discussed over the telephone and on e-mail. Greek music becomes popular as it is consumed on diasporic television and radio, discussed on e-mail, and downloaded on the Internet. As many admit, information about what is going on is much more broadly available than in the past.

Young People and Diasporic Public Space: Beyond the Formal

Most young participants feel strongly about their diasporic identity, even though these sentiments are not reflected in their limited participation in the formally organized community publics. All young participants asked, say that they will make sure they bring up their children within the Greek culture, whatever they mean by that. How about the Greek language? 'I am definitely going to speak Greek to my children . . . especially when I shout to them and curse!,' says a 20-year-old female. Cursing and words that relate to food or ethnic and religious celebrations—for example Πασχα/*Pascha*, meaning Easter—always come out in Greek without any effort. In the most intimate relations of their lives, in the way they express strong feelings and in references that have to do with a public, shared culture, Greek language often frames the immediate discourse of second and third generations.

Most of the teenagers asked in both cities are attracted to diasporic references that seem relevant to their own life. Contemporary Greek music and dancing are very popular among young men and women, as they are part of their entertainment choices in clubs and parties. Dancing lessons form one of the most successful structured community activities that attract young Greek Cypriots. Often young Greek Cypriots choose to attend them without any pressure from their families or the community. Knowledge of Greek dancing and the latest Greek music are assets for gainingpopularity among young people. Greek music and dances become some of the primary identity references for second and third generations to their diasporic identity. Dancing reflects the performative character of identity; it is a demonstration of ethnicity and an attempt for public recognition of the young people in the community.

The most structured diasporic media use is primarily domestic and private. Diasporic media are used at home, either because their parents consume them, or because they themselves choose to catch up with the latest Greek hits. The only exception is the public consumption of Greek music. In public, it is the mainstream media they are seen consuming. In the context of their age group, watching an English-language soap opera or listening to mainstream youth radio is socially expected and accepted performance. It is not only diasporic identities that are performative; age and gender identities are as well.

THE CONSTRUCTION OF A GENDERED PUBLIC: THE CASE OF TWO COMMUNITY CENTERS

In illustrating the diasporic public cultural space in London and New York, one cannot ignore the gender divisions of the public—especially in the case of the first generation and the formal community spaces. The everyday uses and divisions of the Greek Cypriot public are illustrated in a case study that involves two specific community centers—a male-dominated one and a women's center. In both cases, the focus is on the participants' engagement with the media and with diasporic communication in the local and the transnational mediated scapes. Both centers are based in North London, the area with the highest concentration of Greek Cypriots in Britain.

A Male-dominated Community Center

The Cypriot Community Centre is probably the most significant—symbolically and as a living space—public place for the British Greek Cypriot diaspora.[28] Symbolically, its existence reinforces the belief that Greek Cypriots form a distinctive, active and strong community. As a real space, it has various uses, either as an everyday hangout and meeting point, or as a place where people go to attend specific activities and functions. The Cypriot Community Centre attracts many members of the group, though subgroup representation is unequal. It is a place where the construction of diasporic identities and media consumption can be studied in their publicness—in the rituals and routines, in patterns of sociality, in people's choice of being members of a public that projects ethnicity as the ultimate bond. Within this context, I studied how this dominant ideology is taken on board, especially when it relates to the real commonality of experience of the core group of middle-aged, migrant, male, working-class habitués. I examine how it is negotiated in their everyday juggling of identity, which takes its meanings within the diasporic community, the multicultural locality and particularly in this centre, which is attended by Turkish Cypriots as much as by Greek Cypriots. Participants' attitudes in relation to identity and community were studied ever a year-long participant observation. Identities are formed through the repetitive and ritualistic performance of ethnicity, in direct and mediated dialogue with other members of the group. Performance takes place around a game of cards, lunch, and in the communal consumption of diasporic television.

The vast majority of the habitués usually gathering at the Centre are men above the age of 50. The demography of the place largely reflects the demography of a traditional Cypriot coffee-shop, which excludes women. Men gathering here perceive this place as a male traditional space as well; their visiting the centre is largely an act of nostalgia, which most of the people born in the diaspora are indifferent to. When I asked one of them why his wife and other women do not frequent the centre, he was annoyed and surprised by the question: 'Our wives don't go to such places. If they did, we wouldn't have married them!' Women attending male-dominated public places are considered as somehow decadent, according to Cypriot traditions, traditions now retreating in Cyprus.[29] Overall, male domination has restricted women from embracing this and other places of its kind in both London and New York City. One of the many Cypriot community centers in Astoria, where extensive participant observation took place, was very similar in its demographics and its character to the one in London. In both centers the usual habitués are middle-aged men. They like playing cards and backgammon, gossiping and discussing politics—especially Cypriot politics. Television is always present and usually in the background, but moves on the foreground when chosen programs are on—especially football and news.

The Cypriot Community Centre in London is highly mediated. Greek/Greek Cypriot and Turkish satellite television is offered as one of the main daily entertainment choices. For most habitués, satellite broadcast consumption in the center becomes part of the extensive television consumption characterizing their everyday life at home and outside. The availability of satellite television there has not created an audience for media, but an audience for diasporic television. Diasporic channels are competing with British television for the particular audience, even though consumption of mainstream and particularistic television is not mutually exclusive. But for the center's habitués, who choose to spend a lot of their time in a space saturated with Cypriot references, diasporic media consumption is much more meaningful and important—at least as part of the public performance of identity—than for many other Cypriots. They turn to the satellite channels for renewing their images of Cyprus, for building their knowledge around Cypriot politics, for forming their own practice and ideology in relation to Cypriot contemporary reality, for engaging in discussions with other Cypriots in the center, in the locality, in transnational spaces. Besides, this is a group of people who are more resistant to the mainstream culture than they are to the Cypriot one. In their ideology, Cyprus remains the primary reference within an imagined community. Nostalgia is renewed through diasporic media. Nevertheless, sometimes these media also remind them that their perception of the *homeland* is illusionary. This becomes obvious in the men's frequent condemnation of contemporary values and morals in Cyprus. Another consequence of satellite television's availability is the emergence of an inclusive public space for many. Especially the men who do not play games[30] and still want to participate in a community center, find a space for inclusion around the communal television viewing. Television here, almost as much as at home, becomes a permanent referent in the foreground and the background of everyday life. Media talk also is a common denominator. Discussing viewing and evaluating the media is part of their appropriation.

Media Talk

One of the first things realized when conducting media research is that audiences do not usually talk about media consumption; they talk about news, specific programs, their plot and characters. The majority of the people asked, find it difficult to discuss their media choices, even though most are heavy media consumers. However, many engage in an ideological abstract discussion that recognizes the importance of diasporic media. Populist media effects approaches take two forms. The dominant one praises the media for their community, educational and political role in national and transnational scale. The visibility and popularity of the media are good enough reasons for most participants to applaud them. In the words of a 60-year-old participant:

> On LGR we listen to our own language . . . we learn what's going on. Without it, we'd be lost. Before LGR and cable [TV] we were like shipwrecked. Now, we have to remind ourselves that we are in foreign parts.

The opposite, minority critical side, also tends to adopt a demotic media effects approach. One habitué, who considers himself to be a member of the educated elite, says that the role of electronic media is stronger among people with lower political criteria and little education: 'These people would talk about anything as long as it's on television or on radio. But they wouldn't go further to analyze politics. As soon as a story isn't in the news anymore, they stop caring.' Communication practices, however, as observed in this center and in other public and domestic settings, reveal that media consumption is reflexive and diverse. It relates to the particular diasporic identities, people's multiple identities and commitments, as well as to the context of their everyday life and the particular context where media consumption takes place.

Media use in the community center is ritualistic, as it fits the particular group and time and space structures of the center. It follows similar patterns day after day and there is an unwritten rule for respecting these patterns. For example, when the evening news starts on the Cypriot satellite channel, silence replaces chatting and joking. The silence and devotion of the habitués to their viewing does not last for more than half an hour, but during this half hour the small screen becomes a stage for a performance, with the habitués being both participants and audience. The information gained during this short viewing, and the more casual viewing that follows for a few more hours, feeds discussions and debates in the public community stage. For men especially, awareness of political developments—in Cyprus and in Britain—is necessary for participating in public debates. Media's presence and significance for public life lasts much longer than the actual television viewing and radio listening.

Not only diasporic, but also gendered (diasporic) identities are constructed around media consumption (and around the conceptualization of media consumption). The majority of men asked say that they listen to and watch news and current affairs more than any other program. This reflects the process of a male identity construction, an identity shared by this group and one that requires from men to be informed about public affairs. It also reflects diasporic awareness, as the political information habitués seek relates to Cyprus first and to the host country only secondarily. Though it is less common for men to admit they listen to and watch entertainment programs, this is largely the case both in the center and at home. Overall, media talk reflects both individuals' expectations from the media and their communal performance of identity, which is negotiated in public discourse. What people say about their media consumption does not necessarily reflect all its dimensions; yet, it is invaluable in studying what dimensions people choose to project.

The Cypriot Community Centre becomes a space where the identities of the migrant male habitués to a larger extent, and the identities of the other groups that attend it to a smaller extent, become publicly exposed, renewed and communally performed. The processes that take place are complex and multiple. In this space, especially for the first generation, relations of the country of origin are reproduced, with the domination of the Greek Cypriots over other Cypriot groups. The powerful presence of Greek television reproduces these analogies, even if now they are hybrid, and in new, diasporic terms: Greek Cypriots and Turkish Cypriots share the same public space, something that is only an exception in present divided Cyprus. Also, both Greek and Turkish media co-exist and compete, making the diasporic dimension of communication more obvious: sometimes celebrated and others contested. Nevertheless, this center is only a component of the broader diverse public space. Diasporic identities are shaped through relations and cultural references inside the centre, as well as outside it. The Cypriot Community Centre remains a cultural *minority* center in the British context. As people are aware of their minority status, the performed identities in the center become conditional. Public performances outside are not necessarily replicas of performed identities in it.

The Female Public Space—A Hybrid Space Between the Domestic and the Public

Moving from the male-dominated Cypriot Community Centre to a local Greek Cypriot Women's Centre, the dynamics change. The practices in this place are very different to those observed above. This place becomes a space where the public is appropriated to resemble the domestic. It is also a space where use and value of the opportunities outside the home are cherished, where time and activities are well structured. Television viewing here is unusual and a luxury. Media talk on the other hand is usual and appreciated as a bonding activity. The women's center is run by an organization offering Greek Cypriot women a space for socializing and for attending various activities. The services offered include fitness and traditional dancing classes, English language classes, and counseling. This is a pleasant place where women are friendly and turn into hospitable hosts, and where lively discussions take place, especially during the breaks between different activities. These women like to talk to each other, and they grab every opportunity for socialization. This is one of the reasons for not using the media at the center. Even though most of the participants are heavy media—both diasporic and mainstream—users at home, they hardly use them in this public space. The media found here are old and limited, apparently because there is no demand. Women prefer to get involved in other activities.

The core group includes almost exclusively middle-aged, migrant generation, working-class women. The small group of young women participating in the activities of the center—especially fitness and dancing classes— come in the evenings and after work, but they do not spend much more time than their class attendance requires. However, for the older women, this is a social space of extensive and committed presence. For many, this is an extension of their home. They usually gather in the center's kitchen, a space that is much preferred compared to the living room—an obvious similarity with the domestic routines and habits. In the kitchen, catching up and gossip unravels over cups of coffee and herbal tea enjoyed before or after a class. Sharing a home-made cake brought over by one of the members is common practice. As diasporic identities depend on specific gender identifications and vice versa, demonstrating good cooking or housekeeping skills to others is a performative way of reinforcing specific Greek Cypriot female identities in public. The kitchen looks very similar to a domestic kitchen, but as a room it reflects the cross between female working and leisure space; it reflects the cross between the domestic and the public. As most socializing takes place around the kitchen's table, women reproduce a familiar setting. As, on the other hand, public talk never touches sensitive and private issues, it is filtered by the publicness of the center.

Taking into account the profile and the socialization of most migrant women, the value they put in their participation in public activities comes as no surprise. For most, the domestic space is their primary everyday life space. Home is the space for work, leisure, for socialization with family members and friends.[31] The public is an alternative space, where they can get involved in activities they do not experience at home. Here they can enjoy contact and interaction with a large group of women; they can participate and benefit from group activities and services offered by others to them, and not by themselves to others, as is usually the case at home. Taking all this into account, the women's organization is still and primarily a 'use space' for most. Women come here in order to participate in specific organized activities. Socializing takes place parallel to that. It is very rare for a woman to visit the center exclusively for meeting others.

This extensive structuring of time is very different to the male-dominated Cypriot Community Centre, where men go to in order to socialize and to enjoy their leisure time without any sort of structured activities.[32] It seems that this difference relates primarily to the ideologies regarding female and male socialization and gendered time. As argued in research focusing on the domestic economy and the media (e.g., Morley, 1986; Seiter et al., 1989; Lull, 1990), women rarely enjoy exclusive leisure time. Similarly, a sense of 'use of time' and 'wasted time' saturates women's activities within the public space. There is a sense that leisure time should not be 'wasted time.' Also, within this female diasporic group, there is a widespread sense of gendered guilt for socializing with large groups of women. This is stereotyped as an opportunity for gossip. In their talk, participants are eager to exclude themselves from this stereotype, revealing the conflict between the desire to belong in a female public while at the same time rejecting it. This contradiction reveals the lived conflict in the performance of Greek Cypriot female identities in public. During a focus group discussion, one of the center's members used derogative terms for other women in the center: 'Look at them! They never shut up! Like chickens, they cackle all the time. . . . Oh, they give me a headache. If it wasn't for the yoga classes, I wouldn't bother coming at all' (female, 60). But her distancing remark received an ironic comment from another woman: 'Yeah, right. Like you're never thirsty for gossip yourself!'

Hybridity Is Liberating

The migrant generation women are the ones who have experienced, not only uprooting but also relocation in a country where they had little chance to get to know and integrate into its public life and social morals. Most of them come from rural areas and have ended up in an unknown metropolis, surrounded by strangers speaking a language they don't understand. For years, they have depended on familial and kin networks, as traditional morality and restrictions to their integration in the mainstream kept them at home. These women, many of whom have painful stories of years of loneliness and despair to share, develop tactics of resistance to the multiple forms of their subordination at a late age. Some of them decide to join English language classes; others confront their traditional role. The words of a 70-year-old who started learning English explain how her decision liberates her from depending on her husband for communication outside the diasporic group:

First, it was the children and work, then I was sick, now it's the grand-children. . . . My husband speaks English so much better than me. When I find a word I can't read I ask him to translate it for me. I tell him: 'All you do is listen and watch Greek television and radio. At least tell me what this English word means.' . . . And he replies to me: 'I am sick of English. I have to use it everyday at work. I come home, I want to speak and listen to my own language.'

Another woman, participating in the English class adds: 'All these years we were shut in our houses, sewing and raising the children. How could we learn English? Just a few words we learned from the TV.' For many, extensive media consumption at home has been for decades their *window to the world*. But in this sense, the actual distant world was the one outside their front door—the British world—mediated by the media; the diasporic world was the familiar one, the one that did not need mediation.

Most of the women gathering at the center during the evening are in general younger than the majority of pensioners who attend morning-classes. Some of them are well dressed and well spoken, revealing their middle class profile. Some of those attending the traditional dance classes do so not because this is an diasporic space they feel more familiar with, compared to nondiasporic spaces. They attend the center's activities once or twice a week because they choose to get involved in community activities. They share a sense of 'the need to know our culture,' as one says. For them, though, diasporic culture is just one of the components of their everyday life. During one of our discussions before a class, a woman admits that she is embarrassed not to know any Greek dances, and another says that she enjoys dancing because it is a great component of 'our cultural heritage.' 'For me it is also a night out,' argues a middle-class woman, 50. She adds that she does not usually socialize with Greek Cypriots because she lives and works in a different environment. Her attendance of the center started when she saw an advertisement for its dancing classes in the Greek press and she decided to join.

Female Public Media Consumption: It's All About Talk

Media talk among women is a usual, easygoing form of interaction. Media are some of the cultural references they all share; thus they can mediate a discourse they all share. What happened in the latest episode of a Greek or a British soap opera, celebrity news and media technology changes at home—including the installation of satellite, cable, or buying a new mobile phone—are usual topics of discussion. Political information received through the media is rarely on the agenda, unlike in the male-dominated Cypriot Community Centre, because this is not considered to be 'women's talk.' Media talk being such a casual and usual part of everyday life meant that it was not difficult to get women involved in discussions about the media. What was more difficult to achieve was the involvement of the participants in media talk that would surpass the specificities of talk about a particular series or media personalities, or the generalization of stereotyped comments about what is 'good' or 'bad' about the media. However, demotic critique to the stereotypical evaluation of the media is sometimes expressed in talk relating to one's own consumption practices. During a focus group discussion, the broader role of diasporic media for learning and using the Greek language became a concern, sparking lively debates. A woman questioned the effects of the media: '[Diasporic] media are good, they offer something important to us, our language, our culture . . . but no matter what, our children won't speak the language just by watching a series or two on Greek television. You have to talk to them in Greek at home, that's the only way. . . . ' The only woman in the same group of six who does not have transnational television at home is even more skeptical, questioning the value of my own research: 'There are other much more important things you should focus on [rather than the media] . . . for example, there's a need to develop youth centers, things like that.' She also raises the issue of alternatives in media choices: 'There are so many channels out there to watch, there is no time for Greek TV. Especially for the young . . . do you think they'd bother watching them?' This comment provokes a vivid discussion. A second generation participant said: 'You can't just let them [their children] do whatever they want! When I want the Greek channels, I put them on!' A younger member of the group says that some members of her generation have difficulties understanding diasporic media but 'we have to try to understand them and that's good . . . it helps us learn the language.' Those who support the cultural role of diasporic television are happy to give examples of their engagement with it. 'Both my daughter and I love the music programs on ERT.[33] I often tape them and then play them again and again!' A 24-year-old participant uses a similar example, which illustrates the significance of communication technologies in expanding distribution and sharing of diasporic media products. 'I don't have satellite at home, but my aunty does. She tapes films and soaps and then we get the tapes and watch them . . . '

While this discussion takes place in the lounge, the television is playing on the background. *Eastenders*[34] was on a while ago, and a couple of women switched on the television to watch it. Like at home, *Eastenders* is very popular among these women. Here, as much as at home, television and cultural references overall are never exclusively diasporic. This is why, the women participating in the previous discussion soon change the subject and start talking about dieting and about relevant information they got from mainstream women's magazines. Similarly, many satellite television owners emphasize the fact that, apart from Greek satellite channels, they can receive 30-40 other channels from across the world. Most of them agree that this expands their horizons, even though they admit that they never really watch them, as they do not understand the different languages of broadcasting. In their discourse, the potential and the symbolic value of being part of a global public becomes more important than the actual participation in it.

For the women of the center, public space is a continuation of their domestic life, because the values saturating their evaluation of space and time use and leisure opportunities are similar. Although there is a continuation, the exclusively female public space of the Women's Centre is a window to the world, beyond the home and beyond the dependence on male members of the family for participating in the public. But this window to the world, which takes them outside the house, is rather different to another "window" they have in their own houses: the media. In the domestic space, television and radio mediate their experience of the world that is beyond their reach—symbolically and literally. Within this context, it comes as no surprise that most of them have cable and satellite transnational television at home: it is the primary medium for their access to the globalization process; it is one of the primary methods for participation in a hybrid imagined community. At the same time, going out of their homes means that experience becomes immediate; that their participation in the (diasporic) local community is direct and nonmediated. The opportunity to enjoy experiences different from their usual domestic ones, and the socialization that comes with it, temporarily weakens the value of the media use as a particular act. On one level, public experience in the women's center becomes much more local and immediate than the dual and simultaneously local and global experience of the Cypriot Community Centre. On a different level though, media talk and diasporic talk in general shape a multilayered experience that cannot be singularly understood within a local public context. Regular media talk and diasporic talk continuously explore definitions of identity and diaspora through negotiations and renegotiations of geographical borders in time and space, mobility and variety in particularistic and multiethnic communication. They create new understandings of Greek Cypriotness, which can actually have different faces at different stages of people's lives and among people of the same network and family.

SEVEN

GLOBAL CITY AND ITS NEGLECTED DETAIL

Lefebvre (1996) tempts us to discover the city by reflection and to listen to its rhythms and music. Benjamin (1997) incites us to view the city from the street level and to let ourselves become knowledgeable and reflexive *flâneurs*. Massey entices us to observe the meetings of cultures and the global interconnections of the city in the multiple and hybrid urban histories (1999). The tradition of everyday urbanism turns to the senses and to sensual metaphors to capture the transitivity and the experiential character of the city, its life and its interconnections. The suggestion of everyday urbanism to observe the city as a participant and as a flâneur, and to pay attention to the encounters and the meetings of urban cultures and urban dwellers have inspired this study. This chapter tries to make sense of the lived diasporic urban experience and to argue for the significance of the diasporic for the global city and of the global city for the diasporic. Visualizing the city as a process, as a site where encounters and intersections of activities, networks and belongings take their shape, enable us to grasp the city's multiplicity. The urban is not a point bounded within its specific territory or within the nation, but a point for encounters and formations through meeting and mixing. The city, as it hosts diverse populations and activities, shows that identities and communities are not fixed in place and that communities and identities are in process; they are coming and becoming rather than being. '[P]laces . . . are best thought of not so much as enduring sites but as moments of encounter, not so much as "presents," fixed in space and time, but as variable events; twists and fluxes of interrelation' (Amin and Thrift, 2002: 30).

The particular dynamics of the city and of urban life allow different populations to live together, different cultures to coexist and intermix in new urban, multicultural and hybrid schemes and scenaria. Studying diasporic cultures in the urban context where they are experienced, and where many of the media develop and are consumed, means contextualizing diasporic (media) cultures in the space where they become possible. As J. Donald (quoted in Robins, 2001: 89) notes, the city poses 'the internal impossible question of how we strangers can live together.' As we live together, hybrid cultures, identities and alternative scenaria for inclusion and participation emerge, next to others of exclusion, discrimination and racism. All these coexisting, even if conflicting, dynamics need to be taken into account in any reflexive analysis of diaspora and the media.

Diasporic populations are integral part of the contemporary urban economic and cultural life, even if their contribution is not acknowledged as such. The city, where diasporic populations usually live, is the space where the private and the public and the experience of mediation take their meanings in relation to urban cultural practices and in the co-existence with other city dwellers. The mobile foreign subjects, who are not foreign anymore, challenge the purity of the nation and the suburban privatized closure and instead participate in the construction of diverse, creative and anarchic urban cultures. Diasporic populations' participation in the formation of a working-class cosmopolitanism (Werbner, 1999), brings dialogue and new encounters between strangers, between people of different backgrounds, in the city. In the urban meetings and mixings, in the public performance of diverse cultures and in the anarchy of the coexistence and competition for ownership and participation, publicness and exposure come back in public life and in cultural representation. The different kinds of music heard and imposed around town, the large satellite dishes insulting middle-class/white aesthetics, the loud, colorful and tasteless hybrid spaces hosting Internet cafés, combined with hair salons and/or grocery shops, create aural and visual cultural fusions and spatial amalgams, in cacophony as much as in harmony.

GLOBAL CITY'S AND THE NEGLECTED NUANCES

The city reflects the movement of the Others from the periphery of the empire to its core (the metropolis—the city). As migrants and diasporas move to the center, they occupy a symbolic and physical space that is powerful in its presence and in the active alteration of what it used to be through participation in economic, cultural and social life. The white majority moves to suburbia and to the 'pure' white neighborhood/enclaves of the city. The diasporic populations remain in the center, or, when they move to suburbia, they tend to keep symbolic, mediated and experienced close links with the urban core. The urban zone of the initial migrant landing keeps its symbolic role as a key node in the diasporic network (Van Hear, 1998). The city becomes a dynamic space for participation and negotiation of boundaries set by the dominant national and diasporic discourses of belonging. Urban politics and cultural demographics challenge the homogenizing ideology of the nation and suburbia. Satellite dishes, loud music, piracy of audiovisual products and of airwaves reflect some of the elements of the struggle, creativity and competition between the urban/suburban/national/transnational cohabiting classes (Lefebvre, 2003).

Over four-fifths of migrants settle in metropolitan areas, and the cities that receive the largest numbers of newcomers are those most involved in global trade (Muller, 2000). Hannerz (1996) identifies four categories of people playing a major role in the making of contemporary world cities: the transnational managerial category; the various third world populations—migrant and diasporic people; those involved with culture in the narrow sense; and tourists. Migrant and diasporic populations find themselves in cosmopolitan cities, which are part of networks of global cities, shaped in and through their interconnections (Sassen, 1991, 1999). These populations are actively involved in the translocal networks of global cities; cosmopolitan cities are nodes in diasporic networks, and diasporic populations become nodes in global cities' networks. Although global cities' literature recognizes the migrant underclass as one of the main active economic and social actors in the global city (Sassen, 2001), it tends to study migration as part of the capitalist economic activity alone. Researched only as workers or as an underclass, migrant and diasporic groups' multiple contributions to the global city remain understudied. Even so, the global cities' literature is helpful for the present discussion for at least two reasons. Firstly, it addresses the meeting of the local and the global in the metropolitan urban. Additionally, it acknowledges the fact that major metropoles like London and New York are nodes in transnational networks—thus global cities cannot exist without media and communication technologies. It can thus be argued—and this argument will continue in the following chapter—that cultural formations and relations of power within the urban need to be studied across urban and translocal networks, and not only within bounded nation-states. As the identity of places is partly formed in their interaction with other places (Massey, 1993), the need to study the interconnections between people, economies and cultural formations within and between cities becomes important for understanding both the urban and the transnational diasporic.

The Greek Side of New York City

In American social sciences, the city has always been recognized as a central reference point for the analysis of migration and ethnicity. Since the Chicago School's influential sociological research (Park et al., 1925 [1984]), the city has been discussed as a context both for alienation and for community. City changes with migration, and migration and settlement take their shape in the context of urbanization and suburbanization. As the migrants and their offspring become more prosperous, they move to suburbia; then new migrants move into the inner city (Alba, 2000). Different sections of the American city are named as little colonies of the locally dominant ethnic groups. The history of ethnic segregation of the American cities continues at present. In New York City, segregation has actually seen a slight increase between 1970 and 1990 (Massey and Denton, 2000). This segregation is somehow different from the British case. In the British case, particular ethnic groups might dominate particular locales, but the territorial boundedness is more flexible and the ideology of cultural coexistence is stronger than in the American case. The paradox of the American case is that the ideology of the melting pot goes hand in hand with extensive segregation and territorial separation of the various ethnic—and class—groups. Even so, the dominant British ideology of multiculturalism often appears as idealization of reality. Territorial segregation, which is based first on class and then on ethnicity, is more extensive than the dominant ideology of inter-cultural relations implies.[35] Thus, the case of a New York City urban locale discussed in the following sections might be distinct to the American city to certain extent, but it has many similarities to the British case.

In both global cities, new intercultural relations emerge in urban encounters, especially as for many working-class minority people, everyday interaction with members of other migrant and diasporic groups is much more extensive than interaction with the majority white population (Song, 2003). Many of the employees in the Greek restaurants of Astoria, for example, are Latin American, and next to the *Greek Astoria* there is a growing *Latin American Astoria*—and for decades there has been an *Italian Astoria*.[36] The constant interaction between the different groups leads to a hybridization of all cultures, specific to the Western cosmopolis. In terms of numbers, even the parts of Astoria, that are considered to be Greek are not dominated by a Greek population anymore (Georgakas, 1999). However, two points need to be made. Firstly, the visual and performed identity of the specific urban location can remain connected to a particular culture, even if demographics change. Power dynamics, in terms of intercultural relations and cultural (self-)representation, do not only correspond to numerical dominance but also to symbolic dominance. Additionally, the visual and performed identity of a place might be so significant that it can reproduce a sense of a core in the imagination of the community it claims to represent (in this case Greek Americans across the United States and also the broader Greek diaspora). This is what happens in Astoria, as with other similar original ethnic enclaves in the United States (Drucker and Gumpert, 1997). The original inhabitants and their offspring often move to suburbia. Astoria, however, remains a significant symbolic, cultural and political center that people visit and keep links with.

Astoria is part of Queens, New York City. Queens is demographically and geographically an essential part of the city, though it hosts a much more humble cosmopolitanism than Manhattan's. Here, performative ethnicity is visual and gaudy. Shop fronts overemphasize diasporic distinctiveness in stereotyped visual representations. When approaching Astoria, waving Greek flags, large Greek Orthodox churches with distinct Byzantine-inspired architecture and business names become visual reflections of the domination of Greek spatial ownership. Overexposure of exaggerated diasporic and religious characteristics reflects the emphasis of the politics of (self-)representation on popular culture and consumption culture. *Greek Astoria*, like other ethnoculturally distinct urban areas, has been a point of reference and of return for the resident migrants and the suburbanized majority of Greeks and Greek Cypriots. Astoria has been the cultural center for the Greek (Cypriot) diaspora. It has a long history of hosting Greek migrants since the arrival of the first large migrant waves of the early 20th century. Migration from Greece continued in time, but shrank in scale (Angelopoulos, Goutos and Notaras, 1967; Georgakas, 1999). Greek Americans have established their presence in New York City and the United States for four to five generations and are now spread all over the state of New York and the rest of the country. Greek Cypriots form a distinct subgroup within the Greek American community. They were a later addition to the established Greek community, thus they have not (yet) spread to the far corners of the state or of the country. The vast majority of Greek Cypriots arrived in the United States during and after the 1950s, and many arrived after 1974 as refugees and as expert migrants. Most of them landed in the established Greek American community. Significant numbers of Greek Cypriots live either in Astoria or in one of the suburban areas close by.

Astoria is the hub of Greek food shopping and Greek entertainment; diasporic performativity and distinctiveness primarily develop around consumer culture (and religion). Religion seems to be the second component of performed and demonstrated Greekness in public. Large Greek Orthodox churches, religious icons in shops and community centers, crosses in front windows, all become elements of demonstrated commonness—the community element—and of distinctiveness against the Other. Religious and consumer practices have something in common; they are both public performances of commonness and identity. The culture of exposure and the performance of exaggerated (stereotyped) Greekness characterize much of public life here. Even the Cypriot community leaders—almost exclusively middle-aged and male—are celebrities in their own community and benefit from a celebrity aura as they lobby and socialize with American, Greek and Cypriot politicians. However, the celebrity aura is situational and it does not apply across Greek (Cypriot) subgroups. Youth has its own celebrities: the Greek pop stars, Greek DJs in the local clubs and media celebrities.

GLOBAL CITY'S CULTURAL EXPRESSIONS AND DIASPORIC URBAN EVERYDAY

The global city's rich cultural production mirrors the meeting and mixing of diverse cultural ingredients. But it also reflects the increased cultural interdependence between the center and the periphery, which results in cultural inspiration and production. Hannerz (1996) develops a sequential model, with three phases of the cultural production and articulation, that depends on diversity. In the first phase, 'the items of meaning and meaningful form at issue flow fairly freely within some subcultural community, as long as the latter is large and cohesive enough to offer sufficient moral and other basically non-material support' (1996: 136). In phase two, commodification and division of labor within a specific community increase and distinctive subcultural items are consumed within a specific community as alternatives to the mainstream. At the third stage, which sometimes happens parallel with stage two, cultural commodities become more public and surpass the limited consumption within a specific community/subculture. At this stage, they pass directly into commoditization in the wider cultural market. Hannerz's model is helpful, especially in the context of a cosmopolitan consumption mapping. The global city reflects the world in the diverse cultural items and repertoires offered. The reflection is disturbed, on one hand, in the market absorption of the distinct form and the commodification of cultural meanings and, on the other, in the translation that takes place in the urban diverse environment where the subcultural is always in a dialectic relation to the whole (and to the other subcultural). The world is reflected, even in disturbed versions, in the global city's culture. It does so as reciprocal cultural encounters and exchanges take place between the global city and other parts of the world and as cosmopolitan consumption is shaped based on the charm of the cultural meetings of the proximate and the distant.

The so-called ethnic enclaves, or multicultural neighborhoods, have become fundamental components of the global cities, reflecting key elements of each city's cultural, social and economic profile. Such neighborhoods are appropriated and integrated in the city's life as they turn into centers for culinary, musical and nightlife explorations. Ethnic enclaves and multiethnic neighborhoods reflect a dimension of global cities often undermined in the relevant literature. Such neighborhoods and localities combine diasporic cultural continuity with the new, liberating and consumerist cultural elements of the capitalist city. The combination of the old and the new, of the familiar and the diverse cultural repertoires, leads to the emergence of hybrid and mixed cultures that reflect the diversified, transnational, urban identities of the diasporic subjects.

> It is the street that in the big city offers incomparably more choices and possibilities than in the village or hamlet, what we call "seductions," "temptations," opportunities, appeals, whether we're talking about objects or people. Encounters or solicitations and adventures.. (Lefebvre, 2003: 90)

In wandering around the city and in observing its life from street level, the city's cultural expressions are revealed in the nuances of the urban everyday. As Lefebvre (2003) suggests, the urban street and the coexistence of difference can be liberating and creative. Cultural moments reflecting the struggle around the liberating potential of the city were revealed during the conduct of this study. Mothers and priests do their best to control youth's mobility in the urban, in their struggle to protect the Greek offspring from the "corruption" of the big city and the "immorality" of the Western metropolis. But for the youth, escaping familial and institutional surveillance is a chance to explore their city and develop as urban cultural hybrids. 'I don't really have Greek friends. I have friends of all different backgrounds. When we go out, we go to all sorts of places. We go to clubs in Manhattan. We also go to Greek clubs in Astoria. My friends have grown to like Greek music. Sometimes, Greek clubs are fun!,' says a 20-year-old American-born student in New York City. The urban concentration of distinct cultural communities destabilizes the cultural and demographic hegemonic relations of the nation-state. Greeks and non-Greek residents of the *Greek* areas of London and New York dance to the Greek pop tunes, consuming Greek food and challenging the national law by trying their luck with underage drinking and smoking in urban youth spaces. Cafés and bars in the urban locale liberate the youth from old generations' traditionalism on one hand and from the national exclusionary discourses of cultural clarity on the other. Much of the cultural interplay takes place around consumption. Phases two and three of Hannerz's (1996) creative expressions of diversity take place at the same time, and hybrid urbanity becomes the outcome of the meeting of the mainstream with the subcultural; and the subcultural diasporic is the result of the increased options of the city and the limiting and framing repertoires of consumerism. Consumer culture becomes a performative, visual culture that signifies much of the diasporic distinctiveness in the locale.

The Street. Flânerie in Astoria, New York City

The tradition of flânerie invites us to see the city from the street level, through the eyes of the reflexive walker (Benjamin, 1997; Amin and Thrift, 2002). Like for Benjamin, in his trips across European cities, for the flâneur, the city becomes a space for observing and understanding neglected details and nuances, not certainties and ultimate truths. Narratives and auteur mappings of the city become epistemological tools for understanding the urban lived complexity (Amin and Thrift, 2002). The reflexive walker, the flâneur, uses sensory, emotional and perceptual captivations of the city, in the attempt to purposely record and mediate the city's daily rhythms and material juxtapositions (Sheringham, 1996; Amin and Thrift, 2002).

Inspired by the tradition of *flânerie*, I studied lived complexity, visuality and consumerist public life in *Greek Astoria*. Some of the visual and aural material collected are presented in the following paragraphs.

Crossing the river from Manhattan to Queens, the change in the environment and the identity of the urban cultural space is striking. This part of town is not about skyscrapers any more; the buildings are low and humble, the architecture is indistinct, and the noises coming from the elevated train and the motorways make Manhattan's glamor sound distant. The hierarchical position of this part of the city of New York soon becomes clear—it is the workers, the migrants, the ones that rarely cross the river for pleasure who live here. Coming out of the train, I know I am at the right place—first I can see a big sign of the national Greek American newspaper, a sign written in Greek: *Εθνικός Κηρυξ* (*National Herald*). A sign in Greek seems to be all that is needed; it is recognizable to the eyes of the potential readers of the only Greek American daily. As the train stops, I see a Greek flag in a distance and I smell Greek souvlakia (kebab) being grilled at a street stand of the Greek mobile chef. The smell is very familiar; it becomes a sensual translation of a geographically distant cultural language. The senses of smell and of taste compensate for the lack of the Mediterranean colors and override the cold and wet northern atmosphere of New York.

Walking out of the train station, more consistent images, sounds and smells are added to the first scattered signs collected by the senses. Blue and white awnings—in the colors of the Greek flag—cover the front windows of most shops, cafés and restaurants; their names are equally revealing: *Byzantium, Opa, Athena's Nails, Athens Palace.* The reproductions of Greek kitsch on business signs and decorations reflect the effort of the local community to demonstrate a dominant visual gaudy Greekness. Even the sign of *Mercedes Benz* is drawn in ancient Greek-style letters at a local garage. The mechanic talks in Greek to a man passing by—he speaks with the distinct accent of a Greek island. The spoken language is not only Greek, though; this is not a case of reproduction of a pure old and traditional Greekness. There is more to it. *Greeklish* words such as 'car-o' for 'car' become aural reminders of hybridity against cultural purity.

Observing the Greek kitsch, I think of the ascribed Greekness that is produced by the tourist industry and pop culture in a hybrid and often inaccurate mixture of the old and more recent past of the country. This form of kitsch is adopted, adapted and inscribed in New York's diasporic community's self-identification and public image. Is it inscribed for itself or for others? Who needs to read and recognize these visible representations of (some kind of) Greekness? For sure, it develops through an increasingly globalized consumer culture that produces the same symbols and exaggerated identifiers of Greekness—ancient symbols, religious icons—that sell in tourist shops in the center of Athens as much as they do in restaurants and bars at the heart of Astoria.

Strolling down Astoria Boulevard, one comes across a number of Greek and Greek Cypriot community centers: a Greek American football club and the Pancyprian Association being just two of dozens more. These community centers are familiar diasporic spaces and resemble similar places in London. The familiarity takes precedence over difference in the setting of the community centers. A huge television dominating the setting of one of the clubs becomes the most distinct cultural object in the place: big, in prominent position, always switched on. A few middle-aged men sit around the television. It is cold and it is snowing; only a handful habitués have left their homes for a slow night around the community television set.

The center of *Greek Astoria* is inviting on this cold January early evening: lights are on, people walk up an down the icy streets, the smells and the windows of the local restaurants and bakeries are tempting. . . .This is somehow a familiar environment: it doesn't resemble Greece or Cyprus as much as it does resemble the commercial heart of the Cypriot neighbor-

hoods of North London. In Astoria, the atmosphere is similar to the colorful London's Green Lanes, where Cypriot and Turkish shops set the character of the 24-hour local commercial and food culture. There are similarities with another global city space of comparable demographics, London,
but there are also differences. The demonstration of difference is much
more predominated by Greek representations than in the case of the diversified North London. The ethnocultural segregation of the American city
makes urban hierarchies more visible. This is Greek American territory.

Coming out of the train stations of Turnpike Lane in North London
and out of Ditmars Avenue in Astoria, one lands in two different urban
spaces with very similar urban multicultural character. Images in the street
and through the shop and restaurant windows are surprisingly familiar.
They are alike in their projection of public, performative and visible
Greekness, but also in the aesthetics of the multicultural urban hubs they
both represent. On 31st Street, one of the main roads in the heart of *Greek
Astoria*, the consumerist elements of diasporic culture are reflected in the
parade of shops: a few restaurants in a row, a large supermarket, a large
music and video store. All invite their primarily Greek clientele through
the visibility of cultural particularity: in their selection of products and in
the representation of identity in signs, front windows, and proudly demonstrated Greek flags.

The large Greek music and video shop sells almost exclusively Greek
products. It is all about Greek popular culture here; it is all about sharing
the present popular media culture with the *homeland* and across the diaspora. The non-Greek products are only a handful, but they are there for a
clientele that likes Greek but also American mainstream hits. As much of
purchasing of Greek music and films increasingly takes place online, this
shop has a strong virtual presence next to its real tangible one. Though
most of the store sales take place in the shop offices dealing with online
shopping, the main section is still popular with customers. The consumption rituals of browsing, touching and listening to the products that will be
bought over the counter or online take place in this physical space. People
of all ages are in the shop; this is a store that seems to be reaching different kinds of consumers, all having an interest in Greek music and film.
Both the shop and its online service reach a variety of customers, with
diverse tastes and positioned in different locations. This business, which has
become one of the major Internet providers of Greek music, films and
books across the world, brings together the local and the transnational networked diasporic space of cultural consumption.

Greek is still a common language in the street; as with the numerous
stands selling the Greek specialty of souvlakia in the street, sounds, smells,
and images build up the sensual palette of a territory predominantly
Greek. With so many mundane and everyday references constantly sur-

rounding you, it seems inevitable to feel part of a Greek context, if not of a Greek community. As Gumpert and Drucker recorded it:

> It is possible to attend the Greek church (old and new calendar), sit in the waiting room of Greek doctors and dentists (read Greek newspapers and magazines while you wait), eat in Greek restaurants, sit over a dark cup of Greek coffee in a café or zacharoplasteion, attend Greek elementary and high school, play on a Greek soccer team, play cards with friends in a Greek club, shop in Greek stores, buy Greek audio and videotapes, be buried by a Greek undertaker, and never speak English unless an emergency presents itself or one wanders outside into an alien world in which English is a required linguistic skill. It [Astoria] is also an ethnic enclave undergoing change. (1998: 79)

Moving from the heart of *Greek Astoria* and further away from Manhattan, one comes to Ditmars Avenue, the last of three train stops in the line of the Greek territories of Queens. This area leads to the residential parts of Astoria. It is a gate to suburbia, but it is also a transitory position between the diasporic zones of the city. On one hand, it resembles the heart of the ethnic enclave, with Greek cafés and a handful of community organizations. It also hosts a few Greek grocery shops and Greek newsstands and bakeries, the last in the parade of shops of this kind, that are in proximity to the spread out Greek middle classes. Next to the station, two Internet cafés set the distinct diasporic/migrant/working-class identity of the place. In Manhattan, Internet cafés are almost nonexistent, apart from in tourist areas. The two cafés here are popular and busy, resembling Internet cafés of the same kind in multicultural neighborhoods in other parts of New York and in London. These cafés are simple, humble and functional. On the other hand, this part of suburbia reflects the diversity of the boundary between different urban pockets. Astoria, as it expands towards the east, becomes a residential and middle-class hub. In the area around the commercial streets, working-class, new and temporary migrants (e.g., students) concentrate. Parts of it cannot be associated with *Greek Astoria* any more, as, like in any borderland, people of different backgrounds and cultures meet and compete for spatial ownership. *Others* have started coming in. Not everybody speaks Greek in the streets any more: there are Latinos, Eastern Europeans, Indian, Pakistani, Bangladeshi, people from all over the world, who some Greeks see as invaders. They own some convenience stores, they work in the kitchens of the Greek restaurants, they are employed in the Greek shops and live in the surrounding houses and flats rented out by the—often Greek—owners who have now moved to suburbia.

The Diasporic Suburbia

At present, there is a visible mobility from the urban original point of arrival of migrant populations to diasporic suburban new hubs. As studied elsewhere (e.g., Moskos, 1990; Chimbos, 1999; Karpathakis, 1999), suburban mobility and resettlement have not led to full assimilation and disconnection from the broader diaspora, though inevitably they have led to cultural, moral and social change. Even when migrating to the suburbia, diasporic populations remain in cultural closeness to the urban. The city grounds diasporic experience in its multipositioned and multinodal history and present. Drucker and Gumpert talk about a two-step diaspora (1997). They refer to the mobility of migrant populations, first from the country of origin, then to the ethnic enclave, and finally to suburbia. Although the more affluent younger generations tend to move to suburbia, they tend to maintain strong links with the urban enclave and participate in its activities, either directly or through their use of media and communication technologies, as many have said. In the new suburban life, media and communication technologies become increasingly important for sustaining the links that growing geographical distanciation introduces. The links of the suburban Greek (Cypriot)—or interethnic—family to the community core become more selective and partial:

> . . . the story of the Greek Americans in the suburbs is still unfinished. Yet a serious answer would recognize the presence of deep continuities. American-born Greeks have clearly carried forth the communal institutions founded by their forebears. There are times when one could swear that every Greek in town knows every other one, or at least everyone else's Auth Helen or Cousin George. True, not many Greek Americans of the second generation speak Greek among themselves, and many of the third generation do not understand it very well. But in their deepest inclinations of conduct, religious approach, social bias, feeling for family, and affection for the old country, there are heavy signs of immigrant shaping. (Moskos, 1990: 149)

Continuity in suburbia does not mean that identity and cultural life there is the same as in the metropolitan city. Middle-class suburban social life tends to be conservative, assimilationist, hostile to difference and to diversity. When it comes to specific diasporic identifiers, it is also much less diverse than in the urban. The suburban colonies (Drucker and Gumpert, 1997) tend to reproduce themselves around a small number of symbols and institutions, such as churches and the community schools often run by the churches. In the metropolitan urban space, the relation to diaspora is more dynamic, contested and changing in contestations and often tense interactions. The urban is characterized by tense coexistence of various groups not only defined by ethnicity; all of them struggle for visibility and spatial ownership and for representation. Finally, in its nature and in the publicness of the urban social life, the city inevitably implies diversity, and this also applies inside the diasporic groups, which are components of the urban. No migrant/diasporic group is homogenous when it comes to the cultural identities of its members and the social and economic positions they take within the city. For example, Astoria residents, in their majority, are Greek speaking, first generation, working class. Greeks/Greek Cypriots in Long Island, New York, are middle class, English speaking, second and third generation. Some of the divisions of the city tend to be less ethnically and more socially defined. However, in the multicultural urban, class identities are partly shaped in dialogue with diaspora and in relation to the ethnic hierarchies of the specific global city.

Dwellers in Multicultural Cities

The city allows us to think of connections, mobility and participation beyond the restrictions of the nation-state. The mixed populations of the city require rights in local and translocal spaces, and their condition requires 'new citizenship rules based on mobile and transferable rights of personhood.' (Amin and Thrift, 2002)

The multicultural global city is a point of encounters between different populations. These encounters are not just components of everyday life; they also are part of the ideological apparatus of everyday life. The urban diasporic populations tend to live in locales inhabited by diverse populations, and they are actors in the often highly contested politics of the multicultural city. Otherness and identity take their shape in the meeting of three positions: the dominant ideologies in the nation-state where diasporic populations live; the particular ideologies that relate to the diasporic journey and the politics it carries; and the everyday encounters in the city. A 50-year-old participant, who distances himself from what he sees as the Cypriot hostility to diversity, argues for the politics of difference in the multicultural city. He says that in London, unlike Cyprus, diversity is respected.

Here [in London] people live peacefully together. You can find Cypriots, Chinese, Arabs, Indians, Blacks, all living in the same building. And they still don't have any problem with each other. It's all a matter of habit. We [Greek Cypriots] always teach our children the wrong message. First of all, our Church teaches children that our reli-

gion is the best when all religions are as good. Then some of the teach-
ers in the Greek schools teach them the most nationalistic stuff about
the Greeks. . . . But our children are born in this country [Britain], they
grow up with different customs, different language and food. How do
people in Cyprus expect them to be just like them? Just the fact that
they speak the [Greek] language should be appreciated.

In these words, the global city's multiculturalism is celebrated and cherished. For this participant, the lived urban diverse experience seems to lead
to the formation of a reflexive diasporic identity that is conditional and
dialectically shaped in the context of the global city. This flexible identity,
however, seems to become much less flexible when diversity comes home:

I am not a chauvinist but I don't want my grandchild to be called
Mohammed. My children know my desire to marry Cypriots and I
believe that they are not going to hurt me. . . . I told my kids: marry one
of our own kind and if you don't have a good time divorce him [/her].

This man's talk represents the hybrid and conflicting nature of diasporic
subjectivity. At the beginning, his experience in the global city is dominant
in shaping his ideas of other groups and his critique of Greek Cypriot culture. As he goes on, though, the traditional ideology of ethnic separation
becomes more dominant. Contradictory talk often characterizes diasporic
ideologies and everyday life in the Western metropoles. Islam—and in this
case the reference is specifically to Turkish culture and religion—refers to
the immediate, yet distant, Other of the *homeland*. Another middle-aged
man expresses an almost identical approach to the reality of bringing diversity home. In terms of defining the broader territory of his life he says: 'We
don't have a problem with any race. With the Turks as well. They come
here, we are friendly to most of them. The conflict took place in Cyprus.
Here we all live peacefully together.' But again, his approach changes when
the Other gets closer. When a friend of his says that it took him a while to
get used to the idea of having two English daughters-in-law, he feels he has
to comfort him: 'Well, if you have many children you don't mind if one
marries a foreigner. But otherwise, it's a problem.' Interethnic tensions
become even more extreme when it comes to nonwhite groups. One participant disowned his daughter for marrying an Afro-Caribbean man. And
the words of another are chilling: 'If my daughter married a black guy . . .
in a way it would be better if I lost her. Of course, they are humans too,
but, oh no, Holy Mary. . . .' Constructing images of Otherness and symbolic boundaries between Us and the Others is central in the process of self-
identification. Once Otherness comes closer, dealing with diversity
becomes stiffer. The above examples might show a hostile rejection of the

Other—especially the one who is visibly different, either because of appearance or religion—but they do not necessarily reflect the action the participant take in their encounters with the Others. These briefly presented cases also illustrate the specific dynamics of each global city locale. Although diversity and transnational networks cut across global cities, the demographic specificities define the particular encounters and ideologies of its players. Greek Cypriots in London, for example, constantly come across the familiar Other of the *homeland*—Turkish Cypriots. Their encounters with Turkish Cypriots in the global city force them to reassess their ideologies of We-ness and Otherness. In the American case, however, there is almost no encounter between Greek Cypriots and Turkish Cypriots, and ideologies of We-ness and Otherness are largely formed through the definition of the Other as very different, hostile and distant. At the same time, what is often observed is conditional change of outlook. Words and actions are often contradictory in the diverse global city, and they also shift depending on the politics of the individual, the family, the group, the city, and the nation. The resolution is conditional, and it comes in the struggles and the negotiations that inevitably take place in everyday life and as people move in and out of exclusive diasporic spaces.

INTERCITY LINKS

> *They [diasporic minorities] participate, through cable television, video, and other technologies in the steady noise of home entertainment produced in and for the United States. Thus the work of the imagination through which local subjectivity is produced and nurtured is a bewildering palimpsest of highly local and highly translocal considerations.* (Appadurai, 1996: 197)

The cosmopolitan city is the hub of most diasporic populations, but both global cities and diasporic populations exist and are formed in their interconnections with other places and in their participation in transnational networks. There is an emerging homology of the global city network and the diasporic actors—including diasporic people, their media, sounds and images, foods, technologies of communication, multicultural neighborhoods' hybrid cultures—observed in the study of transnationalism. 'World cities are places in themselves, and also nodes in networks; their cultural organization involves local as well as transnational relationships' (Hannerz, 1996: 128). But global cities are not only nodes of economic and large scale global networks. There are various links of smaller scale or invisible to the mainstream, between the global cities and other local points across the world. In the case of transnational communities, one kind of such links develops between the cosmopolitan city and the much smaller-scale town or village in the country of origin. 'Priests and pastors learn to make regular pilgrimages to their town's "colonies" abroad in order to minister to their parishioners and seek their support for various works. Indeed, church repairs are commonly the first sign of the change of fortune of a town with migrants' civic committees abroad' (Portes, 2001: 191). The town of origin becomes an often overlooked node in transnational networks, next and in its interaction with the global city. These interconnections between cities and towns in the country of origin and country of settlement have an impact in both sides. Cultural signifiers and social life in the locality of origin are affected by developments in the diaspora and the other way around. The importance of this connection is that it is two-way and involves multiple forms of mobility and cultural exchange between the two places. The example of the priests visiting 'colonies' in the metropolitan Western cities, as well as travel for leisure that takes place between the two positions, are examples of the multiple directions human and communication flows follow. In the case of the Greek Cypriot diaspora, visits of religious and political leaders seeking political and financial support from, what they literally consider as the colonies are frequent, well organized and strategically sustained through transnational networks. On the opposite side, increasing numbers of Greek Cypriots living in the diaspora invest money in holiday homes by the Cypriot coast and in turning the old village home of their grandparents into a holiday home. The pilgrimage that Portes talks about (2001) goes both ways. It is religious, political, as well as touristic and commodified. Places in both sides of the transnational conversation are culturally formed and conceptualized in the eyes of their inhabitants and visitors through ongoing exchanges and their outcomes. The intercity links between the point of diasporic departure and of diasporic settlement are just one element of diasporic transnationalism. The multiple levels and meanings of diasporic transnationalism unravel in the following chapter.

EIGHT ─────────────────────

DIASPORIC TRANSNATIONALISM

Home is no longer one place, it is locations. (bell hooks cited in Amin and Thrift, 2002: 46)

Diasporic transnationalism is less about place and more about space. It is less about the boundary and more about imagination. It invites us to consider the possible emergence of contradictory yet viable forms of transnational imagined communities, especially through selective and partial participation. Although there is a temptation to interpret the often observed attachment of dispersed people with a transnational community as a reproduction of the imagined community of the nation in global scale, the diasporic case is significantly different from both the nation and the primordial bounded community. The diasporic condition has significant particularities, many of which are shaped in the context of globalization. 'Practices of displacement might emerge as *constitutive* of cultural meanings rather than as their simple transfer or extension,' argues Clifford (1997: 3). Diasporic consciousness is not just about being 'Chinese' or 'Greek' or 'British' or 'French' according to people's settlement; 'it is also about feeling global' (1997: 257). Diasporic consciousness, Clifford continues, is about the possibility of gaining 'a sense of attachment elsewhere, to a different temporality and vision, a discrepant modernity' (1997: 257). Diasporic continuity is as much about the imagining of a common origin and a common fate as it is about the transnationalization of possible common imaginings, which are particular and specific to a group but also global in their relevance. Diasporic continuity is about the interrelation between universalism and particularism—it is about the global and the transnational as much as it is about the particular identity and community.

The intensification of mobility and thus of diasporic scattering, the development of communication technologies and networks across the world and the relocation of diasporic populations in global cities where capitalism thrives are all key conditions of globalization with reflection to the diasporic formation and change. It is in the context of diasporic scattering and development of networks across the world, especially across global cities, where diaspora is re-imagined (Bhabha, 1990) and where transnationalism is defined.

Transnationalism and Its Relevance

Theories of transnationalism address the development of dense networks across borders (Portes, 1997) and 'the process by which transmigrants, through their daily activities, forge and sustain multi-stranded social, economic, and political relations that link together their societies of origin and settlement, and through which they create transnational social fields that cross national borders (Basch, Schiller and Blanc-Szanton, 1994: 6). Importantly, such theorizations of transnationalism emphasize (a) the significance of mediation and networking; (b) the relevance of everyday life; and (c) the interconnection between different spheres of social life—cultural, economic and political.

In a recent analysis, Portes (2001) maps the consequences of immigrant transnationalism in three points. As he argues, although transnational connections and development of consistent social, political and economic relations across space still form a minority of activities and relations within migrant and diasporic populations, there is every reason to expect its growth in the future. The first point that he highlights is that immigrant transnationalism 'is not driven by ideological reasons but by the very logic of global capitalism' (2001: 187). Transnationalism expands as there is a continuous demand for migrant labor, which becomes increasingly mobile as transportation and communication technologies advance long-distant initiatives. The second point relates to issues of integration; immigrant transnationalism, Portes continues, alters the process of integration of migrants and their offspring in the country of settlement. Though often considered as an obstacle to integration, transnational activity can actually support successful adaptation. This happens as transnational connections resist processes of assimilation—and thus, disempowerment and subordi-nation—and advance active and informed participation in the society of settlement, as there are networks of reference and support resisting mar-ginalization and exclusion. Data used by Portes shows that transnational entrepreneurs are better educated and more economically successful than either purely domestic entrepreneurs or wage workers. The third reason for the study of transnationalism is its importance for the sending countries. Increasingly, sending countries realize the political and economic signifi-cance of keeping links with the migrants, and the migrants themselves often get engaged in supporting political causes and economic develop-ment in their country of origin, as already shown in the previous chapter.

Portes' analysis points out the growing significance of thinking through transnationalism and studying transnational networks and connections in their expressions and implications for diasporic life and multicultural soci-eties. Though such approaches of transnationalism allow us to think beyond the national boundedness of identity and community and instead through connections and mediation, they are still primarily constrained within the binary of the country of origin and the country of settlement. Theorists of transnationalism such as Portes (1997; 2001), Basch, Schiller and Blanc-Szanton (1994), Smith and Guarnizo (1998) have still to inte-grate in their analysis the multiple connections between migrant and dias-poric communities across the world and the multiplicity of settlement and resettlement. Similarly, empirical research on multipositioned diasporic connections is just at the beginning. The connections between singular points in the diaspora and the country of origin still dominate the litera-ture. These connections, though important, are only part of the multiple transnational flows and networks and the transnational social fields. Diasporic communities have autonomous connections among them-selves—for example between London and New York—which are the out-come, on one hand, of the multiple points of settlement and resettle-ment—mobility and settlement in different places at different points of the diasporic journey—and, on the other, of the growing communication and transportations links between various positions across the globe. Furthermore, apart from the experienced connections, imagining the dias-pora as a multipositioned global community settled in different places across the world is equally important.

THE LOCAL, THE GLOBAL AND TRANSNATIONAL MEETINGS

Changing geographies are at the core of a growing literature in social sci-ences. Changes in geographical relations and their meanings do not only alter economies and elite connections; they also transform imaginary spaces for larger populations who are in the production and the consumption side of increased mobility and growing mediation of networks and communities. '[O]ur sphere of experience is glocal (our roots are our antennae). A cosmopolitan sociology needs to investigate the "imagined presence" of distant others and distant worlds' (Featherstone, 2002: 4). The changing human and nonhuman geographies have been primarily analyzed within the extensive literature on the local/global nexus (Morley and Robins, 1995; Sreberny-Mohammadi, 1997; Lull, 2000; Featherstone, 2002; Rantanen, 2004). The global and the local contain more and more in their interrelation the real and the symbolic dimensions of the home, the public, the city and as a consequence, the community. Though the literature on the local/global nexus has a tendency to reproduce binary relations, it has been radical in surpassing the centrality of the nation-state and the limitations of Euclidian geography. The literature on transnationalism, global cities and networks has learned from the debates on the global and the local. Definitions of identity and community as bounded within places and as being singularly defined by national sets of values, rights and duties, loyalties and opportunities is long gone. Empirical research, like the present one, has illustrated how diverse sets of values, rights and loyalties coexist and compete within the particular and the infinite of the global/local nexus. People live in local places, but their everyday life is shaped in the context of discourses, cultures and relations that are formed in the dialogue between the local, the national and the transnational. 'The local is created in the consumption of global discourse,' argues Strathern (1994: x). In changing geography, social relations, movements and communications are transformed and come together in places that become unique points of their intersection. Geographical places become meeting places:

> Instead then, of thinking of areas with boundaries around, they can be imagined as articulate movements in networks of social relations and understandings . . . but where a large proportion of those relations and understandings . . . are constructed on a far larger scale. . . . And this, in turn, allows a sense of place which is extroverted, which includes a consciousness of its links with the wider world, which integrates in a positive way the global and the local. (Massey, 1993: 239)

Massey stretches out a basic element of (inter)spatial meetings—the hybridization of human relations, of identities and of places. The city becomes a hybrid place where distinct and parallel experiences of travel, settlement and cultural formations meet in a multiplicity of histories which are not bounded in one place, but formed through movement in space (Massey and Denton, 2000). Like relations and identities, communication becomes hybrid (Friedman, 1995).

A diasporic form of mediated interaction that is hybrid in its nature—it is interactive and it shifts between the local and the global—is that of radio phone-in programs. Phone-in radio programs are some of the most popular broadcasts in local radio stations in North London and in Astoria. Their content varies and it includes the dissemination of information and gossip relating to the local community—that is community public events, marriages, family celebrations, birthdays—and the production of transnational dialogical spaces of communication. Often, popular programs of the kind are real-time co-productions between radio stations in London, Nicosia, Melbourne and New York. News about marriages, deaths, travels of individuals and families between cities travel across the vast distances that separate various diasporic communities. Some listeners religiously follow these special broadcasts and they sometimes use them as a public platform for reconnecting with relatives and friends who have settled elsewhere in the globe and whom they lost touch with. Greetings and messages travel in airwaves and through satellite and international phone connections. The distant diasporic subjects come closer to a community, publicly declaring its connections and its interests in sustaining transnational networks. Radio producers turn into global missionaries who carry the responsibility of reconnecting old friends and distant relatives.

This example is only one case that illustrates the significance of inter-spatial connections for the diaspora. Media connections across space are not only a technological possibility; they are active appropriations of communication technologies that bring the past, the present and the future of the diasporic being and becoming together. Naficy argues that media assist people to construct hybrid identities, not by producing absences, but by producing 'multiple presences of the home and the past and of the here and the now' (1993: 121). Furthermore, communication technologies and the emergence of hybrid identities allow people to break out of the clearly defined boundaries of two nation-states: the one they came from and the one they settled into. That does not mean that the nation-state is no longer a player in the process of identity construction. The nation-state remains a major political and administrative power (Hall, 1992; Rex, 1997). But its role is not as permanent or as taken for granted as it used to be. The competition for power and the diversity of the emergent discourses—even if the processes are still unequal—allow for the (re-)invention of new spaces of in-betweeness, where the sense of belonging is negotiated in being here and there without being bounded within here or there (Bhabha, 1996). In-betweeness is inherent to diasporic transnationalism.

THE POPULAR: TRANSNATIONALISM
BEYOND THE POLITICAL

. . . items which make up the fabric of our everyday lives, elements as
diverse as food and memory, can no longer be located locally. . . .
(Featherstone, 2002: 4)

As will be discussed in the next section, the communication of traditional
political ideologies is very central as a strategy for establishing connections
and diasporic networks across the transnational community. For Cypriots
across the world, the division of their original homeland has been communicated by community leaders as the core issue for transnational
Cypriotness. The discourses around the problem, as developed by the leadership in Cyprus and the diaspora, assumes the centrality of the original
homeland and represents the diaspora as a satellite around it. However, this
political ideology is not synonymous to this transnational community's
identity; on the contrary, it is challenged in political talk and in everyday
practices. The popular becomes an area of huge and growing importance in
the ways Greek Cypriots in the diaspora imagine their sense of belonging
and their connection with other Greek Cypriots positioned within the
transnational. Though news from Cyprus is cherished by a segment of the
diasporic audiences—usually male, middle-aged and migrant—it is the
entertainment products that are the most popular, the ones that travel best,
and those that are consumed the most across various diasporic groups. The
popular becomes important in the continuity of diaspora, especially as discourses of loyalty to the nation-state of the *homeland* retreat. The popular
increasingly replaces a nation-centric living and imagining of the diaspora;
music, literature and television are less bounded and anchored in nation-
states and more compatible with transnational networks, in which they are
actually circulated. Politics, on the other hand—especially in the top-down
versions initiated by the *homeland* governments, national media and community leaders—are stubbornly nation-centric.

Media talk often becomes the illustration of resistance to Cyprus-
centric agendas of media and of community leaders. In discussing satellite television especially, diasporic subjects time and again complain
about the diasporic exclusion from satellite broadcasting decision making. This complaint comes with parallel praise of the opportunities to
have access to certain broadcasts and televisual genres from the *homeland* on satellite and other new media. When certain transnational diasporic media products are discussed, complaints are replaced by enthusi-
astic engagement with transnational Greek culture. Music and football
predominate.

Sonic Diaspora

The dominant political discourse of community leaders is increasingly alien and alienating, especially for the young generations born in the diaspora. For them, diaspora tends to be a decentralized transnational experience. Younger generations, which are brought up away from the original *homeland* and have lived in times of globalization, are less familiar with discourses of political loyalty and more familiar with individualistic cultures of global capitalism. For most young people, the ideology of a duty towards anything Greek, including the media, has long become irrelevant. Their diasporic identities are more about their immediate world and their direct experience than about an essential patriotism and an essentialist Greekness. Thus, media and communication technologies, like other community references, matter only when they are applicable to the popular, consumer culture they embrace.

Greek pop music consumption and entertainment choices that emerge around the communal use of Greek music seem to form the strongest cultural identifier of Greekness across transnational spaces for the youth. In both London and New York, more participants expressed interest in Greek music than in any other symbolic reference. 'My kids love Greek music . . . much more than they like American music,' says a young American-born mother. The predomination of music as a reference is also expressed in the words of a 22-year-old American-born man:

> I really like Greek music. When I go on holidays in Greece or Cyprus I make sure I catch up with new releases. I also browse through the Greek music sites. But usually I don't buy music there—it's too expensive! My cousin in Cyprus burns CDs with the latest hits and sends them over. He's well-hooked, so he helps me keep up with all the new stuff. I like listening to Greek music and I also do some mixing myself—usually Greek music with rap.

What is interesting about this person is that apart from his devoted and active engagement with Greek music, he does not engage with much of the diasporic community activity in his locale. His engagement and appreciative talk about Greek pop vis-à-vis his negative talk about Greek American community life shows that music becomes a universal language he can relate to in the context of global consumerism. The church, the coffee shops and the Sunday Greek schools, on the other hand, represent for him a (peripheral) culture he despises. The universal language of pop music is also his language of Greekness; it is his community language that brings him closer with other people of his age across the world. A female participant of the same age group and education—they are both university graduates—shows a very similar sonic association with a transnational cultural community. After condemning the repressive and conservative Greek community life in New York, she says that she adores Greek music and Greek pop culture. The only Greek organized activities she regularly chooses to attend are Greek music club nights.

Sound, even more than mediated image, becomes a major mundane, sensual experience of diaspora for young generations. Greek music is compatible with British and American youth popular cultures, as the musical themes, the quality and the aesthetics of the Greek music industry are not very different from those of the commercial mainstream. During the last few years especially, the Greek music industry, like others of the periphery, has become a competent competitor in global markets. The recent success of Greek artists in Eurovision (the European song contest) and the commercial success of others, such as Anna Vissi and Despina Vandi in global (primarily diasporic) markets, have advanced the transnational appeal of Greek pop. The emergence of online shops selling Greek CDs across the world and the ability to exchange music over the Internet have been two other major developments that have advanced accessibility and popularity of Greek hits. Thousands of Greek albums and hundreds of Greek music (and other) DVDs and videos are available to buy on www.greekmusic. com,[37] and the exchange of tracks on e-mail is a common habit (and bonding activity) of youth shared across geographical territories. Greek music has become a component of global consumer culture as much as American and British pop has. Popular music turns into an integral, ordinary part of everyday life as, at the same time, it becomes a sensual representation of diasporic transnationalism and global consumer culture. The triangular relation music/consumption/aurality emerges as a powerful link within the transnational community. Sound travels well and it translates into the sensual incorporation of Greekness. 'Hearing takes time—it involves quite long-term sense' (Urry, 2000: 101). Musical tastes take time to develop and once they do, they have some permanence and gain the significance of a communal activity. Musical tastes are not choices of solitude but of community.

Football:[38] Always in Home Ground

Next to music, another very popular global media product is football: televised football, aural football, talked-about football and played football.[39] Football consumed in the media, diasporic and mainstream, and played in local and diasporic football clubs and championships is a very popular activity, especially for men. Football and sports programs are among the most viewed broadcasts on diasporic television. Male participants describe how a good match—of Cypriot teams, as much as of international and national football—can become the reason for a great night with friends who get together around the television at home or in public. Live broadcasting on radio, especially as it is now available in real time on the Internet, is another much praised possibility for engaging with the sport and with sports audiencehood. A substantial part of life in male-dominated community centers and coffee shops takes place around viewing and talking about football. 'The other day, there was a good match on TV. So, we had one TV tuned into the [Cypriot satellite television] news and the other into the game,' a habitué of the Cypriot Community Centre in London says with enthusiasm. Some go to extremely costly solutions in order to keep up with Cypriot football. Especially in the United States, where there is limited access through the media to Cypriot football, other communication technologies compensate. 'When Omonia[40] plays, my brother-in-law tapes the game and sends it with DHL. My husband has the tape in his hands the next morning,' a participant in New York explains. Another, the mother of two American-born young boys, expresses her amazement with her sons' interests in Greek and Cypriot football. 'They have their own Omonia gear, which they love to wear. They love that team.' Televisual and aural access to football become an ultimate transnational experience within the (male) diaspora. Football has been a popular leisure activity for Greek (Cypriot) men, even before the development of transnational electronic media. Greek (Cypriot) football clubs in London and New York have been established since the early days of migration. However, the mediated, real-time—or almost real-time— availability of football as a consumption media product signifies something more than the engagement with the sport. Televisual representation of football has privileged vision over participation and information over experience, argues Sandvoss (2003). This might be true when it comes to engagement with football, as sports audiencehood becomes more popular than participation in the football clubs. In terms of diasporic participation, the case is somehow different. Sports audiencehood is universal, cross-generational and transnational—at least for men. Football language is a language shared across boundaries and beyond age, generational, political and geographical differences. Football becomes a global common language within consumer cultures, and in the case of diaspora, it becomes a subconsumer culture that appropriates diaspora, makes it familiar and brings it home.

MEDIA AS A TRANSNATIONAL PUBLIC SPHERE?

Popular culture is gaining ground against politics, but the political sphere is still of major importance and has implications for both the diasporic communities and the nation-states of their origin and settlement. Looking into the possibilities for liberating and participatory diasporic politics, Appadurai argues that there are growing potentials for the development of diverse and inclusive diasporic public spheres (1996). As electronic media become predominant in mediated communication, the excluding abilities of being able to read and write in a common language become less of an obstacle to participation in transnational public spheres, he continues. The potential for decentralized, transnational diasporic spheres emerges as the nation-state loses its monopoly in social, political and cultural exchanges and as images, sounds and people are less bounded and grounded within singular political and cultural territories. Increased mobility and access to media and technologies of various kinds and origins advance diversity and heterogeneity across diasporic communities. Numerous examples of decentralized and participatory engagement with media and communication technologies apply in the case of the Greek Cypriot diaspora. Within fewer than ten years, web sites that address interests of various groups and subgroups have mushroomed: sites promoting peace in Cyprus; women's networks; gay and lesbian diasporic associations; academic networks; artists' discussion groups: professional mailing lists and more. More conventional media, such as television and radio, have also diversified and now include public, state-run, commercial, and community broadcasts and products that integrate technologies and content connecting people in local and transnational spaces. Are all these components of a new participatory diasporic public sphere—or spheres in plural?

'The challenge for this emergent order will be whether such heterogeneity is consistent with some minimal conventions of norm and value, which do not require a strict adherence to the liberal social contract of the modern West' writes Appadurai (1996: 23). Additionally, we can ask: Do transnational mediascapes become participatory public spheres where alternative modernities, which contest capitalism and Eurocentrism, emerge? Has nationalism and top-down politics been replaced by decentralized multipositional direct democracy? The emerging situation is much more complex than a negative or positive reply to these questions would reflect. Nationalistic and cosmopolitan ideologies are in constant tension in the diaspora, and they often take place around the media. The examples discussed in the two following sections illustrate the two parallel, competing tendencies of transnational diasporic politics.

Networks, Politics and Critical Proximity

Constant and simultaneous exchange of political information from the country of origin and other parts of the diaspora feeds the confidence of belonging in a large cultural and political community of common interests: 'We know about the Cyprus problem. We watch all about it everyday' is a confident statement in many people's mouths. The intensification and vast-ness of information exchanged on the Internet and consumed in satellite television offers reassurance of informed participation in a public sphere, which expands across the globe. Many participants—especially men—have a detailed knowledge of Cypriot politics, which they follow regularly. The ability to demonstrate awareness of developments in Cypriot politics is not only an element of performed male identities in public. It is also a transna-tional common language for communicating with other [male] members of the global diaspora—in a way, just like football. During a dinner party at a London Cypriot home, to which family friends visiting from Melbourne were invited, the Cyprus problem dominated talk. Male participants were much more vocal, and women slowly retreated to the background. Demonstration of knowledge and opinionated comments on the matter became a performative competition of male Cypriot identities.

Engagement with the Cyprus problem reflects a genuine interest among diasporic populations in a crucial political issue that divides their original *homeland*. Besides, for many of them, migration was an outcome of political divide in Cyprus, as they lost their homes and properties after Turkey's military invasion. This genuine interest has been embraced by the leadership in Cyprus, which realized the power of diasporic lobbying in Britain and the United States (Demetriou, 2002). The Greek American lobby is very active in Washington, and in New York, political representa-tives—Greek Americans and others—face constant pressure from the Greek American electorate for a solution in Cyprus. The lobby in London has regular meetings and campaigns in the British Parliament. Part of the Greek Cypriot leadership's strategy for keeping close links with the dias-pora has been the establishment of media connections. The phenomenon is not unique to the Greek Cypriot case and has been addressed in relation to the (re-)established relation between the country of origin and the dias-pora and the emergence of competing nationalisms for different diasporic communities (e.g. Indians, Jews, Iraqis). Anderson talks about diasporic engagement with the *homeland*'s politics as being formed through partial knowledge and selective information that leads to long-distance nation-alisms and email nationalism (1994). Appadurai (1996) calls the increased diasporic interest in their original *homeland*'s politics 'new patriotism.' He argues that new media and communication technologies play a key role in the process of connecting and engaging. Satellite television has been at the heart of the matter, and the case of Al Jazeera, challenging Western transna-tional media domination, illustrates in the most visible manner the politi-cal implications of the appropriation of satellite technology from the periphery.

The success of projects aiming at reinforcing transnational nationalisms can be observed in everyday talk. Ideologies about the centrality of the *homeland* is adopted in everyday talk and it is being appropriated as ordinary and natural. A community leader's words during a major conference for the Cypriot diaspora in Cyprus indicate that the building of a shared mediated imagination becomes a goal of action and political mobilization:

> The magic of the satellite service lies, first of all in a symbolic identification of himself (sic) [the Greek Cypriot of the diaspora] with the Cypriot of the homeland. He listens to the same news bulletin; he watches the same images, at the same time. He identifies with him completely. . . . The result is to feel more connected [with Cyprus]. . . .

The words of a member of the diasporic community in London illustrate how banal nationalism (Billig, 1995) becomes transnational in the everyday and ordinary activity of sharing media:

> Now that we watch Hellenic TV, we realize that during the 70s and the 80s we had lost a part of our Greek identity. During the 80s, LGR started filling this gap and now television does as well. With television we know what's happening, even before it happens. It provides full information and keeps us in touch with our homeland. (female, 45)

Awareness of the significance of diasporic media for the political mobilization of the diaspora is evident in both top-down initiatives, by the governments of the original *homeland* and by community leaders, and bottom-up everyday practice, as people turn to the media to keep up to date with political developments. The diasporic and national hegemonic ideologies of transporting nationalism in transnational spaces, however, faces some significant obstacles. Diasporization and transnational connections imply the emergence of networks. The settlement of diasporic populations in different social and cultural contexts, as well as the increased possibility for mobility and interactivity between different nodes within diasporic networks, comes with increased cultural and political autonomy and inevitable ruptures in the umbilical cord—and the ideologies of the umbilical cord—that link the *homeland* and the diaspora. The ideology of banal (transnational) nationalism is often appropriated in everyday narratives, as the above two quotations show. However, the practice of banal nationalism is much more conditional. The diversity of cultural references in diasporic spaces of belonging, competing nationalisms, and global, individualistic capitalism, destabilize nationalistic tendencies within the diaspora. A community activist in New York explained how the attacks of 9/11 and the vastness of mediated images and information that traveled across transnational media, have intensified the tensions between Greece and Greek Americans:

> Greeks have always been patriotic—as Americans, I mean. Of course this is a generalization, but most of them feel grateful towards this country, which offered them so much. After 9/11 they became even more emotional . . . and many of them got really disappointed with the way Greeks reacted to the events. They watched the anti-American sentiment on [Greek] TV and they got angry and sad. Here we were trying to put the pieces of our lives back together and in Greece they said we deserved it. . . . (female, 36)

More exchange of information might lead to tensions, but this does not imply a breakdown of the community. What seems to be more of the case is that communication spaces become spaces of contestations and conflicting articulations of identity. In being more informed about the politics and the culture of the country of origin or of other sections of the diaspora, individuals and groups can construct their attitude of a *critical proximity*: they become aware that, whether they like it or not, they are not just reflections of the country of origin, but they have various positions—sometimes of proximity and sometimes of distance—within transnational networks. High mobility and increased mediation means that 'more and more people are living in a kind of *place-polygamy*. They are married to many places in different worlds and cultures. Transnational place-polygamy, belonging in different worlds: this is the gateway to globality in one's own life' (Beck, 2002: 24).

Networking and Participant Transnationalism

In mediated networks, relations are formed and reformed: they are not just extensions of already existing face-to-face relations or reflections of pregiven dynamics. Diaspora has always depended on increased mediation—once it was letters, word of mouth and monthly bulletins; now it is satellite, telephone, the Internet. The diasporic networks have a unique and persistent dynamic—against mediated communication in the country of origin, for example—and they follow the routes and the rules of human mobility, deterritorialization and relocation. They are networks and not linear one-way flows, as the people who form them are globally spread and locally multipositioned.

A young woman in New York describes an example of how she established a relation with her cousin in London via e-mail communication.

> With email I've really developed a close relationship with my cousin in London. Before email it was just the occasional phone call and a Christmas card. Now we chat very often. You see, it's also the way email is—you don't have to arrange to call someone who's in a different time zone and has family life and all . . . you just write to them and they reply when they have the time. (female, 36)

Her relation with a relative who used to seem far away has not only been eased by e-mail, but, actually taken further and reinvented as a new closeness. This relation has been reconstituted in imaginary, virtual terms that characterize much of the diasporic transnational (emotional) space. A London-based solicitor describes his experience of (re-)invented diasporic connections:

> I used to have a friend in school but then, when we both left Cyprus, we lost touch. Recently I searched for him on the Internet and I found out he's in Florida. We keep in touch since. (male, 47)

There is increased autonomy within the communities of the diaspora, and their autonomy and interconnection often challenge the linearity and the one-way flow between the country of origin and the diaspora (Hanafi, 2005). Especially as diasporic populations get established in the country of settlement, their relation with the original *homeland* becomes less of an inescapable dependence and more of a partial and selective association. For example, Greek Americans who still identify as Greeks define their Greekness much more in relation to their diasporic life and their participation in the American society rather than in relation to contemporary Greece. Their Greekness is in a constant interplay with their American identity. 'I'm proud to be Greek and I'm proud to be American' are the revealing words of a 28-year-old Greek American.

On one hand, mediation and networking advance the sense of proximity to other dispersed populations and to the country of origin. On the other, they amplify the level of critical reflection and selective engagement with the imagined community, as increased information and interaction remind the members of diasporic groups that the original *homeland* is not sacred and pure and that the spread populations who share a common origin are not characterized by cultural sameness. Increased exchange of images and sounds from the country of origin and the other sections of the diaspora become a constant reminder of diversity and of the real and present face of the country of origin and the fellow members of the imagined community.

Imagination, as it relates to imagined communities, unlike fantasy, is not only escape, but also a staging ground for action. Dispersed communities can move to common action (Appadurai, 1996), especially around specific causes that grasp the common imagination. A very good recent example is that of the spread Greek Cypriot diaspora. As external—especially American—pressure to reach a solution to the Cyprus problem became more intensified, the otherwise diverse dispersed communities—of the United Kingdom and the United States, for example—adopted common and organized strategies of pressuring and lobbying the international power that plays a role in the way the problem will be solved.

Diasporic communities surpass geographical boundaries. Participation, inclusion but also exclusion from the community is not in this case (or any more) framed within singular geographical boundaries or within inescapable dualities of dependence: diaspora/*homeland* or migrants/host country. Geographical boundedness and dualities are being constantly challenged in the actual diasporic experience, which builds upon a number of complex, and even competing, links and relations. The links and flows cut across many different places and follow many different directions. Thus, members of diasporic groups sustain relations with friends in the country of origin, but also relations with friends in the local multicultural community. Diasporic belonging is nonexclusive and, in times of increased transnationalism, high mobility and intense mediation, it can only be conditional and parallel to other forms of belonging. People use diasporic as well as nondiasporic media; they appropriate technologies in order to renew repertoires of diasporic identity, but also in order to fulfill age group interests, professional or other political interests, hobbies and friendships in and across places. The emphasis on the diversity of spatial contexts, cultural content and communication flows is a reminder of the growing significance of network structures and the transnational mechanisms of sharing images, sounds and information and their consequences for imagining a multipositioned and inevitably diverse community. In this context, boundaries have not faded away; this is not time for celebrating liberating cosmopolitanisms. Boundaries are still there, though they are now more symbolic than physical; they are more diverse, as they are defined as much by exclusionary mechanisms within global capitalism as they are by national and diasporic exclusionary discourses. Diversity, dispersal and difference come closer together in the context of an imagined community, even if often through tense relations. Diasporic populations, which are part of global networks as much as of locales, actively shape a sense of commonality and (imagined) community in their engagement with transnational communication. Media offer what Urry calls 'interpretative tools' to make sense of 'what would otherwise be disparate and apparently unconnected events and phenomena' (Urry, 2000: 180) but they also shape discourses and network links of imagined (co-)presences and imaginative mobility.

CONCLUSIONS

Everyday ethnographic practice, experimentation with *flânerie*, and four years of sharing mundane daily practices, media consumption, immediate, symbolic and imagined spaces and locations with a transnational diasporic group, brought this research to life. The focus of the research was the relation between media and communication practices and identity and community construction. In order to understand the relation, I turned to everyday and lived experience. Participants' own voices are heard and their presence is seen in the extensive data presented and analyzed. I hope that the result is a reflexive engagement with the data that recognizes emic and etic meanings of action and consumption, of talk and nontalk, of performed commonality and difference. While having dinner with a London Cypriot family, I saw an appropriation of media, when a young girl jokingly compared her father to a Cypriot sitcom character. In my long evenings at the Cypriot Community Centre, I realized that many interpersonal relations develop around communal television viewing—the performative bonding activity that initiates social interaction and ideologies of Greek Cypriotness. In wandering in local shopping centers, I observed cross-generational female networks reconfirming their community belonging in vocal and vibrant practices of consumption. In everyday ordinariness, identities are constructed and performed—identities that have to do with diasporic particularity and identities that don't. Participants' identities are the incomplete outcome of the diasporic journey, of the experienced and imagined deterritorialization and reterritorialization. At the same time, they are the unfinished product of participation in consumption (media) cultures, (various) transnational communities of origin and interest, and cosmopolitan Western urban societies.

Diasporas are cosmopolitans of a different kind to the high-flying, jet-setting cosmopolitans in control of global capitalism. Diasporic populations are usually the invisible cosmopolitans and the unnoticed participants in the formation of transnational (media) cultures; they are initiators of urban and transurban networks, which are antagonistic towards the nation-state, which diversify urban spaces in creative and communication practices, which develop parallel, competing and complimenting elements of mediated consumer cultures. Diasporas build transnational networks, develop particularistic cultural formations and construct distinct identities in mediation—in the mixing denied by the ideology of boundedness and separation of the nation-state and the modernist separated spheres of economic, cultural and political life. Diasporas are postmodern—and in a way, premodern—formations, as they construct messy, intermixing and anarchic political, cultural and economic spheres. Networks of family and kin, of economic and political interests and of cultural activities, become merged, fused and confused. In their (con)fusion, they reflect a range of ideologies: from the most conservative traditionalist and nationalistic, to the cosmopolitan celebration of capitalism and the cosmopolitan resistance to nationalism and profit. The contradictions, oxymora and struggles of diaspora are expressed in public transnational dialogues and debates, which tend to be highly mediated. Contradictory dynamics of diaspora reflect the lack of clear-cut order in cosmopolitan spaces and in transnationally connected cultural and political spheres:

> I doubt that cosmopolitan societies are any less ethical and historical than national societies. But cosmopolitanism lacks orientation, perhaps because it is so much bigger and includes so many different kinds of people with conflicting customs, assorted hopes and shames, so many sheer technological and scientific possibilities and risks, posing issues people never faced before. There is, in any case, a greater felt need for an evident ethical dimension in the decisions, both private and public, that intervene in all aspects of life and add up to the texture of cosmopolitan societies (Beck, 2002: 20)

Contemporary transnational connections and the persistence of diaspora as a relevant cultural category can only be understood in the context of transnationalism, competing cosmopolitanisms, and intense mediation.

SAME SYMBOLS–DIFFERENT MEANINGS: DIASPORA AND TRANSNATIONAL APPROPRIATION

Media narratives and cultural symbols circulated in networks and in com-munication flows produce and reproduce (imagined) belonging in transna-tional diasporic communities. Although there is a growing circulation of same symbols across large distances and diverse geographical and cultural contexts, the meanings of these symbols are not necessarily common across the transnational populations that share them. The construction of differ-ent meanings through the consumption of the same symbols, observed in actual practices and talk, reveals how transnational media cultures bring into being diasporic commonality without achieving transnational similar-ity and homogeneity. Diasporic commonality raises 'the possibility of same-ness' (Gilroy, 1995: 26), without this sameness ever actually *being*—rather, it is always a process of *becoming*. Continuity is implied in the process of *becoming*. It refers to what Gilroy (1993a) calls the *changing same*—it is the continuously changing *outcome* of the meeting of the roots with the routes (Gilroy, 1995). Continuity depends on shared memories and myths and on the communal imagining of a shared journey, a shared experience of deter-itorialization and reterritorialization (either directly or as a narrative). Continuity also depends on the dual spatial[41] and temporal[42] standpoint that brings the past and the future together in diasporic imagination and identification.

The appropriated meanings are the outcome of communal, subcom-munal, conflicting interpretations and of different processes of imagina-tion. Commonality can host diversity, while at the same time framing and sometimes restricting and repressing its expandability. To make this argu-ment more precise, I return to one of the examples extensively discussed in the previous chapters. When Greek pop music hits are consumed in Athens, Nicosia, London, New York and Melbourne, the content is the same; their communal, simultaneous, mass, transnational consumption is enabled by communication technologies, especially satellite and the Internet. People of different backgrounds and generations, who have var-ious interests and diverse identities and locations, consume the same product; however, the meanings of their consumption vary. For some, this is a cherished association with the contemporary culture of the *homeland*; for others, this is just a commodity consumed like any other pop music product; for a few, the music becomes a tool enabling familial or kin sociality. For most, it tends to become all these at different times and con-texts. In the diversity and shifting appropriation of music, an imagined condition of commonality and community develops. People who are oth-erwise very different find themselves sharing the same symbols (e.g., music), which are interpreted into a common language of communication and community.

Diversity in the interpretation and appropriation of meanings relates, first of all, to the diversity inherent in identity. Diasporic identities do not exist outside particular and complex social experience, especially as it relates to class, gender, sexuality, age and generation; rather they emerge and they are in an unending interplay of change through dialogue and negotiation with other identities. Diasporic identities are positioned in time and space and in relation to We-ness, Otherness, in the uneasy dialogue with the country of origin and the diaspora in its transnational expressions. Theorizations such as those of Hall (1981, 1986, 1991, 1992, 1997), Gillespie (1995), Gilroy (1993a, 1995, 2001), Brah (1996), Baumann (1996), Ahmed (1999), and Fortier (1999, 2000), engage with identity in analyses beyond the essentialization of certain identity politics, traditional race and ethnicity studies, and popular ideologies of ethnic fixity. Essentialisms, which consider ethnicity and diaspora as being either bounded within inescapable dependence upon a distant *homeland* or doomed to fade out through inevitable assimilation, fail to grasp the negotiations, conflicts and unease of the diasporic condition in relation to both the country of origin and the country of settlement.

The experience of the generations born in the diaspora illustrates most visibly the limitations of such approaches; these generations are more likely to challenge the set boundaries and ideologies around identity and community within the domestic, the public, the multicultural global city and in transnational diasporic and nondiasporic spaces. A middle-class 40-year-old female who lives alone and talks about the tendency of the older generations to reject her because of her choice not to get married, finds parallels in her life and that of George Michael.[43] 'It's people's narrow-mindness that pushed him [George Michael] away from the community,' she says. Whether or not this is true for George Michael, it is true for some of the members of the group, who give up the effort to sustain diasporic belonging through difference and completely detach themselves from the community, *disappearing* into the broader society. Her choice of finding parallels with a figure of universal[44] recognition who, at the same time, shares a particular identity of Greek Cypriotness with her, shows that she—like many others of her generation—can only see herself as cosmopolitan in the crossroad of the particular and the universal. The adoption of lifestyles and practices, which challenges group norms and dominant values, can become disidentifiers that enable the process of opting out (Song, 2003). The norms and rules that restrict entry and participation of different subgroups usually reflect ideologies of a closed transnationalism, clutching upon national and primordial values. At present, diasporic populations find themselves in the middle of struggles—within their communities and between their communities and the mainstream—over the values that will predominate. Political and social marginalization of diasporic groups tends to benefit regressive ideologies of closure, whereas increased spatial, cultural and social mobility tends to advance hybridization and flexibility of diasporic imagined communities.

For those staying within the community, participation increasingly takes place through links and networks that become ordinary and mundane cultural practices. As younger and older generations, men and women, working class and middle class, share common everyday small things and perform routines, habits and rituals, they construct shared discourses and reproduce particular values, such as religion, family, kinship. Everyday life becomes extensively saturated by cultural references that signify diasporic identity. Commodities, information, flavors and sounds are consumed on television, the radio, in parties and christenings, in travels and telephone calls. As different people share these same symbols, they (re)produce a sense of unforced attachment to transnational familial, kin and friendly diasporic networks.

As much as diasporic symbols become appropriated, so do the values of western, cosmopolitan capitalist societies, in which these populations now live. Diasporic identities are shaped at the meeting of ethnocultural particularism and modern ideologies of universalism.[45] That's why participation and belonging in diasporic families and networks is not incompatible with the ambition of social and economic success. Most working-class migrant parents have aspirations for their children's success and indeed, most of their offspring fulfill this desire. Many participants in New York proudly repeat in their comments that Greeks—including Greek Cypriots—have a reputation across the United States for being economically successful and high achievers in education.[46] The duality of the devotion to the values of the particular community and those of the broader society signifies the shift in the diasporic experience, which is inevitable as new generations take over and as Western universalism becomes a predominant ideology. This same, but changing, diasporic context leads to an intimate distanciation from the original *homeland*, its people and its culture. Although diasporic populations are affiliated with the *homeland* and although they consume its media, their interpretation and their appropriation of images, information and ethics comes with a critical distanciation. They relate to the original *homeland* in the context of a hybrid—decentralized, multinodal, conditional—imagined community. They know that they do not *belong* to the country of origin and they usually have no desire to do so.[47]

Diasporic populations do not only belong to a distinct transnational community; they have multiple identities and positions in local, national and transnational spaces. As Sinclair, Jacka and Cunningham explain, the relation between identity and the media shifts accordingly:

> It becomes possible to think of identities which are multiple. . . . An
> Egyptian immigrant in Britain might think of herself as a Glaswegian
> when she watches her local Scottish channel, a British resident when
> she switches over to the BBC, an Islamic Arab expatriate in Europe
> when she tunes into the satellite service from the Middle East, and a
> world citizen when she channel-surfs on to CNN. (1996: 25)

The playful shift between identities and between media is a constant ordinary condition for the diaspora. None of the hundreds of participants in
this research consumes diasporic media alone—or mainstream media
alone, for that matter. Even participants with minimum knowledge of
English flick between English language channels for a favorite soap opera
or for catching up with (fractions and/or images of) the local and national
news. As particularistic media coexist with others, the appropriation of
both is filtered by the diverse experience of their audiences. Diasporic
media audiences have a media literacy that surpasses the particularistic
consumption, especially as they are used to consume all different kinds of
media in everyday life. Diverse media consumption allows them to develop a reflexive, critical approach towards the media, both diasporic and
mainstream.[48] The diversity characterizing particularistic media consumption and appropriation challenges the limitations of theories of diasporic
homogeneity; it also takes further our comprehension of media consumption's complexity. In the study of diasporic media audiences, we can investigate how consumers participate in co-existing media culture(s)—particularistic, diverse, mainstream—and, at the same time, observe how the
shared, but exclusive to some, diasporic media use reconfirms symbolic
boundaries and particular and distinct identities.

Like media consumption, everyday sociality is diverse. None of the
participants has exclusively Greek social relations. Even if it is a matter of
brief interaction with a grocer or a non-Greek neighbor, the multiplicity of
everyday culture is a daily reminder of diasporic complexity. The constant
coexistence and interaction with the Other—or rather with various
Others—is another characteristic of the diasporic (hybrid) imagined community—which is never secluded and bounded away from the Other.
Diasporic community belonging is conditional and partial, as its members
live and belong to other local, urban, transnational communities—all at the
same time. Diasporic transnationalism is lived locally—in interactions with
the neighbor from Cyprus and the neighbor from the Caribbean—and it is
imagined globally.

In the diaspora, there is not necessarily so much physical mobility, but
there is an increased sense of mobility compared to other populations and
previous times. 'Culture also moves without people moving . . . not least
through the media' (Hannerz, 1996: 131). The mediated and imagined

links to a distant *homeland* and to other people spread across the globe, and the circulation and sharing of similar cultural repertoires feeds the imagined copresence and the imagination of mobility. In the diaspora, the shared sense of belonging builds upon the imagination of copresence, imaginative mobility and the interplay of the local and the global. Diffused audiences are both local and transnational; local in actual performance, transnational in their imagination and connections.

Diasporic Particularity: The Greek Cypriot Case

The experience of deterritorialization and reterritorialization, self-exile and interethnic conflict in Cyprus, as well as the ideologies of whiteness, consumerism and capitalist success integrated in the diasporic discourse, saturates the group's collective memory and imagination. These experiences and ideologies translate into everyday ordinariness as they are (re-)produced in (mediated) narratives that reconfirm belonging in both a distinct diasporic community and the cosmopolitan West. As much as such symbols project the group's distinctiveness, they also remind them that the original *homeland* is not an ideal place to return to. The adventurous, emotional and often painful historical journey of this community has shaped the present diasporic Greek Cypriot condition—a condition of integrated particularity. The historical and cultural context of diasporic Greek Cypriotness involves interesting particularities:

- Cypriots are some of the very few European peoples in Britain and the United States whose migration relates to violent deterritorialization; Cyprus' continuing division renews a collective concern for the *homeland* among the diaspora. This condition resists extensive assimilation, characteristic to many other white European groups.
- Greek Cypriots are European and white, but their migration was primarily part of the late colonial and postcolonial mass movements to the former colonial powers. Their peculiar position creates a condition of in-betweeness, both in relation to the white British/WASPS, as well as in relation to the other ethnic groups. This in-betweeness is shifting and changes in context—for example, Greek Cypriots are "white in multicultural North London, but "colored" in middle-class, white English/WASP-dominated professions.[49]
- The close connection within the diaspora and between the diaspora and Cyprus is not only the outcome of diasporic transna-

tionalism. The Cypriot government and the Greek government have reinvented the diaspora in their political discourse. Like many other governments with thriving diasporic populations, they have realized the political and financial benefits of keeping close relations with diaspora (Portes, 1997; Demetriou, 2002). The establishment of satellite television channels was a landmark in the initiatives connecting diverse populations with the country of origin.

- Though this group is small, its diasporic media are various and many. This creates an interesting condition, as members of the group can choose between, and combine, a number of media and contents, originating in the country of origin, the locale and the broader diaspora. The growing diversity in diasporic media maps is fast becoming the predominant diasporic condition, especially in the case of large diasporic groups—for example, Indians, Arabs, Turkish.

Intensified globalization and rapid changes in information, communication and transportation technologies have challenged old limitations in communication between different locations in the diaspora and between the diaspora and the country of origin. Technologies radically alter communication spaces, though identities and meanings do not change as fast. The allegiance with Cyprus remains strong for the migrant generation, but it is diluted in the case of the generations born in the diaspora. For both the Cyprus-born and the diaspora-born generations, however, the image of the distant *homeland* is now daily renewed in media consumption. Though media representations are always selective, they are still a constant reminder that Cyprus and Cypriots are changing as much as diasporic communities. Diasporic media, next to the increased possibilities of traveling back and forth between Britain/the United States and Cyprus (and other places where Cypriots live), as well as regular telephone communication, the exchange of consumer products, and the possibility of owning property in both countries, create new allegiances that surpass the estrangement that the reality of the diaspora-born generations assumed in the past.

At the same time, the establishment of regular communication between the diaspora and the country of origin reveals the differences between the Greek Cypriots of *here* and of *there* and forms a condition of transnational critical proximity. Diaspora is the unifying thread that brings diversity into a whole of commonality, formed away from the *homeland*. For the first generation it is defined as a relation of center-periphery, with Cyprus as the core, and for the new generations it is defined as a transnational decentralized experience; centripetal and centrifugal forces coexist and often conflict. For all generations though, diasporic identities are primarily grounded in their particular urban locales and in the cosmopolitanism of a life less bounded within nation-states and more shaped through connections and parallel spatial and cultural attachments.

Diverse diasporic meanings come together in sharing common discourses and imagined commonalities. 'Common discourse is forged out of diverse meanings rather than shared ones,' argues Stromberg (1986: 51). A crucial element of the discourse of community is the communal sense of deterritorialization. Diaspora is centrally dependent on the fact that there is a country somewhere far away that people have as a reference and can imagine as being a cultural source. For that same reason, they can identify with others who experienced this deterritorialization, either directly, or as a narrative. Additionally, a centrally important symbolic issue reconfirming Greek Cypriot particularity is the ongoing division of the original *homeland*. The Cyprus problem is a shared concern, and the hope for its solution has become a common cause. Although it is experienced differently by different people and generations, the Cyprus problem is a concern crossing geographical and cultural differences. Information regarding the division that dominates diasporic media news is a daily reminder of the problem and a daily renewed issue that informs everyday community discourse. This symbolic unifying agenda indicates that, apart from experience, Greek Cypriotness is an ideology (Mavratsas, 1999). Part of this ideology is the concern to preserve and renew a sense of continuity, uniqueness and community.

The ideology of particularity relates to the common origin and the transnationalism of a common diasporic journey, but it also relates to the context of the *now* and the interactions of *here*—the cosmopolitan city spaces. *Whiteness* is particularly important in this context. In the multicultural settings of North London and Astoria, New York City, Greek Cypriots identify themselves as one of the few *white* minorities. *Whiteness* and Europeanism are projected by a community that wants to distant itself from other Third World migrants and has aspirations for social success. Younger generations are directed to professions that guarantee success in the mainstream: law and accountancy more than any other. Their lifestyle usually reflects the attempts to adapt to the mainstream middle-class norm. The younger generations' social success and their performance of the social color *white* often make the boundaries between diasporic Cypriotness and (middle-class) *Whiteness* difficult to draw. Usually the two coexist, without this coexistence being necessarily a deliberate choice—it is more of an everyday tactic, as tactic is defined by Goffman, as opposed to strategy (1959)—for their wellbeing. In most cases, the two identities put individuals and groups in situations of continuous negotiations.

More than being a case of *either* (being Greek Cypriot)/*or* (being British/American), identities involve shiftings and combination of cultural choices in their performance. Greek Cypriot *Whiteness* allows the group's members to achieve this in a playful performance of parallel belonging in a particular community and the broader (capitalist/ cosmopolitan/global) society. As a result, there are special tactics and particular codes and behaviors, so that, for example, it is all right to act American in a non-Greek environment, while there are expectations of respect of Greek rituals and traditions within the community. This negotiation makes it easier for the youth to accept and celebrate diaspora without giving up other cultural choices. This does not mean that there are no conflicts and extremities; diasporic identities always involve exclusions and exorcizing of incompatible difference.

THE SPATIALITY OF THE DIASPORIC EVERYDAY

Home is a special, intense and emotional space and symbol for diaspora. It relates to deterritorialization and loss as much as it relates to imagination and the desire for intimacy and security. Home can be different things at different times, reflecting the diversity and (con)fusion of the spatial, cultural and emotional spheres of diasporic belonging—or the different levels of diasporic belonging. Home can be the domestic natural space, the immediate family, a private home, the refuge from the outside world. It can be the local space where everyday life evolves—the place to which people always return. It can also be the country of origin, the symbolic Home, the source, or, the highly symbolic and mediated transnational context, which shelters diaspora against exclusionary national spaces. More than any one of these, it tends to be all of the above. Diasporic Home is a symbol of cosmopolitan and intimate transnationalism. The diasporic inhabitants of its real and imaginary form constantly cross boundaries—less physically and more in their imagination and in mediated everyday. They develop a sense of familiarity and seek ontological security in their struggles to combine the ideologies and cultural practices attached to their different spheres of belonging—the diasporic home, the local community institutions, the capitalist economic life, global consumption cultures, and transnational identifications (with relatives, other young people, places, property, etc). Communication and transportation technologies and mediation allow access and interplay between symbolic and real spaces that constitute the Home. They also allow a daily interplay between various spaces of belonging—these being the home, the public, the city and the transnational.

Diasporic spatiality is not experienced in the same way by all members of a group. The meanings of space—of intimacy and networking, of imagined space and lived place, of spatial interconnections and participation in its various components—are conditional. Social positionings shape the lived and imagined diasporic space. Generation has been extensively discussed as a key social factor. The level of attachment to the country of origin, the access and use of media and communication technologies, the different cultural and economic capital of the migrant laborers vis-à-vis their middle-class offspring are some of the key elements that define the relation between generation and diasporic space. Spatiality is not only generational, though. Gender is another social element of importance. The division between the private and the public is experienced differently by men and women, especially in the case of the migrant generation. Traditional conceptualizations of home as a workplace for women and as a leisure space for men are reproduced in the Greek Cypriot domestic. A sense of duty that saturates women's life in the domestic informs and forms distinct diasporic roles. Women usually take the role of the agent of diasporic particularity, which must be communicated to the young generations. The sense of a mother's and wife's duty also affects the position of women in public. Public is much more functional, domesticated, and mediated by familial relations for women than for men.

This division is also reflected in media consumption. For women, media use tends to be a private affair, whereas for men it usually is both private and public. For women, the global and local public is mediated by the media at home; for men, it is the participation in the public that mediates the local and the global. For them, media are only part of their overall participation in the (diasporic) public sphere. The traditional boundaries separating the private and the public that are imposed to women are increasingly penetrable and penetrated. Female heavily mediated daily routines bring the world to the home. At the same time, entry in the public expands, both through the media and through physical mobility. Hybridization of identities and of access to diasporic space is the outcome of increased mediation and negotiation of the boundedness of home and of the community.

Female roles, both as represented in the mainstream and the diasporic media, challenge perceptions for themselves and the others. Media construct shared discourses and agendas that women share among themselves in public and with their families at home. Participation in community centers, churches, and associations brings women out of the house, but their relation to the public is still shaped by specific gender expectations and rules. For women, the public tends to be domesticized and privatized. Public sociality depends heavily on visiting friends' and relatives' homes. Within this public-private space, it is common to reproduce specific roles in repetitive and ritualistic performances of diasporic female identity. For both women and men, sociality at home and in public is most often connected to communal media consumption: family, friends, members of community centers regularly communicate around screens and in media talk. Media consumption becomes both a mediator of sociality and a shared diasporic activity.

The public space is not only ethnoculturally specific, especially when it becomes urban public. People walk in streets of multiethnic neighborhoods, they work in multicultural settings, they go to the shops and the cinema, they attend schools and clubs. Urban life is cosmopolitan, multicultural and transnational in more than one way: it is not only about diasporic cultural references, but also about the circulation of cultural products, images and flavors that characterize the global city and that are beyond *one* diasporic particularity. Being diasporic in the global city is a conditional meeting of a distinct—for example, Greek—particularity with other particularities—for example, Chinese, Mexican—in the context of shared universalisms—for example, consumer culture, capitalism, democracy. Diasporic particularity is never completely bounded, and much of its content is actually the outcome of dialogue/opposition with the Others close by (i.e., the other minority groups, the majority population, other religions and competitors for spatial ownership).

Diasporic particularity is constructed in the urban locale, in interaction, and in opposition to the Other urban cosmopolitans. It is a particularity that is imagined, more than lived, as a clear-cut and bounded difference. More than anything, it is symbolically and ideologically constructed against the neighbor, the Other of the city, of the nation, of globe societies. Diasporic particularity—identity and community—is projected as a universal, unquestioned position across spaces and over time. The ideology and the actual practice tend to contradict each other to such an extent that imagination becomes a key, necessary component of belonging and of diasporic continuity.

Particular spatial positioning in the local, the national and the diasporic context disrupt popular perceptions of the homogeneity of the diaspora. The coexistence with significant Others of the *homeland* and new Others, the dominant perceptions about difference and *ethnic* color, the politics and policies of ethnic and interethnic relations, position diasporic groups in their particular local and national context. Communication between here and there, between the country of origin and with the rest of the diaspora, does not erase difference in context. The diversity of the diasporic everyday experience leads to the construction of multiple diasporic identities. Mediation and imaginary traveling are ingrained in the development of diasporic (imaginative) multipositionality. As much as electronic media have surpassed the strict boundaries separating the public and the domestic and brought the world into the home, they have also brought the distant *home(land)* close and the distant relative and friend into the living room and the community center. In their temporality, banality and taken-for-grantedness, media as part of popular culture are not only compatible with the everyday—they are part of it. The media speak everyday language, they produce and reproduce everyday humor, as the repeated comments of many participants emphasized. Media representations, agendas and discourses inform diasporic discourse, and in their dailiness they produce and reproduce symbols of community and identity.

Media and Diasporic Identities—A Matter of Compatibility

As the emphasis turns to media culture as context, it allows an understanding of the relation of the media and identities as discursive and neverending. Identities are shaped within the context of media culture. Thus, their multiplicity cannot but be informed by, and their commonality constructed around the shared media consumption. In the cultural process of media consumption, audiences participate in the construction of meanings. What does this mean? The relation between media and identities is dialectical and homologous, especially as it unravels in the context of everyday life. The functions and values of the two meet dynamically in everyday life and although, or perhaps because, conflicts and inconsistencies exist, they reach a level of constant, dialectic compatibility. When, for example, young British Greek Cypriots choose the local Greek radio, they listen to programs addressing their age group; they choose the programs that are as bilingual as they are; they choose the ones broadcasting (Greek) pop music—a genre they enjoy in their listenings—diasporic or not. As much as their multiple identities (teenage- Greek-British) bind their media consumption, these identities are renewed and continuously reframed within the media and media(ted) culture.

The media saturate everyday life, and inevitably identities learn and are shaped in highly mediated worlds. The media inform us about what is important, what is fashionable, acceptable and attractive. As these perceptions are appropriated, adopted and adapted in everyday consumption, the multilayered homology and the dynamic compatibility between the media and identities take their shape. Diasporic media are not as much a taken-for-granted part of everyday life as are the mainstream media and the values they represent. Thus, the homology of diasporic media and identity is formed in a specific context, where the particular(istic) media establish their presence and become meaningful components of everyday communication and cultural practice. This context is community, a community lived and imagined in multiple spaces and in their interconnection. Maybe now more than ever, diasporic communities are truly transnational. Diasporic transnationalism is about the impossibility of restraining communities within national frames and the impossibiity of thinking of identity outside imagined and highly mediated cultural spaces.

NOTES

1. The concept of *homeland* appears in italics throughout this book—unless it is used by participants themselves—as it is a symbolic, ideological concept. It is a concept that addresses issues of imagination, longing and belonging and less so a specific geographical place.
2. The term 'mediated' refers to communication achieved in and by the media, such as television, radio and the Internet and the term 'non-mediated' refers to communication that takes place outside the media. The two concepts are used to emphasize this antithesis. However, this conceptualization does not assume that the media are the only mediators of communication. As it is argued later on, it is recognized that communication is always mediated (by language, etc.).
3. Of course, not all Greek and Greek Cypriots in the US wholeheartedly adopted these ideologies. The comment refers to the dominant discourses and hegemonic ideologies within the group.
4. Greekness and Cypriotness are ideological constructs and not taken-for-granted biological referents. However, as ideological constructs they are powerful in the construction and definition of identity. As will be shown, Greekness becomes a more ecumenical cultural reference in the United States than Britain. This is the outcome of the numerical predomination of Greeks (from Greece) in the country. In Cyprus, a sense of a Cypriot cultural distinctiveness remains, as people from Cyprus are numerically predominant among all migrants of Greek cultural backgrounds.
5. The national Census does not register Cypriots in a separate category; thus demographic information about British Cypriots is very limited. The only group that is visible in the Census are the people born in Cyprus (Storkey, 1994).

6. *New ethnicities* is a useful term introduced by Stuart Hall, who relates the concept to the hybridity of ethnicities in the Western multicultural world (see especially Hall, 1992).

7. There are dozens of village associations in Britain and the United States. These organizations bring together migrants and their offspring who originate in the same village in Cyprus.

8. The present research project learns from the ethnographic media studies tradition, including such studies as Radway, 1984; Morley and Silverstone, 1990; Ang, 1991; Buckingham, 1993; Gillespie, 1995; Livingstone, 1996; Seiter, 1999, and many others.

9. Although both diversity and the dual social/psychological diasporic journey always characterize ethnicity, the multiplicity and (relative) fluidity discussed in this book develops in the specific historical and spatial context of Western advanced capitalism. Belonging might (often) be a choice in western multicultural societies, but probably not in other parts of the world (Modood *et al.*, 1997), where it is an inescapable and dominant identification. The context of this research is London and New York, two of the most cosmopolitan global cities of the Western world.

10. Part of this critical adoption of ethnography is the use of methods that are not traditionally considered as ethnographic, next to the purely ethnographic methods of participant observation, unstructured interviewing and discussions. Though ethnographic methods were dominant, other methods used include short interviews based on a questionnaire and the analysis of quantitative data. These methods were adjusted to the ethnographic perspective of this study; i.e., they were used as part of a methodological triangulation.

11. The complexity of the relation between Greece and Cyprus has a history of thousands of years. The majority population in Cyprus is ethnically Greek and speak Greek. However, after Cyprus gained its independence from the British Empire (1960) it became a state, separate from Greece. Numerous historical events have led to the development of a love and hate relationship between Greeks and Greek Cypriots, as well as to a growing sense of cultural and political autonomy of Cyprus from Greece. These relations and identities are renegotiated in the transnational context of diaspora.

12. 'Asians' in the British context refers to South Asian people.

13. An inventory of diasporic Greek and Cypriot media available in London and New York City is presented in the Appendix.

14. Cyprus Broadcasting Corporation—Satellite: Public television from Cyprus.

15. See young people's comments in the next chapter; they say that they enjoy some sitcoms on CBC-SAT because they remind them of their parents and grandparents. See also participants' comments of preference to CBC-SAT against ERT-SAT; as they argue, the language of the former is considered as more familiar than that of the latter.

16. The photographer asked his subjects to pose with an item they chose as representative of their identity.

17. Town in Northern Cyprus, occupied and now controlled by the Turkish army.

18. The Turkish invasion of northern Cyprus started with the war in July 1974.

19. The reference to home here signifies its conventional meaning as a place that relates to a house. It has already been argued, though, that for diasporic populations, the concept of home has multiple meanings, either as a utopic construct, or as a space of belonging that includes but is not constrained in the domestic.
20. Religious celebration at the beginning of summer.
21. See for example research by Radway (1984[1987]); Lindlof (1987); Gray (1987, 1992); Ang and Hermes (1991); Liebes and Ribak (1991); Seiter (1999).
22. Both teenagers call themselves Greek and passionately talk about the Cyprus problem and the *homeland*.
23. Sitcom on Cypriot satellite TV.
24. Participants are not only used to switching back and forth between Greek and English language channels. They are also used to switch into and out of different media models and aesthetics—i.e., public service television such as the BBC and commercial British, American and Greek channels. Diversity of media consumption has advanced media literacy and critical viewing, though it does not necessarily lead to the most thoughtful choice. Often participants express their opinion about what is good or bad about each channel and each broadcasting model. They are, for example, aware of the better quality of BBC programming, though they tend to choose commercial channels over public British/America/Greek/Cypriot service channels. Preferences in terms of genres and media aesthetics tend to cut across both the mainstream and the particular viewing choices.
25. Diasporic cultural space in a broader sense includes all the places and activities in which diasporic people get engaged. The diversity of places and activities beyond the *exclusive* diasporic space are not underestimated; on the contrary, they are acknowledged as crucial in the construction of multiple and hybrid identities. However, for the purpose of this study, this chapter pays more attention to the *exclusive* diasporic space.
26. Casual alcohol drinking among young people is not demonized among Greek and Greek Cypriot populations, as it is considered acceptable in small quantities and on special occasion.
27. Traditional male-dominated coffee shops.
28. Participant observation in a similar male-dominated center, the Pancyprian Association, took place in Astoria. There, as well as in the case of the London Cypriot Community Centre, middle-aged, working class men gather to play cards, socialize and watch satellite diasporic television. There were many similarities observed in the two places, though there are also significant differences. The most important difference relates to the bicommunal character of the London centre—Greek Cypriots and Turkish Cypriots co-exist—vis-à-vis the domination of Greek (Cypriots) in the Astoria community centre. Everyday interaction with the immediate Other—Turkish Cypriots—has implications for constructing We-ness.
29. This, of course, raises methodological questions about my presence and interaction with the men in the centre. While my gender and age inevitably played a role in the relation built between the researcher and the participants, the

long-term conduct of the study—nine month intense ethnography and three more years living in the field—limited the restrictions and preconceptions towards the other on both sides.

30. Playing cards and backgammon are two of the most common activities in traditional Cypriot coffee-shops.

31. As noted elsewhere, socialization for women even beyond their own home usually revolves around visits in other people's homes.

32. Watching television at specific times is the most structured that activities in the Cypriot Community Centre get.

33. Public television channel broadcasting from Greece.

34. Popular British soap opera.

35. The British official ideology regarding ethnic and interethnic relations promotes multiculturalism and recognition of diversity within the British society. However, in recent years and especially after 9/11, this ideology has been under attack (Georgiou, 2002). Also, recent research (Kyambi, 2005) shows that ethnic segregation in British cities is on the rise.

36. These concepts appear in italics, because they refer to a symbolic imaginary space rather than to the real spatial demographics. None of these neighborhoods is exclusively inhabited by a single group. The group that is considered as dominant in certain urban areas is rarely the majority in this area. This is certainly the case when it comes to Greeks and Greek Cypriots in both London and New York City (Moskos, 1990; Georgiou, 2001).

37. This website is attached to the largest music store in Astoria, New York. However, the physical location of the store becomes irrelevant, as the site sells music, videos, DVDs, gifts and even religious icons to a global clientele. One can buy almost every album that is available in the Greek market. The latest venture of www.greekmusic.com is an online bookstore. Book sales remain a marginal activity in comparison to the massive music sales.

38. Football refers to what is also called soccer.

39. There are numerous Greek and Greek Cypriot football clubs in Britain and the U.S. In London, there is an established championship with diasporic Greek (Cypriot) teams competing among themselves. Also, these teams often play against other local (diasporic) teams, such as Irish or Turkish Cypriot teams.

40. Premier league Cypriot football team.

41. Common origin; common settlement in global diasporic spaces and new countries.

42. Past traced in an original *homeland*; present and future grounded in a new country and in transnational diasporic spaces.

43. The well-known pop artist of Greek Cypriot ancestry chooses not to keep links with the Greek Cypriot community. The revelation of his homosexuality after his arrest in an LA public lavatory caused tense debates within the group, with some members defending his right to sexual choice and others considering his homosexuality as insulting to his 'community of origin'.

44. Universal, as beyond diasporic and national differences.

45. Diaspora and diasporic media are particularistic projects, as they promote distinctiveness of a specific culture within broader national and transnational contexts. On the other hand, diaspora and its media depend on universalistic ide-

ologies of capitalist progress and financial success, freedom of communication, and human rights. The particularism-universalism continuum (Balibar and Wallerstein, 1991; Robertson, 1992) is an inherent contradiction of diasporic condition. Nevertheless, it is a contradiction that allows diasporic particularism to remain relevant to people living in Western capitalist societies (Georgiou, 2005b).

46. Greeks and Jews are the ethnic groups with the highest educational and economic achievements in the U.S. (Moskos, 1990). Many participants expressed their admiration, but also an antagonism, towards Jewish Americans. The expressed sense of resemblance with the Jewish community, in terms of social success and aspiration, reflects the tense association between two *white* minority groups competing for power in the (dominantly *white*) country of settlement.

47. Even though dominant discourses—especially powerful among the migrant generation—reproduce ideologies of the umbilical cord, when it comes to actual practice, no such unconditional attachment to the *homeland* is actually observed. For example, when many participants asked why they do not move to Cyprus, they said that they had no choice because of family, property, work, or other obligations in the diaspora.

48. Research with different diasporic audiences for the After September 11 research project (2002) also showed that the more diverse media—national, transnational, mainstream, diasporic, etc.—audiences consumed, the more reflexive they were in their engagement with them.

49. This point relates to participants' descriptions of their own experience in such settings.

APPENDIX

An inventory of Greek and Greek Cypriot media available in London and Astoria, New York City.

London

Radio
London Greek Radio (LGR)

Television
Hellenic TV
CBC SAT (Cyprus Broadcasting Corporation satellite programme)
ERT SAT (Greek public television)
NOVA (Cable network offering access to more than 14 Greek channels and many global media. Connection to NOVA outside Greece is illegal, yet increasingly popular).
A number of Greek and Cypriot channels have live broadcasting on the web though availability and access is often difficult and inconsistent.

Press
Παροικιακη/Parikiaki (weekly)
Τα Νεα/Ta Nea (fortnightly)
Ελευθερια/Eleftheria (weekly)

These are the main diasporic media consumed; there are numerous other regular and irregular publications (in the form of newsletters and magazines) produced in London, Greece, Cyprus and elsewhere in the diaspora. Additionally, there are numerous Web sites with live broadcasting and other information and communication options that the members of the group use more and more. Newspapers from Greece and Cyprus are imported daily, but they are not regularly bought, especially as the cost is quite substantial. However, they are often read by first-generation migrants who have access to them in public libraries and community centres.

Astoria, New York City

Radio
Aktina FM
COSMOS FM
Hellas News

Television
ERT SAT (Greek public television available on cable and satellite)
MEGA Cosmos (Commercial Greek channel available on satellite; installation of satellite dish is necessary)
ANT1 Satellite (Commercial Greek channel available on satellite; installation of satellite dish is necessary)
A number of Greek and Cypriot channels have live broadcasting on the web though availability and access is often inconsistent

Press
Εθνικός Κηρυξ/National Herald (daily)
Greek News (weekly)

These are the main diasporic media consumed; there are numerous other regular and irregular publications (in the form of newsletters and magazines) produced in London, Greece, Cyprus and elsewhere in the diaspora. Additionally, there are numerous web sites with live broadcasting and other information and communication options that the members of the group use more and more. Newspapers from Greece and Cyprus are regularly imported, but not broadly used.

REFERENCES

Abercrombie, Nicolas and Brian Longhurst (1998) *Audiences: A Sociological Theory of Performance and Imagination*. London, Thousand Oaks, CA, New Delhi: Sage

After September 11 Research Project (2002) http://www.afterseptember11.tv/

Ahmed, Sara (1999) '"She'll Wake Up One of These Days and Find She's Turned into a Nigger": Passing Through Hybridity' in *Theory, Culture and Society*, 16 (2): 87-106

Aksoy, Asu and Kevin Robins (2000) 'Thinking Across Spaces: Transnational Television from Turkey' in *European Journal of Cultural Studies*, 3 (3): 343-365

Aksoy, Asu and Kevin Robins (2003) "The Enlargement of Meaning: Social Demand in a Transnational Context" in *Gazette*. 65 (4-5): 365-388

Alasuutari, Pertti (1999) 'Introduction: Three Phases of Reception Studies' in P.Alasuutari (ed.) *Rethinking the Media Audience*. London: Sage

Alba Richard D. (2000) 'The Melting Pot: Myth or Reality' in S. Steinberg (ed.) *Race and Ethnicity in the United States: Issues and Debates*. Malden, MA: Blackwell

Alia, Valerie (2002) 'Scattered Voices, Global Vision: Indigenous Peoples and the New Media Nation' in Karim Karim (ed.) *The Media of Diaspora*. London and New York: Routledge

Amin, Ash and Nigel Thrift (2002) *Cities: Reimagining the Urban*. Cambridge: Polity

Anderson, Benedict (1983(1991)) *Imagined Communities: Reflections On the Origins and Spread of Nationalism*. London: Verso

Anderson, Benedict (1994) 'Exodus' in *Critical Enquiry*, 20 (2): 314-327

Ang, Ien (1985[1993]) *Watching Dallas: Soap Opera and the Melodramatic Imagination*. London, New York: Methuen

Ang, Ien (1991) *Desperately Seeking the Audience*. London, New York: Routledge

Ang, Ien (1996) *Living Room Wars: Rethinking Media Audiences for a Postmodern World*. London and New York: Routledge

Ang, Ien and Joke Hermes (1991) 'Gender and/in Media Consumption' in James Curran and Michael Gurevitch (eds.) *Mass Media and Society*. London: Arnold

Angelopoulos, A., M. Goutos, G. Notaras *et al.* (1967) *Essays on Greek Migration*. Athens: Social Sciences Centre

Anthias, Floya (1992) *Ethnicity, Class, Gender and Migration: Greek Cypriots in Britain*. Aldershot: Avebury

Anthias, Floya (1998) 'Evaluating "Diaspora"': Beyond Ethnicity' in *Sociology*, 32 (3): 557-580

Anthias, Floya (2001) 'The Concept of "Social Division" and Theorising Social Stratification: Looking at Ethnicity and Class' in *Sociology*, 35 (4): 835-854

Anthias, Floya and Nira Yuval-Davis (1992) *Racialized Boundaries: Race, Nation, Gender, Colour and Class and the Anti-racist Struggle*. London, New York: Routledge

Appadurai, Arjun (1990) 'Disjuncture and Difference in the Global Cultural Economy' in M. Featherstone (ed.) *Global Culture: Nationalism, Globalization and Modernity*. London: Sage

Appadurai, Arjun (1996) *Modernity at Large: Cultural Dimensions of Globalization*. Minneapolis and London: University of Minnesota Press

Back, Les (1996) *New Ethnicities and Urban Culture: Racism and Multiculture in Youngs Lives*. London: UCL Press

Balibar, Etienne (1991) 'The Nation Form' in E. Balibar and I. Wallerstein *Race, Nation, Class*. London: Verso

Ballis-Lal, Barbara (1986) 'The "Chicago School" of American Sociology, Symbolic Interactionism, and Race Relations Theory' in J.Rex and D.Mason (eds.) *Theories of Race and Ethnic Relations*. Cambridge: Cambridge University Press

Barbesino, Paulo (1996) 'The Community of Society: From Virtual Community to Virtual Community'. Brighton: University of Sussex, CulCom Working Paper

Barth, Fredrik (1969) *Ethnic Groups and Boundaries*. Boston, MA: Little, Brown and Co

Basch, Linda, Nina Glick Schiller, and Cristina Szanton Blanc (1994) *Nations Unbound: Transnational Projects, Postcolonial Predicaments and Deterritorialized Nation-States*. Langhorne, PA: Luxembourg: Gordon and Breach.

Bauman, Zygmunt (1996a) 'From Pilgrim to Tourist—or a Short History of Identity' in Stuart Hall and Paul Du Gay (eds.) *Questions of Cultural Identity*. London: Sage

Bauman, Zygmunt (1996b) 'Modernity and Ambivalence' in M. Featherstone, (ed.) *Global Culture: Nationalism, Globalization and Modernity*, London, Thousand Oaks, CA, New Delhi: Sage

Bauman, Zygmunt (1998) *Globalization: The Human Consequences*. Cambridge: Polity

Bauman, Zygmunt (2000) *Community: Seeking Safety in an Insecure World*. Cambridge: Polity

Baumann, Gerd (1996) *Contesting Culture: Discourses of Identity in Multi-ethnic London*. Cambridge: Cambridge University Press

Beck, Ulrich (2000) 'The Cosmopolitan Perspective: Sociology of the Second Age of Modernity' in *British Journal of Sociology*, 51 (1): 79-105

Beck, Ulrich (2002) 'The Cosmopolitan Society and its Enemies' in *Theory, Culture and Society*, 19 (1-2):17-44

Bell, C. and H. Newby (1971) *Community Studies.* London: George Allen and Unwin

Bell, Vicky (1999) 'Performativity and Belonging: An Introduction' in *Theory, Culture and Society*, 16 (2): 41-64

Ben-Amos Dan and Liliane Weissberg (eds.) (1999) *Cultural Memory and the Construction of Identity*. Detroit: Wayne State University Press

Benjamin, Walter (1997) *One Way Street*. London: Verso

Berland, J. (1992) 'Angels Dancing: Cultural Technologies and the Production of Space' in Grossberg, Nelson and Treichler (eds.) *Cultural Studies*. New York: Routledge

Betteridge, Jenie (1997) 'Answering Back: The Telephone, Modernity and Everyday Life' in *Media Culture and Society*, 19(4): 585-603

Bhabha, Homi (1990) 'The Third Space': An Interview with Homi Bhabha in Rutherford, J. (ed.) *Identity: Community, Culture and Difference*. London: Lawrence and Wishart: 207-221

Bhabha, Homi (1990) 'Introduction: Narrating the Nation' in H. Bhabha (ed.) *Nation and Narration*. London: Routledge

Bhabha, Homi (1994) 'Frontierlines/borderposts' in A. Bammer (ed.) *Displacements: Cultural Identities in Question*. Bloomington, IN: Indiana University Press

Bhabha, Homi (1996) 'Culture's In-Between' in Stuart Hall and Paul Du Gay (eds.) *Questions of Cultural Identity*. London: Sage

Billig, Michael (1995) *Banal Nationalism*. London: Sage

Bodroghkozy, Aniko (1995) '"Is This What You Mean by Color TV?": Race, Gender and Contested Meanings in NBC's Julia' in Gail Dines and Jean M. Humez (eds.) *Gender, Race and Class in Media: A Text Reader*. Thousand Oaks, CA, London, New Delhi: Sage

Bourdieu, Pierre (1984) *Distinction: A Social Critique of the Judgement of Taste*. Cambridge, MA: Harvard University Press

Boyarin, Jonathan (ed.) (1994) *Remapping Memory: The Politics of Time Space*. Minneapolis, London: University of Minnesota Press

Boyarin, Daniel and Jonathan Boyarin (1993) 'Diaspora: Generation and the Ground of Jewish Identity' in *Critical Inquiry*, 19 (4): 693-725

Brass, Paul (1986) 'Ethnicity and Political Stalemate' in Ali Banuazizi and Myron Weiner (eds.) *The State, Religion and Ethnic Politics: Afghanistan, Iran and Pakistan*. Syracuse, NY: Syracuse University Press

Brah, Avtar (1996) *Cartographies of Diaspora: Contesting Identities*. London: Routledge

Bryce, Jennifer W. (1987) 'Family Time and Television Use' in T.R. Lindlof, (ed.) *Natural Audiences: Qualitative Research of Media Uses and Effects*. Norwood, NJ: Ablex

Buckingham, David (1987) *Public Secrets: EastEnders and Its Audience*. London: BFI

Buckingham, David (1993) *Children Watching Television: The Making of Television Literacy*. London: Falmer Press

Butler, Judith (1990) *Gender Trouble: Feminism and the Subversion of Identity*. London: Routledge

Butler, Judith (1993) *Bodies That Matter: The Discursive Limits of 'Sex'*. London: Routledge

Calhoun, Craig (1980) 'Community: Towards a Variable Conception for Comparative Research' in *Social History* 5(1): 105-129

Calhoun, Craig (1998) 'Community without Propinquity Revisited: Communications Technology and the Transformation of the Urban Public Sphere' in *Sociological Inquiry* 68(3): 373-97.

Cashmore, E. (1988) *Dictionary of Ethnic and Race Relations*. New York: Routledge

Castells, Manuel (1996) *Information Age: Economy, Society and Culture: Rise of the Network Society Vol 1 (The Information Age: Economy, Society & Culture)*. Oxford: Blackwell

Castells, Manuel (2001) *The Internet Galaxy: Reflections on the Internet, Business and Society*. Oxford and New York: Oxford University Press

Chambers, Iain (1994) *Migrancy, Culture, Identity*. London and New York: Routledge

Chimbos, Peter D. (1999) 'The Greeks in Canada: An Historical and Sociological Perspective' in R.Clogg (ed.) *The Greek Diaspora in the Twentieth Century*. London and New York: Macmillan

Clifford, James (1994) 'Diasporas' in *Cultural Anthropology* 9(3):302-337

Clifford, James (1997) *Routes: Travel and Translation in the Late Twentieth Century*. Cambridge, MA: Harvard University Press

Clifford, James and George E. Marcus (eds.) (1986) *Writing Culture: The Poetics and Politics of Ethnography*. Berkeley: University of California Press

Cohen, Anthony P. (1985) *The Symbolic Construction of Community*. London: Open University

Cohen, Anthony P. (1994) *Self-Consciousness: An Alternative Anthropology of Identity*. London: Routledge

Cohen, Phil (1993) 'Subcultural Conflict and Working-class Community' in Ann Gray and Jim McGuigan (eds.) *Studying Culture: An Introductory Reader*. London, New York: Arnold

Cohen, Robin (1994) *Frontiers of Identity: The British and the Others*. New York: Longman

Cohen, Robin (1996) 'Diasporas and the Nation-State: From Victims to Challengers' in *International Affairs* 72(4): 507–520

Cohen, Robin (1997) *Global Diasporas: An Introduction*. London: UCL Press

Constantinides, Pamela (1984) 'The Greek Cypriots: Factors in the Maintenance of Ethnic Identity' in J. L. Watson (ed.) *Between Two Cultures*. Oxford: Basil Blackwell

Cormack, Mike (1998) 'Minority Language Media in Western Europe: Preliminary Considerations' in *European Journal of Communication*, 13(1): 33-52.

Cormack, Mike (2000) 'Minority Languages, Nationalism and Broadcasting: The British and Irish Examples' in *Nations and Nationalism*, 6(3): 383–398

Cottle, Simon (ed.) (2000) *Ethnic Minorities and the Media: Changing Cultural Boundaries*. Buckingham, Philadelphia: Oxford University Press

Crow, Graham (1994) *Community Life: An Introduction to Local Social Relationships*. Hemel Hempstead: Harvester Wheatsheaf

Crow, Graham and Graham Allen (1994) *Community Life: An Introduction to Local Social Relations.* London Harvester Wheatsheaf

Dayan, Daniel (1998) 'Particularistic Media and Diasporic Communications' in T. Liebes and J.Curran (eds.) *Media, Ritual and Identity.* New York: Routledge

Dayan, Daniel (1999) 'Media and Diasporas' in J. Gripsrud (ed.) *Television and Common Knowledge.* London, New York: Routledge

Demetriou, Madeleine (2002) 'Politicising the Diaspora: Contested Identities among the Greek Cypriot Community in Britain'. Unpublished Thesis. Canterbury: University of Kent

de Certeau, Michel (1984) *The Practice of Everyday Life.* Berkeley, Los Angeles and London: University of California Press

Dines, Gail and Jean M. Humez (eds.) (1995) *Gender, Race and Class in Media: A Text Reader.* Thousand Oaks, London, New Delhi: Sage

Drucker, Susan and Gary Gumpert (1997) *Voices in the Street: Explorations in Gender, Media, and Public Space.* Cresskill, NJ: Hampton Press

Drzewiecka, Jolanta A. and Kathleen Wong (Lau) (1999) 'The Dynamic Construction of White Ethnicity in the Context of Transnational Cultural Formations' in Thomas K. Nakayama and Judith N. Martin (eds.) *Whiteness: The Communication of Social Identity.* Thousand Oaks, CA, London, New Delhi: Sage

Durham Peters, John (1999) 'Exile, Nomadism, and Diaspora' in Hamid Naficy (ed.) *Home, Exile, Homeland.* London: Routledge

Dyer, Richard (1988) 'White' in *Screen* 29(4): 44-64

Eade, John (2000) *Placing London: From Imperial Capital to Global City.* New York and Oxford: Berghahn Press

Fanon, Frantz (1986) *Black Skin, White Masks.* London: Pluto Press

Fischer, Michael M.J. (1986) 'Ethnicity and the Post-Modern Arts of Memory' in James Clifford and G.E. Marcus (eds.) *Writing Culture: The Poetics and Politics of Ethnography.* Berkeley: University of California Press

Fiske, John (1982 (1997)) *Television Culture.* London: Methuen

Fiske, John (1990) 'Ethnosemiotics: Some Personal and Theoretical Reflections' in *Cultural Studies* 4 (1): 85-99

Featherstone, Mike (2002) 'Cosmopolis: An Introduction' in *Theory, Culture and Society* 19(1-2): 1-16

Fortier, Anne-Marie (1999) 'Re-membering Places and the Performance of Belonging(s)' in *Theory, Culture and Society,* 16 (2): 41-64

Fortier, Anne-Marie (2000) *Migrant Belongings: Memory, Space, Identity.* Oxford, New York: Berg

Foucault, Michel (1974) *The Order of Things: Archaeology of the Human Science.* London: Tavistock

Frankenberg, Ruth (1997) 'Introduction: Local Whiteness, Localizing Whiteness' in R. Frankenberg (ed.) *Displacing Whiteness: Essays in Social and Cultural Criticism.* Durham and London: Duke University Press

Franklin, M.I. (2001) 'Postcolonial Subjectivities and Everyday Life On-line,' *International Feminist Journal of Politics* 3 (3): 387-422

Friedman, Jonathan (1995) *Cultural Identity and Global Process.* London: Sage

Gabriel, John (1998) *Whitewash: Racialized Politics and the Media.* London and New York: Routledge

Geertz, Clifford (1973) *The Interpretation of Cultures*. New York: Basic Books

Geertz, Clifford (1988) *Works and Lives: The Anthropologist as Author*. Cambridge: Polity Press

Georgakas, Dan (1999) 'The America Beyond Ellis Island' in S. Tsemberis, H.J. Psomiades and A. Karpathakis (eds.) *Greek American Families: Traditions and Transformations*. New York, NY: Pella

Georgiou, Myria (2001) 'Crossing the Boundaries of the Ethnic Home: Media Consumption and Ethnic Identity Construction in the Public Space: The Case of the Cypriot Community Centre in North London' in *Gazette*, 63(4): 311-329

Georgiou, Myria (2002) Mapping Minorities and their Media: The National Context: The UK. http://www.lse.ac.uk/collections/EMTEL/Minorities/reports.html

Georgiou, Myria (2003) 'Consuming Ethnic Media, Constructing Ethnic Identities, Shaping Communities: The Case Study of Greek Cypriots in London' in R. A. Lind (ed) *Race/Gender/Media: Considering Diversity Across Audiences, Content and Producers*. Boston, MA: Allyn & Bacon

Georgiou, Myria (2005a) 'Mapping Diasporic Media Cultures: A Cultural Approach to Exclusion' in R. Silverstone (ed.) *From Information to Communication: Media, Technology and Everyday Life in Europe*. London: Ashgate

Georgiou, Myria (2005b) 'Diasporic Media Across Europe: Multicultural Societies and the Universalism-Particularism Continuum' in *Journal of Ethnic and Migration Studies*, 31(3): 481-498

Georgiou, Myria (2006) 'Diasporic Communities On Line: A Bottom Up Experience of Transnationalism' in K. Sarikakis and D. Thussu (eds.) *The Ideology of the Internet: Concepts, Policies, Uses*. Cresskill, NJ: Hampton Press

Giddens, Anthony (1990) *The Consequences of Modernity*. Cambridge: Polity

Gillespie, Marie (1995) *Television, Ethnicity and Cultural Change*. London: Routledge

Gilroy, Paul (1991) *There Ain't No Black in the Union Jack: The Cultural Politics of Race and Nation*. London: Routledge

Gilroy, Paul (1993a) *The Black Atlantic: Modernity and Double Consciousness*. London: Verso

Gilroy, Paul (1993b) *Small Acts: Thoughts on the Politics of Black Cultures*. London: Serpent's Tail

Gilroy, Paul (1995) 'Roots and Routes: Black Identity as an Outernational Project' in H.W.Harris *et al.* (eds.) *Racial and Ethnic Identity: Psychological Development and Creative Expression*. London and New York: Routledge

Gilroy, Paul (1997) 'Diaspora and the Detours of Identity' in K. Woodward *Identity and Difference*. London, Thousand Oaks, CA, New Delhi: Sage

Gilroy, Paul (2001) *Against Race: Imagining Political Culture beyond the Color Line*. Cambridge, MA: Harvard University Press

Goffman, Erving (1959(1990)) *The Presentation of Self in Everyday Life*. London: Penguin

Gray, Ann (1987) 'Reading the Audience' in *Screen* 28(3): 24-36

Gray, Ann (1992) *Video Playtime: The Gendering of a Leisure Technology*. London: Routledge

Gray, Ann and Jim McGuigan (eds.) (1993) *Studying Culture: An Introductory Reader.* London, New York: Arnold

Guarnizo, Michael Peter and Smith Luis Eduardo (1998) 'The Locations of Transnationalism' in M.P.Guarnizo and S.L.Eduardo (eds.) *Transnationalism from Below.* New Brunswick, NJ: Transaction

Guba, E.G. and Y.S. Lincoln (1981) *Effective Evaluation: Improving the Usefulness of Evaluation Results through Responsive and Naturalistic Approaches.* San Francisco: Jossey-Bass

Guibernau, Montserrat and John Rex (eds.) (1997) *The Ethnicity Reader: Nationalism, Multiculturalism and Migration.* Cambridge, Oxford, Malden, MA: Polity Press

Gumpert, Gary and Susan J. Drucker (eds.) (1998) *The Huddled Masses: Communication and Immigration.* Cresskill, NJ: Hampton Press

Gumpert Gary and Susan J. Drucker (1998) 'The Greek World of Astoria' in G.Gumpert and S.J.Drucker (eds.) *The Huddled Masses: Communication and Immigration.* Cresskill NJ: Hampton Press

Gumpert, Gary and Susan J. Drucker (1999) 'The Right to Communicate: Jurisdictions Both International and Virtual'. Paper presented at the *IAMCR Conference*, Leipzig.

Hall, Stuart (1981) 'The Whites of their Eyes: Racial Ideologies and the Media' in G. Bridges and R. Brunt Silver *Linings: Some Strategies for the Eighties.* London: Lawrence and Wishart

Hall, Stuart (1986) 'Popular Culture and the State' in Mercer et al. (eds.) *Popular Culture and Social Relations.* Oxford: Open University Press

Hall, Stuart (1988) 'New Ethnicities' in K. Mercer (ed.) *Black/Film/British Cinema, ICA documents 7.* London: Institute of Contemporary Arts.

Hall, Stuart (1990) 'Cultural Identity and Diaspora' in J. Rutherford (ed.) *Identity: Community, Culture, Difference.* London: Lawrence and Wishart

Hall, Stuart (1991) 'The Local and the Global: Globalisation and Ethnicity' in A. D. King (ed.) *Culture, Globalisation and the World-system: Contemporary Conditions for the Representation of Identity.* London: Macmillan

Hall, Stuart (1992) 'The New Ethnicities' in J. Donald and A. Rattansi (eds.) *Race, Culture and Difference.* London: Sage

Hall, Stuart (ed.) (1997) *Representation: Cultural Representations and Signifying Practices.* London, CA: Thousand Oaks, New Delhi: Sage

Hammersley, Martyn and Paul Atkinson (1995) *Ethnography: Principles in Practice.* London: Tavistock

Hanafi, Sari (2005) 'Reshaping Geography: Palestinian Community Network in Europe and the New Media' in *Journal of Ethnic and Migration Studies* 31(3): 581-589

Hannerz, Ulf (1996) *Transnational Connections: Cultures, People, Places.* London: Routledge

Hannerz, Ulf (2002) 'Flows, Boundaries and Hybrids: Keywords in Transnational Anthropology'. Working Paper on www.transcom.ox.ac.uk

Hartley, John (1999) *Uses of Television.* London, New York: Routledge

Harvey, David. (1989) *The Condition of Postmodernity: An Enquiry into the Origins of Cultural Change.* Oxford: Blackwell

Hassiotis, Anna (1989) *"The Greek Cypriot Community in Camden."* London: London Borough of Camden

Hastrup, Kirsten (1987) 'Fieldwork among Friends: Ethnographic Exchange within the Northern Civilization' in A. Jackson (ed.) *Anthropology at Home*. London: Tavistock Publications

Hastrup, Kirsten (1992) 'Writing Ethnography: State of the Art' in Judith Okely and Helen Callaway (eds.) *Anthropology and Autobiography*. London and New York: Routledge

Hirsch, Eric (1998) 'Bound and Unbound Entities: Reflections on the Ethnographic Perspectives of Anthropology vis-à-vis Media and Cultural Studies' in F. Hughes-Freeland (ed.) *Ritual, Performance, Media*. London, New York: Routledge

Hobson, Dorothy (1989) 'Soap Operas at Work' in Ellen Seiter et al. (eds.) *Remote Control: Television, Audiences, and Cultural Power*. London: Routledge

Holmes, David (1997) "Virtual Identity: Communities of Broadcast, Communities of Interactivity' in D. Holmes (ed.) *Virtual Politics: Identity and Community in Cyberspace*. London: Sage

Holton, R. (1998) *Globalization and the Nation-State.* London: Macmillan

Hughes-Freeland, Felicia (ed.) (1998) *Ritual, Performance, Media*. London, New York: Routledge

Husband, Charles. (1994) *A Richer Vision: The Development of Ethnic Minority Media in Western Democracies*. Paris: UNESCO

Iordanova, Dina (2001) *Cinema of Flames: Balkan Film, Culture and the Media.* London: British Film Institute

Johnson, Parker C. (1999) 'Reflections on Critical Whiteness Studies' in Thomas K. Nakayama and Judith N. Martin (eds.) *Whiteness: The Communication of Social Identity*. Thousand Oaks, CA, London, New Delhi: Sage

Jones, Steven G. (1995) 'Introduction' in S.G. Jones (ed.) *CyberSociety: Computer-Mediated Communication and Community*. London: Sage

Karim, Karim (2002) *The Media of Diaspora*. London and New York: Routledge

Karpathakis, Anna (1999) '"I Don't Have to Worry about Money Anymore, and I Can Live like a Lady": Greek Immigrant Women and Assimilation' in S.Tsemberis, H.J. Psomiades and A. Karpathakis (eds.) *Greek American Families: Traditions and Transformations*. New York: Pella

Kassimati, Koula (1984) Μεταναστευση—Παλιννοστηση: Η Προβληματικη της Δευτερης Γενιας *(Immigration—Return: The Problematics of the Second Generation)*. Athens: National Centre of Social Research

Kearney, Michael (1991) 'Borders and boundaries of state and self at the end of empire,' *Journal of Historical Sociology* 4(1):52-74

King, Russell and Janet Bridal (1982) 'The Changing Distribution of Cypriots in London' in *Studi Emigrazione*, Anno XIX, no.65. Roma: Centro Studi Emigrazione

King, Russell and Nancy Wood (2001) *Media and Migration*. London: Routledge

Koupparis, Christos (1999) Οι Κυπριοι της Βρετανιας—50 Χρονια. Προσφορας 1930–80 *(The British Cypriots—50 Years of Offer 1930-80)*. Nicosia: Theopress

Kuper, Adam (1999) *Culture: The Anthropologist's Account*. Cambridge, MA: Harvard University Press

Kyambi, Sarah (2005) *Beyond Black and White: Mapping New Immigrant Communities*. London: IPPR

Lacan, Jacques (1977) *Ecrits: A Selection*. London: Tavistock

Lee, Minu and Chong Heup Cho (1990) 'Women Watching Together: An Ethnographic Study of Korean Soap Operas Fans in the United States' in *Cultural Studies*, 4 (1): 30-44

Leeuwenburg, Jeffrey (1979) *The Cypriots in Haringey: A Study of Their Literacy and Reading Habits*. London: Polytechnic of North London

Lefebvre, Henri (1991) *Critique of Everyday Life*. London: Verso

Lefebvre, Henri (1996) *Writing on Cities*. Oxford: Blackwell

Lefebvre, Henri [with Stuart Elden and Elizabeth Lebas] (2003) *Henri Lefebvre: Key Writings*. London: Continuum

Liebes, Tamar and Katz, E. (1990) '*The Export of Meaning*.' Oxford: Oxford University Press

Liebes, Tamar and Rivka Ribak (1991) 'A Mother's Battle Against TV News: A Case Study of Political Socialization' in *Discourse and Society* 2 (2): 203-222

Liebes, Tamar and James Curran (eds.) (1998) *Media, Ritual and Identity*. New York: Routledge

Lindlof, T. R. (ed.) (1987) *Natural Audiences: Qualitative Research of Media Uses and Effects*. Norwood, NJ: Ablex

Livingstone, Sonia (1998) *Making Sense of Television: The Psychology of Audience Interpretation*. Oxford: Butterworth-Heinemann

Loizos, Peter (1981) *The Heart Grown Bitter*. Cambridge: Cambridge University Press

Loizos, Peter and Evthymios Papataxiarchis (eds.) (1991) *Gender and Kinship in Modern Greece*. Princeton, NJ: Princeton University Press

Lull, J. (1990) *Inside Family Viewing: Ethnographic Research on Television Audiences*. London: Routledge

Lull, J. (2000) *Media, Communication, Culture: A Global Approach*. Second edition. Cambridge: Polity

Mai, Nicola (2005) 'The Albanian Diaspora in-the-Making: Media, Migration and Social Exclusion' in *Journal of Ethnic and Migration Studies* 31(3): 543-562

Martin-Barbero, J. (1993) *Communication, Culture and Hegemony*. London: Sage.

Massey, Doreen (1991) 'A Global Sense of Place' in *Marxism Today* (June): 24-29

Massey, Doreen (1993) 'A Global Sense of Place' in A. Gray, and J. McGuigan (eds.) *Studying Culture: An Introductory Reader*. London: Edward Arnold

Massey, Doreen (1999) 'Cities in the World' in D. Massey, J. Allen and S. Pile (eds.) *City Worlds*. London: Routledge

Massey, Douglas et al. (1993) 'Theories of International Migration: A Review and Appraisal' in *Population and Development Review*, 19(3): 431-466

Massey, D.S. and N.A. Denton (2000) 'Should the Ghetto Be "Dismantled"?' in S. Steinberg (ed.) *Race and Ethnicity in the United States: Issues and Debates*. Malden, MA: Blackwell

Mavratsas, Caesar V. (1999) 'National Identity and Consciousness in Everyday Life: Towards a Sociology of Knowledge of Greek Cypriot Nationalism' in *Nations and Nationalism* 5 (1): 91-104

McDonald, J. D. (1972) *The Invisible Immigrants*. London: Runnymede Trust

McDonald, Sharon (ed.) (1993) *Inside European Identities: Ethnography in Western Europe*. Providence: Berg

McQuail, Dennis (1997) *Audience Analysis*. Thousand Oaks, London, New Delhi: Sage

Mettis, Charis (1998) Οι Ριζες του Παροικιακου Ελληνισμου της Μεγαλης Βρετανιας *(The Roots of the Diasporic Greeks of Great Britain).* Athens: Athena

Meyrowitz, Joshua (1985) *No Sense of Place.* Oxford: Oxford University Press

Mintoff-Bland, Yana (ed.) (1987) *Nobody Can Imagine Our Longing: Refugees and Immigrants in the Mediterranean.* Austin, TX: Plain View Press

Modood, Tariq, Richard Berthoud et al. (eds.) (1997) *The Fourth National Survey of Ethnic Minorities: Ethnic Minorities in Britain, Diversity and Disadvantage.* London: Policy Studies Institute

Moores, S. (1993) 'Television, Geography, and Mobile Privatisation' in *European Journal of Communication* 8 (3): 365-79

Morley, David (1980) *The 'Nationwide' Audience, Structure and Decoding.* London: BFI

Morley, David (1986) *Family Television: Cultural Power and Domestic Leisure.* London: Comedia

Morley, David (1991) 'Where the Global Meets the Local: Notes from the Sitting Room' in *Screen*: 1-14

Morley, David (1995) 'Theories of consumption in media studies' in D. Miller (ed.) Acknowledging Consumption: A Review of New Studies. London: Routledge: 296-328

Morley, David (1999) 'Bounded Realms: Household, Family, Community, and Nation' in H. Naficy (ed.) *Home, Exile, Homeland: Film, Media and the Politics of Place.* New York, London: Routledge

Morley, David (2000) *Home Territories: Media, Mobility and Identity.* London: Routledge

Morley, David and Kevin Robins. (1995) *Spaces of Identity: Global Media, Electronic Landscapes and Cultural Boundaries.* London: Routledge

Morley, David and Roger Silverstone (1990) 'Domestic Communications: Technologies and Meanings' in *Media, Culture and Society* 12 (1)

Morrison, Tony (1992) *Playing in the Dark: Whiteness and Literary Imagination.* Cambridge: Harvard University Press

Morse, Margaret (1999) 'Home: Smell, Taste, Posture, Gleam' in H. Naficy (ed.) *Home, Exile, Homeland: Film, Media and the Politics of Place.* New York, London: Routledge

Moskos, Charles C. (1990) *Greek Americans: Struggle and Success.* Brunswick, NJ: Transaction

Muller, Thomas (2000) 'The Immigrant Contribution to the Revitalization of Cities' in S. Steinberg (ed.) *Race and Ethnicity in the United States: Issues and Debates.* Malden, MA: Blackwell

Naficy, Hamid (1993) *The Making of Exile Cultures: Iranian Television in Los Angeles.* Minneapolis: University of Minnesota Press

Naficy, Hamid (ed.) (1999) *Home, Exile, Homeland: Film, Media and the Politics of Place.* New York, London: Routledge

Nakayama, Thomas K. and Judith N. Martin (eds.) (1999) *Whiteness: The Communication of Social Identity.* Thousand Oaks, CA, London, New Delhi: Sage

Nash, Manning (1989) *The Cauldron of Ethnicity in the Modern World.* Chicago and London: University of Chicago

Nassari, John (1998) *Photographic Exhibition: First Person/Second Generation.* London: PhotoInsight

Nightingale, Virginia (1996) *Studying Audiences: The Shock of the Real.* London and New York: Routledge

Nightingale, Virginia (1995) *9th International Conference for the Cypriots of Diaspora*, Nicosia 28/8 - 1/9 1995

Oakley, Robin (1979) 'The Cypriot Migration to Britain' in Saifullah Khan *Minority Families in Britain.* London: The Macmillan Press

Oakley, Robin (1989) 'Cypriot Migration to Britain Prior to World War II' in *New Community* 15 (4): 509-525

Ogan, Christine (2001) *Communication and Identity in the Diaspora: Turkish Migrants in Amsterdam and their Use of Media.* Lanham: Lexington

Oldenburg, Ray (1999) *The Great Good Place: Cafes, Coffee Shops, Bookstores, Bars, Hair Salons, and Other Hangouts at the Heart of a Community.* Washington, DC: Marlow & Company

Onoufriou, Andreas (2002) 'In Search of Voices: Policing the Borders of Legitimate Sexuality and Gendered Subjectivities among Cypriot Students'. Unpublished Thesis. London: University of London

Osborne, Peter and Lynne Segal (1997) 'Gender As Performance: An Interview with Judith Butler' for Radical Philosophy' in K. Woodward (ed.) *Identity and Difference.* London, Thousand Oaks, CA, New Delhi: Sage, Oxford University Press

Panayiotopoulos, Prodromos (1996) 'Challenging Orthodoxies: Cypriot Entrepreneurs in the London garment Industry' in *New Community* 22(3), 437-460

Papastergiadis, Nikos (1998) *Dialogues in the Diaspora: Essays and Conversations on Cultural Identity.* London and New York: Rivers Oram Press

Park, Robert E., Ernest W. Burgess and Roderick D. McKenzie (1925[1984]) *The City.* Chicago: The University of Chicago Press

Pasquier, Dominique et al. (1998) 'Family Lifestyles and Media Use Patterns' in *European Journal of Communication*, 13(4), 503-519

Portes, Alejandro (1997) 'Immigration Theory in the new century: some problems and opportunities' *International Migration Review* 31(4): 799–825

Portes, Alejandro (2001) 'Introduction: The Debates and Significance of Immigrant Transnationalism' in *Global Networks* 1(3): 181-193

Rabinow, P. (1977) *Reflections on Fieldwork in Morocco.* Berkley: University of California Press

Radway, Janice (1984[1987])) *Reading the Romance: Women, Patriarchy, and Popular Culture.* New York: Verso

Rantanen, Terhi (2004) *The Media and Globalization.* London: Sage

Rex, John (1997) 'The Nature of Ethnicity in the Project of Migration' in M.Guibernau and J. Rex (eds.) *The Ethnicity Reader: Nationalism, Multiculturalism and Migration.* Cambridge, Oxford, Malden, MA: Polity Press

Riggins, Stephen Harold (1992) *Ethnic Minority Media, An International Perspective.* London: Sage

Roberts, John Michael (2003) *The Aesthetics of Free Speech: Rethinking the Public Sphere.* London: Palgrave

Robertson, Roland (1992) *Globalization: Social Theory and Global Culture.* London, Thousand Oaks, New Delhi: Sage

Robins, Kevin (2001) 'Becoming Anybody: Thinking Against the Nation and Through the City' in *City*, 5(1): 77-90

Robins, Kevin and Frank Webster (1999) *Times of Technoculture: From the Information Society to the Virtual Life*. London, New York: Routledge

Rosaldo, Renato (1989) *Culture and Truth: The Remaking of Social Analysis*. Boston, MA: Beacon Press

Rothenbuhler, Eric W. (1998) *Ritual Communication: From Everyday Conversation to Mediated Ceremony*. Thousand Oaks, CA, London, New Delhi: Sage

Rutherford, Jonathan (ed.) (1990) *Identity: Community, Culture, Difference*. London: Lawrence and Wishart

Safran, William (1991) 'Diasporas in Modern Societies: Myths of *Homeland* and Return' in *Diaspora*, 1(1)

Said, E. (1985) *Orientalism*. Harmondsworth: Penguin

Sandvoss, Cornel (2003) *A Game of Two Halves: Football, Television and Globalisation*. London: Routledge

Sassen, Saskia (1991) *The Global City: New York, London, Tokyo*. Princeton: Princeton University Press

Sassen, Saskia (1999) *Guests and Aliens*. New York: New Press

Sassen, Saskia (2001) *Globalization and Its Discontents*. New York: New Press

Saussure, de Ferdinand (1983) *Course in General Lingu*istics. London: Duckworth

Schlesinger, Peter (1987) 'On National Identity: Some Conceptions and Misconceptions Criticised' in *Social Science Information*, 26 (2)

Schlesinger, Peter (1991) *Media, State and Nation: Political Violence and Collective Identities*. London: Sage

Schwirian, Kent et al. (eds.) (1977) *Contemporary Topics in Urban Sociology*. NJ: General Learning Press

Seed, Patricia (1999) 'The Key to the House' in H. Naficy (ed.) *Home, Exile, Homeland: Film, Media and the Politics of Place*. New York, London: Routledge

Seiter, E., H. Borchers, G. Kreutzner, E. M. Warth (eds.) (1989) *Remote Control: Television, Audiences and Cultural Power*. London and New York: Routledge

Seiter, Helen (1999) *Television and New Media Audience*. Oxford: Oxford University Press

Sennett, Richard (1970) *The Uses of Disorder: Personal Identity and City Life*. New York: Norton

Sheringham, M. (1996) 'City Space, Mental Space, Poetic Space: Paris in Breton, Benjamin and Reda' in M. Sheringham (ed.) *Parisian Fields*. London: Reaktion

Shome, Raka (1999) 'Whiteness and the Politics of Location: Postcolonial Reflections' in Thomas K. Nakayama and Judith N. Martin (eds.) *Whiteness: The Communication of Social Identity*. Thousand Oaks, CA, London, New Delhi: Sage

Siapera, Eugenia (2005) 'Minority Activism on the Web: Between Deliberative Democracy and Multiculturalism in *Journal and Ethnic and Migration Studies*, 31(3): 499-519

Silverstone, Roger (1993) 'Time, Information and Communication Technologies and the Household' in *Time and Society* 2(3), 283-311. London, Newbury Park and New Delhi: Sage

Silverstone, Roger. (1994) *Television and Everyday Life*. London: Routledge

Silverstone, Roger (1996) 'Future Imperfect: Information and Communication Technologies in Everyday Life' in W. Dutton (ed.) *Information and Communication Technologies—Visions and Realities*. Oxford: Oxford University Press

Silverstone, Roger (1999) *Why Study the Media?* London, Thousand Oaks: CA, New Delhi: Sage

Silverstone, Roger (2004) Regulation, Media Literacy and Media Civics' in *Media, Culture and Society*, 26(3): 440-449

Silverstone, Roger and Eric Hirsch. (1994) *Consuming Technologies: Media and Information in Domestic Spaces*. London: Routledge

Sinclair, John, Elizabeth Jacka, and Stuart Cunningham (eds.) (1996) *Peripheral Vision: New Patterns in Global Television*. Oxford and New York: Oxford University Press

Smart, Barry (1993) *Postmodernity*. London and New York: Routledge

Smith, Anthony D. (1981) *The Ethnic Revival of the Modern World*. Cambridge: Cambridge University Press

Smith, Anthony D. (1990) 'Towards a Global Culture' in *Theory, Culture and Society* 7 (2-3)

Smith, Anthony D. (1997) 'Structure and Persistence of Ethnie' in M. Guibernau and J. Rex (eds.) *The Ethnicity Reader: Nationalism Multiculturalism and Migration*. Cambridge, Oxford, Malden, MA: Polity Press

Smith, M. P., and L. E. Guarnizo (eds.) (1998) *Transnationalism from Below*. New Jersey: Transaction Books

Song, Miri (2003) *Choosing Ethnic Identity*. Cambridge: Polity

Sreberny-Mohammadi, Annabelle (1996) 'The Global and The Local in International Communications' in J. Curran and M. Gurevitch (eds.) *Mass Media and Society*. London: Arnold

Sreberny-Mohammadi, Annabelle et al. (eds.) (1997) *Media in Global Context*. London: Edward Arnold

Sreberny, Annabelle (2002) 'Collectivity and Connectivity: Diaspora and Mediated Identities' in G. Stald and T. Tufte (eds.) *Global Encounters: Media and Cultural Transformations*. Luton: University of Luton

Steinberg, Stephen (ed.) (2000) *Race and Ethnicity in the United States: Issues and Debates*. Malden, MA: Blackwell

Storkey, Marian (1994) 'Identifying the Cypriot Community from the 1991 Census'. London: London Research Centre

Strathern, Marilyn (1994) 'Forward' in Roger Silverstone and Eric Hirsch (eds.) *Consuming Technologies: Media and Information in Domestic Space*. London: Routledge

Stratton, Jon (2000a) *Coming Out Jewish: Constructing Ambivalent Identities*. London and New York: Routledge

Stratton, Jon (2000b) 'Not Really White—Again: Performing Jewish Difference in Hollywood Films Since the 1980s'. Unpublished paper presented at the *3rd Crossroads in Cultural Studies Conference*. Birmingham

Stromberg, Peter G. (1986) *Symbols of Community: The Cultural System of a Swedish Church*. Tucson: University of Arizona Press

Thompson, John (1995) *The Media and Modernity: A Social History of the Media.* Stanford: Stanford University Press

Tsaliki, Liza (2002) 'Globalization and Hybridity: The Construction of Greekness on the Internet' in Karim Karim (ed.) *The Media of Diaspora.* London and New York: Routledge

Tufte, Thomas (2000) *Living with the Rubbish Queen: Telenovelas, Culture and Modernity in Brazil.* Luton: Luton University Press

Tufte, Thomas and Maja Riis (2001) 'Cultural Fields and Borderlands of Identity: Exploring Media and Ethnicity, Culture and Community' forthcoming in the *Gazette,* 63(4): 331-350

Turkle, S. (1995) *Life on the Screen: Identity in the Age of the Internet.* New York, Simon and Schuster

Urry, John (2000) *Sociology Beyond Societies: Mobilities for the Twenty-First Century.* London and New York: Routledge

Urry, John (2002) 'Mobility and Proximity' in *Sociology,* 36(2): 255-274

van der Pennen, T. (1998) 'The Neighborhood: About Community and Social Integration' in G.Gumpert and S.J. Drucker (eds.) *The Huddled Masses: Communication and Immigration.* Cresskill NJ: Hampton Press

Van Hear, Nicholas (1998) *New Diasporas: The Mass Exodus, Dispersal and Regrouping of Migrant Communities.* London: UCL Press

Werbner, Pnina (1999) 'Global Pathways: Working Class Cosmopolitans and the Creation of Transnational Ethnic Worlds' in *Social Anthropology* 7(1): 17-35

Williams, Raymond (1961) *The Long Revolution.* London: Chatto & Windus

Williams, Raymond (1980) *Problems in Materialism and Culture: Selected Essays.* London: Verso

Willis, Paul and Mats Trondman (2000) 'Manifesto for Ethnography' in *Ethnography* 1(1)

Woodward, Kathryn (ed.) (1997) *Identity and Difference.* London, Thousand Oaks, New Delhi: Sage, Oxford University Press

Zoupaniotis, Maria, Press Councilor, Cyprus High Commission, New York. Interview with the Author. New York, 7/1/04.

AUTHOR INDEX

SUBJECT INDEX

Printed in the United States
64105LVS00002B/73

9 781572 737242